Verse by Verse Commentary on

PSALMS
119-150

Enduring Word Commentary Series

By David Guzik

The grass withers, the flower fades,
but the word of our God stands forever.
Isaiah 40:8

Commentary on Psalms 119-150

Copyright ©2020 by David Guzik

Printed in the United States of America
or in the United Kingdom

Print Edition ISBN: 978-1-939466-54-9

Enduring Word

5662 Calle Real #184

Goleta, CA 93117

Electronic Mail: ewm@enduringword.com

Internet Home Page: www.enduringword.com

Contents

Psalm 119 – The Greatness and Glory of God's Word

This long psalm deserves a long introduction. The author is unnamed; older commentators almost universally said it is a psalm of David, composed throughout his entire life. More modern commentators sometimes conclude that it is post-exilic, coming from the days of Nehemiah or Ezra. It may be that David was the author, but we can't say this with certainty, and it is not necessary to know; if it were important, God would have preserved the name of David to this psalm. No matter who the author was, it was likely written over some period of time and later compiled, because there is not a definite flow of thought from the beginning of the psalm to the end. The sections and verses are not like a chain, where one link is connected to the other, but like a string of pearls where each pearl has equal, but independent value.

Psalm 119 is arranged in an acrostic pattern. There are 22 letters in the Hebrew alphabet, and this psalm contains 22 units of 8 verses each. Each of the 22 sections is given a letter of the Hebrew alphabet, and each line in that section begins with that letter. The closest parallel to this pattern in Scripture is found in Lamentations 3, which is also divided into 22 sections, and a few other passages in the Hebrew Scriptures use an acrostic pattern.

Since this is a psalm glorifying God and His word, it refers to Scripture over and over again. Psalm 119 is remarkable for how often it refers to God's written revelation, His word. It is referred to in almost every verse. The Masoretes (a group of Jewish scholars between the 6th and 10th centuries AD) said that the word of God is mentioned in every verse except Psalm 119:122. Other people analyze this differently (with disagreement about verses 84, 90, 121, and 132). But Scripture is mentioned in at least 171 of the 176 verses.

In this psalm there are eight basic words used to describe the Scriptures, God's written revelation to us:

- **Law** (*torah*, used 25 times in Psalm 119): "Its parent verb means 'teach' or 'direct'; therefore coming from God it means both 'law' and 'revelation.' It can be used of a single command or of a whole body of law." (Derek Kidner)

- **Word** (*dabar*, used 24 times): The idea is of the spoken word, God's revealed word to man. "Proceeding from his mouth and revealed by him to us..." (Matthew Poole)

- **Judgments** (*mispatim*, used 23 times): "...from *shaphat*, to *judge, determine, regulate, order*, and *discern*, because they *judge* concerning our words and works; show the *rules* by which they should be *regulated*; and cause us to *discern* what is *right* and *wrong*, and *decide* accordingly." (Adam Clarke)

- **Testimonies** (*edut/edot*, used 23 times): This word is related to the word for *witness*. To obey His **testimonies** "...signifies loyalty to the terms of the covenant made between the Lord and Israel." (Willem VanGemeren)

- **Commandments** (*miswah/miswot*, used 22 times): "This word emphasizes the straight authority of what is said...the right to give orders." (Derek Kidner)

- **Statutes** (*huqqim*, used 21 times): The noun is derived from the root verb "engrave" or "inscribe"; the idea is the written word of God and the authority of His written word: "...declaring his authority and power of giving us laws." (Matthew Poole)

- **Precepts** (*piqqudim*, used 21 times): "This is a word drawn from the sphere of an officer or overseer, a man who is responsible to look closely into a situation and take action.... So the word points to the particular instructions of the Lord, as of one who cares about detail." (Derek Kidner)

- **Word** (*imrah*, used 19 times): *Imrah* is similar in meaning to *dabar*, yet a different term. "The 'word' may denote anything God has spoken, commanded, or promised." (Willem VanGemeren)

The theme of the glory of Scripture is diligently explored in this psalm, but always in connection with God Himself. Derek Kidner remarks: "This untiring emphasis has led some to accuse the psalmist of worshipping the Word rather than the Lord; but it has been well remarked that every reference here to Scripture, without exception, relates it explicitly to its Author; indeed, every verse from 4 to the end is a prayer for affirmation addressed to Him. This is true piety: a love of God not desiccated by study but refreshed, informed and nourished by it."

"This wonderful psalm, from its great length, helps us to wonder at the immensity of Scripture. From its keeping to one subject it helps us to adore the unity of Scripture; for it is but one. Yet, from the many turns it gives to the same thought, it helps you to

see the variety of Scripture…. Some have said that in it there is an absence of variety, but that is merely the observation of those who have not studied it. I have weighed each word, and looked at each syllable with lengthened meditation; and I bear witness that this sacred song has no tautology in it, but is charmingly varied from beginning to end. Its variety is that of a kaleidoscope: from a few objects a boundless variation is produced. In the kaleidoscope you look once, and there is a strangely beautiful form. You shift the glass a very little, and another shape, equally delicate and beautiful, is before your eyes. So it is here." (Charles Spurgeon)

Being such a long psalm – and the longest chapter in the Bible – this psalm has been of great historical interest. There have been many lengthy works written on this psalm; one of them is by Thomas Manton, a Puritan preacher and writer, who wrote a three-volume work on Psalm 119. Each volume is between 500 and 600 pages, with a total of 1,677 pages. There are 190 chapters in his work, more than one chapter for each verse.

"Luther professed that he prized this Psalm so highly, that he would not take the whole world in exchange for one leaf of it." (Charles Bridges) Some great people have memorized this whole psalm and found great blessing in doing so: John Ruskin (19th century British writer), William Wilberforce (19th century British politician who led the movement to abolish the slave trade in the British Empire), Henry Martyn (19th century pioneer missionary to India), and David Livingstone (19th century pioneer missionary to Africa).

Matthew Henry – the great 18th century Bible commentator – was introduced to Psalm 119 as a child. His father, Philip Henry, told his children to take one verse of Psalm 119 every morning to meditate on, and thereby go through the entire psalm twice in the year. Philip said to his children, "That will bring you to be in love with all the rest of the Scriptures." Perhaps that practice was why Matthew Henry loved the Bible so much that he wrote commentary that is used still today.

George Wishart was the Bishop of Edinburgh in the 17th century (not to be confused with another Scot by the same name who was martyred a century earlier). Wishart was condemned to death for his faith. But when he was on the scaffold, he made use of a custom that allowed the condemned person to choose one psalm to be sung, and he chose Psalm 119. Before two-thirds of the psalm had been sung, his pardon arrived and his life was spared.

A. Aleph א: The blessedness of those who walk in God's word and the longing to do so.

1. (1-2) Blessing declared.

Blessed *are* the undefiled in the way,
Who walk in the law of the LORD!

Blessed *are* those who keep His testimonies,
Who seek Him with the whole heart!

a. **Blessed are the undefiled in the way**: In beginning to describe man's blessedness, the psalmist starts with the idea that being **undefiled in the way** is a blessing.

i. Many people – ancient and modern – think the life lived **undefiled in the way** is *boring* at best. The idea is that if there isn't any defilement in it, then it can't be any fun. Yet the one who walks in God's word knows the true blessedness of living and enjoying an undefiled life.

ii. We can simply say that God is blessed; He wants us to share His blessedness. His word shows us the way to share His blessedness, and it is found by being **undefiled in the way**.

iii. Survey and polling data constantly demonstrate that those who live lives in general conformity to God's standards are happier, enjoy life more, and are more content. Yet the illusion remains for many that a *defiled* life is more "fun."

iv. We need God to show us the way to a happy life, and it is centered on being **undefiled in the way**. "The reason we are not happy is that we sin, and the main reason we sin as much as we do is that we do not know the Bible well enough.... Apart from being instructed by God, human beings do not know how to achieve happiness." (Boice)

b. **Who walk in the law of the LORD**: In the mind of the psalmist, there is a strong and definite connection between being **undefiled in the way** and walking **in the law of the LORD**. To **walk in the law of the LORD** is in fact to be **undefiled in the way**.

i. We wouldn't *know* what a pure life was without God telling us. Certainly, some aspects of a pure life are revealed in human conscience and known widely among humanity. Yet there are other aspects of the pure life that we learn only from the word of God.

ii. **The law of the LORD**: Here the author of Psalm 119 uses, for the first time, a phrase referring to the written revelation of God. The many various ways he referred to God's written revelation shows us how much he knew, loved, and respected God's word.

iii. **The law of the LORD**: The word here used is *torah*. "Here the great word *Torah* is used, the word which to the Hebrew stood for the Law, being the word employed to describe the first division of the Bible, that which we call the Pentateuch." (Morgan)

iv. "To enjoy this beatitude a holy walking must become habitual. This sacred exercise is very different from sluggish piety. 'Blessed are the undefiled in the way who walk in the law of the Lord.' A man may sit down in the road without soiling his skin or fouling his apparel, but that is not enough. There must be progress – practical action – in the Christian life; and in order to experience blessedness we must be doing something for the Master." (Spurgeon)

c. **Blessed are those who keep His testimonies**: To **keep His testimonies** is virtually the same as to **walk in the law of the LORD**. Here is an example of the parallelism common to Hebrew poetry, used for both explanation and emphasis.

i. **Keep** means *doing*, not only *hearing*. "Neither is it enough that we understand or ponder God's precepts, but we must practise them, if we would be happy." (Trapp)

ii. "Blessedness is ascribed to those who treasure up the testimonies of the Lord: in which is implied that they search the Scriptures, that they come to an understanding of them, that they love them, and then that they continue in the practice of them. We must first get a thing before we can keep it. In order to keep it well we must get a firm grip of it: we cannot keep in the heart that which we have not heartily embraced by the affections." (Spurgeon)

iii. "But let me not shrink from the question, do I '*keep his testimonies*' from constraint, or from love? Surely when I consider my own natural aversion and enmity to the law of God, and the danger of self-deception in the external service of the Lord, I have much need to pray." (Bridges)

d. **Who seek Him with the whole heart**: If one will **seek** God **with the whole heart**, it *must* include diligent study of God's written revelation. There are good and important ways to seek God other than through His word (such as in prayer, worship, fasting, serving, and so forth). Yet if these do not include seeking God in and through His word, these other practices can be misdirected.

i. **With the whole heart**: Yet, we do not miss the emphasis on the **heart**. "God is not truly sought by the cold researches of the brain: we must seek him with the heart. Love reveals itself to love: God manifests his heart to the heart of his people. It is in vain that we endeavour to comprehend him by reason; we must apprehend him by affection." (Spurgeon)

ii. The **whole heart** is vital. God is one; and we will not know Him closely until we seek Him with the **whole heart**. This is a challenge to the *divided* heart, not to the *broken* heart. "Strange to say, in scriptural phraseology, a heart…may be broken but not divided; and yet again it may be broken and be whole." (Spurgeon)

2. (3) Blessing described.

They also do no iniquity;
They walk in His ways.

a. **They also do no iniquity**: The idea from verses 1-2 is repeated; these ones *keep His testimonies*, they are *undefiled in the way*, and **they also do no iniquity**. There is a purity and goodness that marks their lives.

b. **They walk in His ways**: They have *learned* **His ways** from the written revelation; but with His word, God also gives grace and power to **walk in His ways**.

3. (4-8) Blessing desired.

You have commanded *us*
To keep Your precepts diligently.
Oh, that my ways were directed
To keep Your statutes!
Then I would not be ashamed,
When I look into all Your commandments.
I will praise You with uprightness of heart,
When I learn Your righteous judgments.
I will keep Your statutes;
Oh, do not forsake me utterly!

a. **You have commanded us to keep Your precepts diligently**: The psalmist connects **commanded** *obedience* with the blessings to the obedient. He shows that the reason God **commanded us to keep** His **precepts diligently** is not only because it honors Him, but also because it is the path to blessing.

i. With the words "**You have commanded us**," we see that the psalmist begins to address God in prayer; a position he will hold through most of the psalm. This shows that he was not only a student of Scripture, but also a man of prayer.

ii. "Because it was a hard thing to rightly understand this word in all its parts, and harder to put it in practice, he therefore intermixed many prayers to God for his help therein, thereby directing and encouraging others to take the same course." (Poole)

iii. **To keep Your precepts**: "God has not commanded us to be diligent in *making* precepts, but in *keeping* them. Some bind yokes upon their own necks, and make bonds and rules for others: but the wise course is to be satisfied with the rules of holy Scripture." (Spurgeon)

b. **Oh, that my ways were directed to keep Your statutes**: This is not only a pious wish; it is also a prayer for the ability to obey God's word. Apart from His work in us, we lack the ability to keep those commands.

i. Here the psalmist gets *personal*. This isn't a theological treatise on written revelation; it is an interaction with the Living God regarding His primary way of showing Himself to us. "It may be considered as the journal of one, who was deeply taught in the things of God, long practiced in the life and walk of faith." (Bridges)

ii. "We do not get very far into the psalm before we discover that he is very much like ourselves, at least in the respect that he has not yet gotten to be like the happy, blessed ones he is describing. He wants to be, but he is not yet." (Boice)

iii. "Without thee I can do nothing; my soul is *unstable* and *fickle*; and it will continue *weak* and *uncertain* till thou *strengthen* and establish it." (Clarke)

c. **Then I would not be ashamed, when I look into all Your commandments**: The psalmist felt the shame that comes when the standard of God's word is compared to our lives. He prayed for the power to live an unashamed life.

i. "'Shame' is the fruit of sin; confidence is the effect of righteousness." (Horne)

ii. "There is a twofold shame; the shame of a guilty conscience; and the shame of a tender conscience. The one is the merit and fruit of sin; the other is an act of grace." (Thomas Manton, cited in Spurgeon)

iii. "...*unto all thy commandments;* so as not to be partial in my obedience, not to allow myself in the practice of any known sin, or in the neglect of any known duty." (Poole)

iv. "Sincerity therefore must be the stamp of my Christian profession. Though utterly unable to render perfect obedience to the least of the commandments, yet my desire and purpose will *have respect unto them all*." (Bridges)

d. **I will praise You with uprightness of heart**: The psalmist found it not only important to **praise** God, but to do it with **uprightness of heart**. He did not want to offer God the *image* of praise or a *moment* of praise when the rest of his life was not upright.

> i. "Be sure that he who prays for holiness will one day praise for happiness. Shame having vanished, silence is broken, and the formerly silent man declares, 'I will praise thee.'" (Spurgeon)

e. **I will keep Your statutes**: This was a promise to **keep** – in the sense of *guarding* – the **statutes** (*huqqim*), the engraved, inscribed, written word of God.

> i. We never forget that in a real sense, only Jesus could say **I will keep Your statutes**. "The many strong expressions of love toward the law, and the repeated resolutions and vows to observe it, will often force us to turn our thoughts to the true David, whose 'meat and drink it was, to do the will of him that sent him.'" (Horne)

f. **Oh, do not forsake me utterly**: We sense the note of *desperation* in the psalmist. He knows and loves God's word, yet is also very conscious of his inability – apart from the work of God in his life – to *live* God's word. If God did **forsake** him, he would be lost.

> i. "*Forsaken* we may be – but not *utterly*. David was *forsaken*, not like Saul. Peter was *forsaken*, not like Judas, *utterly* and for ever.... Mark his dealings with you. Inquire into their reason. Submit to his dispensation. If he *forsakes*, beg his return: but trust your *forsaking* God." (Bridges)

> ii. The heart that sings **do not forsake me utterly** is a heart that longs to be close to God. "Apparently unconsciously, that is without intention, the song reveals the fact that a man who obeys the will of God as revealed, comes to a personal fellowship with God. From beginning to end, the singer sang as one who had personal knowledge of God and direct dealing with Him." (Morgan)

B. Beth ב: Purity of life and meditation on God's word.

Each line of this second section of Psalm 119 begins with the Hebrew letter Beth, which also means "a house." Some have suggested that this section tells us how to make our heart a home for the word of God.

1. (9) A young man finds a cleansed life through God's word.

How can a young man cleanse his way?
By taking heed according to Your word.

a. **How can a young man cleanse his way?** This was no less a difficult question in ancient times than in our own. The **young man** has his own particular challenges in living a pure life.

i. This is a question that some – even some who are numbered among the people of God – never seem to ask for themselves. Sadly, some people never have a concern for moral purity. They echo the prayer of Augustine before his conversion: "Lord, make me chaste – but not yet."

ii. The world tells us, "Have your good time when you are young; get it all out of your system. When you are older you can settle down and be religious and proper." Boice comments on this thinking: "God's answer is quite different. God says, If you are going to live for me, you must begin at the earliest possible moment, without delay, preferably when you are very young."

iii. Even when one has the desire for moral purity, there are many things that may make it difficult for a young man to **cleanse his way**.

- Youthful energy and a sense of carelessness.
- The lack of life wisdom.
- The desire for and gaining of independence.
- Physical and sexual maturity that may run ahead of spiritual and moral maturity.
- Money and the freedom that it brings.
- Young women who may – knowingly or unknowingly – encourage moral impurity.
- The spirit of the age that both expects and promotes moral uncleanness for young men.
- The desire to be accepted by peers who face the same challenges.

iv. "Why is the *young man* so especially called to *cleanse his way*? Because God justly claims the first and the best." (Bridges)

v. God wants to spare the **young man** (and the older man) the bondage of sin. *Experience* has the power to shape our *habits*. Surrender to any temptation; transfer it from the realm of mental contemplation to life experience, and that temptation instantly becomes *much more difficult to resist in the future*. Each successive experience of surrender to temptation builds a habit, reinforced not only spiritually, but also by brain chemistry. Such ingrained habits are more and more difficult to break the more they are experienced; and it is almost impossible to break such habits without *replacing* them with another habit.

vi. Significantly, the words **his way** come from the Hebrew word *orach*. "*Orach*, which we translate *way* here, signifies a *track*, a *rut*, such as is made by the wheel of a cart or chariot." (Clarke) A **young man** the tracks for the rest of his life.

vii. Of course, it is not *only* the **young man** who has these challenges; older men and women of every age have their own challenges in living pure lives. Yet these are often more severely felt in the life of the **young man**.

viii. "From the heartfelt prayers of the surrounding verses it would seem that the *young man* is the psalmist himself in the first place. He is praying rather than preaching." (Kidner)

b. **By taking heed**: A life of moral purity does not happen accidentally. If one does not take **heed**, the natural path is toward impurity and degeneration. One must **take heed** in order to be pure.

c. **According to Your word**: This is *how* one takes heed. The foundation for a morally pure life is found in God's **word**.

- God's word shows us the standard of purity, so we know what is right and what is wrong.
- God's word shows us the reasons for purity, so we understand the wisdom and goodness of God's commands.
- God's word shows us the difficulty of purity, and reminds us to be on guard.
- God's word shows us the blessings of purity, and gives us an incentive to make the necessary sacrifices.
- God's word shows us how to be born again – converted, so our inner man may be transformed after the pattern of ultimate purity, Jesus Christ.
- God's word shows us the way to be empowered by the Holy Spirit, so that we have the spiritual resources to be pure.
- God's word is a refuge against temptation, giving us a way of escape in the season of enticement.
- God's word is a light that clears away the deceptive fog of seduction and temptation.
- God's word is a mirror that helps us see our spiritual and moral condition, and thus walk in purity.
- God's word gives us wise and simple commands, such as to "Flee youthful lusts" (2 Timothy 2:22).
- God's word washes us from impurity, and actually cleanses our life in a spiritual sense (Ephesians 5:26, John 15:3).

- God's word is the key to the renewing of our minds, which in turn is the key to personal, moral, and spiritual transformation (Romans 12:1-2).

- God's word gives a refuge against condemnation when we have been impure, and shows us how to repent and come back to a pure life.

- God's word shows us how to conduct our lives so that we are an encouragement to others in purity.

  i. Jesus spoke specifically of the power of His word to cleanse and keep us pure: *You are already clean because of the word which I have spoken to you* (John 15:3). *Sanctify them by Your truth. Your word is truth* (John 17:17).

  ii. The impact is clear: if you want to **cleanse** your **way**, then you must also **take heed according** to God's word.

  iii. "Young man, the Bible must be your chart, and you must exercise great watchfulness that your way may be according to its directions. You must take heed to your daily life as well as study your Bible, and you must study your Bible that you may take heed to your daily life. With the greatest care a man will go astray if his map misleads him; but with the most accurate map he will still lose his road if he does not take heed to it." (Spurgeon)

  iv. This idea is communicated in Proverbs 2:10-12: *When wisdom enters your heart, and knowledge is pleasant to your soul, discretion will preserve you; understanding will keep you, to deliver you from the way of evil, from the man who speaks perverse things.*

  v. We remind ourselves that Jesus answered temptation with the word of God (Matthew 4:1-10). "He who became man for our salvation, passed through this state of youth, undefiled, that he might, as it were, reclaim and consecrate it anew to God." (Horne)

2. (10-11) How one takes heed of God's word.

With my whole heart I have sought You;
Oh, let me not wander from Your commandments!
Your word I have hidden in my heart,
That I might not sin against You.

a. **With my whole heart I have sought You**: Here the psalmist declares his dedication to God, and at the same time recognizes his weakness in being able to maintain such a dedication (**Oh, let me not wander from Your commandments**).

i. **With my whole heart I have sought You** reminds us that Scripture was no mere textbook to the psalmist; it was how he **sought** and met with God. "His heart had gone after God himself: he had not only desired to obey his laws, but to commune with his person." (Spurgeon)

ii. **Let me not wander** helps us put in perspective the many claims to purity and devotion in this psalm (and others). They are understood in the light of *dependence upon God*, not in the sense of self-righteous pride.

iii. "The path of purity is that of caution conditioned by the Word of God. This caution is further manifested in the distrust of self, and earnest seeking to be kept in the way of God's commandments." (Morgan)

iv. "When the soul is thus conscious of 'following the Lord fully,' there is a peculiar *dread of wandering*. In a careless or half-hearted state, wanderings are not watched, so long as they do not lead to any open declension." (Bridges)

b. **Your word I have hidden in my heart**: The psalmist knew the value of taking God's word and *hiding* it in his heart. It is **hidden** in the sense that it is on the *inside*, where no one can see it, and it is *safe* so that no one can take it away.

i. We can be assured that before this word was **hidden in** his **heart**, it was received in his *mind*. The psalmist heard and read the word of God, and thought about it continually, until it became ingrained in both his mind and his heart.

ii. "Memorizing is precisely what is called for, since it is only when the Word of God is readily available in our minds that we are able to recall it in moments of need and profit by it." (Boice)

iii. "If God's word be only in his *Bible*, and not also in his *heart*, he may soon and easily be surprised into his *besetting* sin." (Clarke)

c. **That I might not sin against You**: Here the psalmist states one *benefit* from having God's word **hidden in** his **heart**. It is a defense against sin, for all the reasons discussed above and more.

i. "The personal way in which the man of God did this is also noteworthy: 'With my whole heart have *I* sought thee.' Whatever others might choose to do he had already made his choice and placed the Word in his innermost soul as his dearest delight, and however others might transgress, his aim was after holiness: 'That *I* might not sin against thee.'" (Spurgeon)

3. (12) A prayer for instruction.

Blessed *are* You, O LORD**!**
Teach me Your statutes.

> a. **Blessed are You, O L**ORD: The psalmist seems to interrupt his thoughts on the connection between God's word and a pure life with this expression of praise. The greatness of these ideas and the reality of them in his life has made this praise necessary.

> b. **Teach me Your statutes**: This demonstrates the humility of the psalmist. Though filled with God's word and a desire for purity, he sensed his constant need for instruction by God. He didn't simply need to *read* God's **statutes**; he pleaded with God to **teach** him.

>> i. This saying is written in the front of some Bibles: "This book will keep you from sin. Sin will keep you from this book." The psalmist understood this principle, and longed for God to be his teacher, and to keep him in God's great book.

>> ii. "We need to be disciples or learners – '*teach me;*' but what an honour to have God himself for a teacher: how bold is [the psalmist] to beg the blessed God to teach him!" (Spurgeon)

4. (13-16) A declaration of commitment.

With my lips I have declared
All the judgments of Your mouth.
I have rejoiced in the way of Your testimonies,
As *much as* in all riches.
I will meditate on Your precepts,
And contemplate Your ways.
I will delight myself in Your statutes;
I will not forget Your word.

> a. **With my lips I have declared all the judgments of Your mouth**: The psalmist understood the importance of not only silently reading or hearing the word of God, but also the importance in *saying* it. To declare God's word (**all the judgments of Your mouth**) with his **lips** was another part of his relationship with and love for God.

>> i. We may confidently conclude that there is not enough – never enough – of this among the people of God. God's people should have His word not only in their minds and hearts, but also upon their **lips**. *Saying it* is powerful and must not be neglected.

ii. "When we make the Scriptures the subject of our conversation, we glorify God, we edify our neighbours, and we improve ourselves." (Horne)

b. **I have rejoiced in the way of Your testimonies, as much as in all riches**: The psalmist understood the true value of God's word; it gave him as much joy as **all riches** might.

i. It could be fairly asked of every Christian: "For what amount would you deny yourself to ever hear or read God's word again?" It is to be feared that many, like Esau, would sell this birthright treasure for the equivalent of a bowl of stew.

ii. "We may also observe here an evidence of adoption. Obedience is not a burden, but a *delight*. The servant may *perform* the statutes of God, but it is only the son who '*delights in them.*'" (Bridges)

c. **I will meditate...and contemplate...I will delight...I will not forget Your word**: The greatness of God's word has led the psalmist to great resolution for his life. His life will be filled with God's word, in his mind (**meditate...contemplate**), in his heart (**delight**), and in his habits (**not forget**).

i. "Meditation is recalling what we have committed to memory and then turning it over and over in our minds to see the fullest implications and applications of the truth." (Boice)

ii. **I will delight**: "The word is very emphatical: *evetva eshtaasha, I will skip about and jump for joy.*" (Clarke)

iii. This giving of the fullness of life to God's word – in mind, heart, and habits – is a good description of what the psalmist meant by *taking heed* in verse 9. The young man will *cleanse his way*, and enjoy the fullness of such a God-honoring life.

iv. We can almost hear a challenge from the psalmist: "You live your compromising, impure life that thinks it knows pleasure and satisfaction; I will cleanse my way and give the fullness of my life to God and His word, and we will see who will be more blessed, more happy, and more filled with life."

C. Gimel ג: The word of God and the trials of life.

1. (17) A prayer for blessing, so that God's word can be kept.

Deal bountifully with Your servant,
***That* I may live and keep Your word.**

a. **Deal bountifully with Your servant**: This is a wonderful request: boldly asking for blessing (**deal bountifully**), while at the same time coming humbly before God (**Your servant**). The servant properly depends upon the master for his bounty.

> i. In saying, **Deal bountifully**, the psalmist was asking for a lot, not just a little. "The believer, like [the psalmist], is a man of large expectations.... We may, indeed, be too bold in our manner of approach to God; but we cannot be too bold in our expectations from him." (Bridges)

> ii. "He begs for a liberality of grace, after the fashion of one who prayed, 'O Lord, thou must give me great mercy or no mercy, for little mercy will not serve my turn.'" (Spurgeon)

b. **That I may live and keep Your word**: This is *why* the psalmist asked for God's blessing. It was not for personal indulgence or even comfort, but so that God's **word** might be *lived* and *kept*. This is a wonderful, God-honoring prayer that is heard in heaven.

> i. As the rest of this section will demonstrate, the psalmist prayed this because of great problems and pressures that had beset him. This section of the psalm shows us that the author was a man who had suffered deeply. He had known persecution (verses 22-23), deprivation and fear for his life (verse 17), seasons when he seemed to get nothing from God's word (verse 18), and loneliness, rejection, and a sense of abandonment (verses 19-20).

> ii. In the midst of these trials, he wanted to **live** – not only surviving, but also a better *quality* of life, especially in regard to God.

> iii. **That I may live**: "[This] is the first of many such prayers.... While some of them could refer simply to surviving an illness or an attack, others are clearly qualitative, speaking of life that is worthy of the name, or in our terms, spiritual life, found in fellowship with God." (Kidner)

2. (18) A prayer for insight, so that God's word can be understood.

Open my eyes, that I may see
Wondrous things from Your law.

a. **Open my eyes, that I may see**: The psalmist recognized that without God's enlightenment, he could not **see** what he could and should from God's word.

> i. "The verb 'open' in verse 18 is used in the Balaam story where the Lord opened Balaam's eyes so he could see the angel of the Lord

standing in the road with his sword drawn. It has to do with removing a veil, or covering." (Boice)

ii. This reminds us that it isn't the word of God that needs changing, as if it were obscure; we are the ones who are veiled and can't understand the word of God apart from the work of the Spirit. Paul's eyes were unveiled when he was converted (Acts 9:18); it was as if scales had dropped from his eyes.

iii. "In order to *keep God's word*, must we not pray to understand it? What then is this prayer? Not – give me a plainer Bible – but *open my eyes* to know my Bible. Not – show me some new revelations beside *the law* – but make me *behold the wonders of the law*." (Bridges)

iv. The psalmist didn't need new revelation; he needed to see the revelation that was already given. He didn't need new eyes; he needed to see more clearly with the eyes he already had.

b. **Wondrous things from Your law**: There are **wondrous things** in Scripture; but they can only be seen when the eyes are opened by God. This means that *prayer* is an important (and often neglected) part of Bible study.

i. Not *everyone* sees the **wondrous things** in God's word, but when he *does* see them, he should regard it as evidence of God's blessing and favor.

ii. Jesus rejoiced that God revealed His wisdom this way: *At that time Jesus answered and said, "I thank You, Father, Lord of heaven and earth, that You have hidden these things from the wise and prudent and have revealed them to babes."* (Matthew 11:25)

iii. God has given man a sense of wonder, and there are certain things that prompt it. The new and unexpected can cause wonder, the beautiful and great can cause wonder, and the mysterious and unknown can cause wonder. God has provided for this sense of wonder by giving us His word. The Holy Spirit can make us alive to the Bible, and helps us constantly see things that are new and unexpected, things that are great and beautiful, and things that are mysterious and unknown. It is a shame that many Christians look for their sense of wonder to be satisfied without looking to the word of God.

iv. Think of all there is in the Bible that *you don't see*. Think of all the wonder, all the treasure that is *there*, but you don't see it. You *can* see some things, though you can't see *everything*, and sometimes you will think you see things that are not really there. Those who see more than you are not necessarily smarter or better; their eyes are just more open.

v. "If we want to see wonderful things in the Scriptures, it is not enough for us merely to ask God to open our eyes that we might see them. We must also study the Bible carefully. The Holy Spirit is given not to make our study unnecessary but to make it effective." (Boice)

3. (19-20) A prayer for revelation, longing for God's word.

I *am* a stranger in the earth;
Do not hide Your commandments from me.
My soul breaks with longing
For Your judgments at all times.

a. **I am a stranger in the earth; do not hide Your commandments from me**: This is the same request as in the previous verse, but made for a different reason. The psalmist wants to know and keep God's word, and prays for it to be so; but now he makes the request because he recognizes that the **earth** is not his home, and he needs communication with his true homeland.

i. When we think of the man who says **I am a stranger in the earth**, we should not think of the man who wanders alone through the wilderness. We should think of the man who lives among others and is surrounded by the vanity of the world's joys, but all the while knows, "I don't really belong here."

ii. "If you are trying to follow God, the world is going to treat you as an alien, for that is what you will be. You cannot expect to be at home in it, and if you are, well, it is an indication that you really do not belong to Christ or at least are living far from him." (Boice)

b. **My soul breaks with longing for Your judgments at all times**: His **soul** longed for God's word so much because he was indeed **a stranger in the earth**; for those who feel perfectly at home in this world, the word that comes to them from heaven is less precious.

i. **My soul breaks**: "We have a similar expression: *It broke my heart, That is heart-breaking, She died of a broken heart.* It expresses excessive longing, grievous disappointment, hopeless love, accumulated sorrow. By this we may see the *hungering* and *thirsting* which the psalmist had after righteousness, often mingled with much *despondency*." (Clarke)

ii. "Spiritual desires are the shadows of coming blessings. What God intends to give us he first sets us longing for. Hence the wonderful efficacy of prayer, because prayer is the embodiment of a longing inspired of God because he intends to bestow the blessing. What are thy longings, then, my hearer?" (Spurgeon)

iii. "Longing lingers not within a lifeless corpse. Where the heart is breaking with desire there is life. This may comfort some of you: you have not attained as yet to the holiness you admire, but you long for it: ah, then, you are a living soul, the life of God is in you." (Spurgeon)

4. (21-24) A prayer for refuge in God's word.

You rebuke the proud—the cursed,
Who stray from Your commandments.
Remove from me reproach and contempt,
For I have kept Your testimonies.
Princes also sit *and* **speak against me,**
***But* Your servant meditates on Your statutes.**
Your testimonies also *are* **my delight**
***And* my counselors.**

a. **You rebuke the proud**: Those who **stray** from God's **commandments** are both **proud** (their disobedience is evidence of willfulness) and **cursed** (no good can come from their disobedience).

i. "Let the histories of Cain, Pharaoh, Haman, Nebuchadnezzar, and Herod, exhibit *the proud under the rebuke and curse of God.*" (Bridges)

b. **Remove from me reproach and contempt**: The psalmist recognized that even **princes also sit and speak** against him; yet he would not turn from meditation on God's word. Instead, he simply prayed, asking God to deal with the **reproach and contempt** that notable people put on him for his love of God's word.

i. **Reproach** is unpleasant; it is the expression of disapproval or disappointment. Yet **contempt** is even worse; it is the feeling that a person or thing is beneath consideration, that he is worthless and useless.

ii. Beyond **reproach** and **contempt**, these enemies also *slandered* the psalmist (**sit and speak against me**). Slander goes beyond our "stranger" status. When the world thinks we are strange and wonders if we belong, it sees us correctly. When they slander us, they tell lies about us and falsely accuse us.

iii. "The best way to deal with slander is to pray about it: God will either remove it, or remove the sting from it. Our own attempts at clearing ourselves are usually failures." (Spurgeon)

c. **Your testimonies also are my delight and my counselors**: The psalmist delighted and trusted in God's word much more than in the high people of this earth (such as **princes**).

i. "Most men covet a prince's good word, and to be spoken ill of by a great man is a great discouragement to them, but the Psalmist bore his trial with holy calmness.... While his enemies took counsel with each other the holy man took counsel with the testimonies of God." (Spurgeon)

ii. **My counselors**: "Yet a mere cursory reading will never realize to us its holy delight or counsel. It must be brought home to our own experiences, and consulted on those trivial occasions of every day, when, unconscious of our need of Divine direction, we are too often inclined to lean to our own counsel." (Bridges)

iii. In this section the psalmist saw many things that hindered his reception of the word of God and his fellowship with God, and he prayed to be protected from them.

- He saw the danger of a dead soul and a cold heart; therefore he prayed, "*Deal bountifully with Your servant, that I may live and keep Your word.*"

- He saw the danger of darkened understanding; therefore he prayed, "*Open my eyes, that I may see wondrous things from Your law.*"

- He saw the danger of living as a stranger in a strange land; therefore he prayed, "*Do not hide Your commandments from me.*"

- He saw his own weakness and instability; therefore he prayed, "*My soul breaks with longing.*"

- He saw the danger of pride, evident in those who attacked him; therefore he recognized that the proud are "*the cursed, who stray for Your commandments.*"

- He saw the reproach and contempt that came upon him, and how those could shake his standing; therefore he prayed, "*Remove from me reproach and contempt.*"

- He saw rulers plotting against him; therefore he prayed, "*Your testimonies are my delight.*"

iv. "He rises superior to these sorrowful circumstances by keeping the testimonies, meditating on the statutes, and so finding delight therein." (Morgan)

D. Daleth ד: Revived from the dust.

1. (25) A prayer for revival from a soul who feels dead.

My soul clings to the dust;
Revive me according to Your word.

a. **My soul clings to the dust**: The psalmist used a strong image to say that he felt near death in his current crisis; **dust** was the place of death, the place of mourning, and the place of humiliation.

i. "Whatever was the cause of his complaint, it was no surface evil, but an affair of his inmost spirit; his *soul* cleaved to the dust; and it was not a casual and accidental falling into the dust, but a continuous and powerful tendency, or *cleaving* to the earth." (Spurgeon)

b. **Revive me according to Your word**: From this low place, the prayer for *revival* came. The psalmist asked for life and vitality to be restored, and he asked that it happen **according to Your word**.

i. Revival comes from a sense of spiritual need and lowliness. True revival – in the Biblical and historical sense – is marked by a shamed awareness of sin and an urgency to confess and make things right (mentioned verse 26).

ii. The psalmist knew what he needed. "One would have thought that he would have asked for comfort or upraising, but he knew that these would come out of increased life, and therefore he sought that blessing which is the root of the rest. When a person is depressed in spirit, weak, and bent towards the ground, the main thing is to increase his stamina and put more life into him; then his spirit revives." (Spurgeon)

iii. **According to Your word** shows us that God *uses* His word in bringing revival. Works that claim to be revival can be measured **according to** His **word**.

2. (26-27) Teach me, make me understand.

I have declared my ways, and You answered me;
Teach me Your statutes.
Make me understand the way of Your precepts;
So shall I meditate on Your wonderful works.

a. **I have declared my ways...teach me Your statutes**: The idea behind **I have declared my ways** is that the psalmist told God *everything* about himself and his life. He confessed fully and freely before God.

i. "Can each one of us now say, in this sense, 'I have declared my ways' to the Lord? For this should be done, not only at our first coming to him, but continually throughout the whole of our life. We should look over each day, and sum up the errors of the day, and say, 'I have declared my ways,' – my naughty ways, my wicked ways, my wandering ways, my backsliding ways, my cold, indifferent ways, my proud ways.'" (Spurgeon)

ii. The psalmist had a wonderful liberty in conversation; he spoke to God as a dear friend. "How often do we treat our Almighty Friend as if we were weary of dealing with him!" (Bridges)

b. **Make me understand the way of Your precepts**: The psalmist understood that he needed more than *knowledge*; he also needed *understanding*. With both he would **meditate on** God's **wonderful works**.

i. **Make me understand**: "It is concerned with a deep understanding, one that goes beyond a mere understanding of the words to a profound understanding of what they reveal about the nature of God, the gospel, and God's ways." (Boice)

ii. "'Teach me thy statutes.' I think the psalmist means this, 'My Lord, I have told thee all; now, wilt thou tell me all? I have declared to thee my ways; now, wilt thou teach me thy ways? I have confessed to thee how I have broken thy statutes; wilt thou not give me thy statutes back again?'" (Spurgeon)

3. (28) A plea for strength from a shrinking soul.

My soul melts from heaviness;
Strengthen me according to Your word.

a. **My soul melts from heaviness**: The problems surrounding the psalmist (as seen in verses 17-24) made his soul heavy, as if it would melt. He felt that he had no strength or stability within.

b. **Strengthen me according to Your word**: Therefore, he prayed for *strength*, and that this strength would come both from and **according to** God's **word**.

i. "The singer is bowed down, overwhelmed. He sorely needs succour and strength. How does he seek it? Not by asking for pity, but by a determined application to the law of his God." (Morgan)

ii. "This *melting heaviness* has not wrought its work, until it has bowed us before the throne of grace with the pleading cry of faith – *Strengthen thou me!*" (Bridges)

4. (29-30) Choosing the way of truth.

Remove from me the way of lying,
And grant me Your law graciously.
I have chosen the way of truth;
Your judgments I have laid *before me*.

a. **Remove from me the way of lying.... I have chosen the way of truth**: The psalmist sensed the common temptation to lie; yet he determined to choose **the way of truth**.

>i. **Remove me from the way of lying**: "...a sin that David, through diffidence, fell into frequently. See 1 Samuel 21:2,8, where he roundly telleth three or four lies; and the like he did, 1 Samuel 27:8,10; this evil he saw by himself, and here prayeth against it." (Trapp)

>ii. **Grant me Your law graciously**: The verb translated **graciously** "...actually has the sense of 'graciously teach,' a single word. The full thought is, If we are to be kept from sin, it must be by the grace of God exercised through the teaching of his Word." (Boice)

b. **Your judgments I have laid before me**: This is *how* the psalmist was able to choose **the way of truth**: He was in close relationship with the word of God.

>i. "Men do not drop into the right way by chance; they must choose it, and continue to choose it, or they will soon wander from it." (Spurgeon)

5. (31-32) Rescue me; enlarge my heart.

I cling to Your testimonies;
O LORD, do not put me to shame!
I will run the course of Your commandments,
For You shall enlarge my heart.

a. **I cling to Your testimonies; O LORD, do not put me to shame**: The psalmist understood that if he were to give himself entirely to God – to **cling** to His word as a shipwrecked man clings to a floating plank in the sea – then he could trust that God would not allow him to be **put...to shame**. This was well-placed confidence.

>i. In the beginning of the section, he is clinging to the dust (verse 25); by the end he is clinging to God's word. In the beginning he is laid low; now he is joyfully running with all his strength in the race God's word sets before him.

>ii. The *clinging* of this verse connects well with the *choosing* of the previous verse. "Having once chosen our road, it remains that we persevere in it; since better had it been for us never to have known the way of truth, than to forsake it, when known." (Horne)

b. **I will run the course of Your commandments**: After beginning low in the dust, now the psalmist is *running*. He has moved in a beautiful progression, from confessing to choosing to clinging to running.

c. **For You shall enlarge my heart**: The psalmist comes back to a familiar theme, not only of the greatness of God's word, but also of his acute sense of weakness and dependence upon God. He must have his **heart** enlarged: made bigger, stronger, better, and more steadfast. His confidence is that God would do this through His word.

> i. "The remedy therefore is in that *enlargement*, which embraces a wider expanse of light, and a more full confidence of love.... He does not say – I will make no efforts, unless thou work for me; but if *thou wilt enlarge – I will run*. Weakness is not the plea for indolence, but for quickening grace.... The secret of Christian energy and success is a *heart enlarged* in the love of God." (Bridges)

E. He ה: A plea for guidance and life.

He *is the fifth letter of the Hebrew alphabet, and it is used at the beginning of verbs to make them causative. Therefore, the prayers in this section have the meaning, "Cause me to learn," "Cause me to understand," "Cause me to walk" and so forth.*

1. (33-35) A prayer for instruction for righteous living.

Teach me, O LORD, the way of Your statutes,
And I shall keep it *to* the end.
Give me understanding, and I shall keep Your law;
Indeed, I shall observe it with *my* whole heart.
Make me walk in the path of Your commandments,
For I delight in it.

a. **Teach me, O LORD, the way of Your statutes, and I shall keep it to the end**: The psalmist here stresses his great *desire* to keep the **way** and word of God. If God would teach him, he would persevere and **keep** the way **to the end**.

> i. "The general desire expressed in this division is that for guidance. It is not an appeal for direction in some special case of difficulty, but rather for the clear manifestation of the meaning of the will of God." (Morgan)

> ii. Only a God-changed heart can pray this. Left to himself, man is unable to keep the way and word of God (much less **keep it to the end**). Philippians 2:13 tells us that it is *God who works in you both to will and to do for His good pleasure*. Here the psalmist prays as one who has received the *will*, and now prays for the *doing* of it.

> iii. We should have the expectation of following God and His word **to the end**. "The end of our keeping the law will come only when we cease to breathe; no good man will think of marking a date and saying,

'It is enough, I may now relax my watch, and live after the manner of men.'" (Spurgeon)

b. **Give me understanding…I shall observe it with my whole heart**: Without this understanding, the psalmist could not follow the desire of his transformed heart. We need **understanding** to persevere in the faith.

> i. "The understanding operates upon the affections; it convinces the heart of the beauty of the law, so that the soul loves it with all its powers; and then it reveals the majesty of the lawgiver, and the whole nature bows before his supreme will." (Spurgeon)

> ii. The psalmist had no doubt that God had *given* His word to us; his only fear was that he would not understand it (or be distracted from it). Yet he was utterly confident that God had spoken and that it could be understood rightly by the prayerful heart and mind.

> iii. "'To the end' means without time limit, and 'with all my heart' means without reservation." (Boice)

c. **Make me walk in the path of Your commandments, for I delight in it**: Despite his **delight** and desire for God's word, the psalmist knows he cannot **walk** in God's **path** without God's empowering.

> i. "We need no instruction in the way of sin…. But for a child of God, this is a prayer for constant use." (Bridges)

> ii. "This is the cry of a child that longs to walk, but is too feeble; of a pilgrim who is exhausted, yet pants to be on the march; of a lame man who pines to be able to run." (Spurgeon)

2. (36-37) God's word and the problem of material things.

Incline my heart to Your testimonies,
And not to covetousness.
Turn away my eyes from looking at worthless things,
***And* revive me in Your way.**

a. **Incline my heart to Your testimonies, and not to covetousness**: The psalmist rightly understood that **covetousness** was a threat to walking in God's way. A heart inclined toward God's word would help him be satisfied in what God provides.

> i. "He is asking God to turn his heart toward the Bible *rather than* allowing him to pursue selfish gain. For the first time he is confessing a potentially divided mind." (Boice)

> ii. The Bible tells us how covetousness has ruined many people.

- Balaam sold out God's people and his own soul because he coveted (Numbers 22, 2 Peter 2:14-16).

- Ahab murdered because he coveted (1 Kings 21:1-13).

- David committed adultery and murder because he coveted (2 Samuel 11:2-17).

- Achan stole and brought Israel to defeat because he coveted (Joshua 7:21).

- Judas stole from his fellow disciples and betrayed Jesus because he coveted (John 12:6 and Matthew 26:14-16).

- Gehazi lied because he coveted (2 Kings 5:20-27).

- Ananias lied to the Holy Spirit because he coveted (Acts 5:1-6).

iii. "It is a handmaid of all sins; for there is no sin which a covetous man will not serve for his gain." (William Cowper, cited in Spurgeon)

b. **Turn away my eyes from looking at worthless things**: The psalmist rightly understood that some things, comparatively speaking, are **worthless things**. They are of no value for eternity and little value for the present age. He prayed that God would empower and enable him to **turn away** his **eyes** and attention from such things.

i. Many lives are wasted because people find themselves unwilling or unable to **turn away** their **eyes** from **worthless things**. The modern world with its media and entertainment technology brings before us an endless river of **worthless things** to occupy not only our eyes and time, but also our heart and minds.

ii. Some things are clearly **worthless**; some things are thought by many to be worthy, but are in fact **worthless**:

- **worthless** because they do no good.
- **worthless** because they do not last.
- **worthless** because they help no one else.
- **worthless** because they build no faith, hope, or love.
- **worthless** because they distract from things that are truly worthy.
- **worthless** because they have nothing to do with Jesus.

iii. The psalmist understood that he had a natural tendency toward **worthless things**, so he prayed for that natural tendency to be counter-acted. "Keeping the eye is a grand means of 'keeping the heart' (Numbers 15:39, Job 31:1)." (Bridges)

iv. Yet the eyes are so powerful that the psalmist had to pray – to pray for power outside himself to turn his eyes from worthless things. Does the psalmist have no eyelids or no muscles in his neck to turn the head? We all sympathize with this prayer; the eyes are so small – yet they can lead the whole person, and often lead to destruction. This is because the eyes lead the heart, lead the mind, and can lead the whole person. He prayed this, "…lest looking cause liking and lusting." (Trapp)

v. He did not gouge out his own eyes or pray God to do it; instead he wanted to look another way, a better way. The best way to look away from sin is to look at something else. "The prayer is not so much that the eyes may be shut as '*turned away;*' for we need to have them open, but directed to right objects." (Spurgeon)

c. **And revive me in Your way**: This is another prayer for revival – this time, to be made alive again in the **way** (or path) of God. The psalmist wanted to walk in God's way, and to do it with a revived heart. He prayed for deadness in one direction – toward **worthless things** – and for life in another direction – toward God's **way**.

i. "As I desire that I may be dull and dead in affections to worldly vanities; so, Lord, make me lively, and vigorous, and fervent in thy work and service." (Poole)

ii. "He goes at once to him in whom were all his fresh springs. Life is the peculiar sphere of God: he is the Lord and Giver of life. No man ever received spiritual life, or the renewal of it, from any other source but the living God. Beloved, this is worth recollecting, for we are very apt when we feel ourselves declining to look anywhere but to the Lord. We, too, often look within." (Spurgeon)

iii. God has many ways to revive us. Spurgeon listed some:

- *God's word*: "There are promises in God's word of such effectual restorative power, that, if they be but fed upon…they will make a dwarf into a giant in the twinkling of an eye."

- *Affliction*: "It is wonderful how a little touch of the spur will quicken our sluggish natures."

- *Great mercies*: "A man may be stirred up to diligence by a sense of gratitude to God for great mercies."

- *Christian example*: "I believe the reading of holy biographies has been exceedingly blessed of God."

- *Warm-hearted ministry*: "We should select not that which tickles the ear most, but that which most enlivens the heart."

3. (38-40) Longing for revival from God's word.

Establish Your word to Your servant,
Who *is devoted* to fearing You.
Turn away my reproach which I dread,
For Your judgments *are* good.
Behold, I long for Your precepts;
Revive me in Your righteousness.

a. **Establish Your word to Your servant**: This is not a prayer for God to change His word in some way; indeed, the word of the LORD is established forever (Isaiah 40:8). This is a prayer for a change in the heart and mind of the **servant** of God, so that the word of the LORD would be established in him.

i. **Establish Your word to Your servant** is much the same idea as what Mary said to Gabriel regarding the word of the Lord that he brought to her: *Let it be to me according to your word* (Luke 1:38).

b. **Turn away my reproach which I dread, for Your judgments are good**: While declaring the goodness of God's judgments, the psalmist also prayed that his disgrace (**reproach**) would be turned away by the merciful God.

i. There is some **reproach** [disgrace] that we face as faithful followers of Jesus. Paul suffered these kind of reproaches (1 Timothy 4:10) and indeed even took pleasure in them (2 Corinthians 12:10). We expect and receive **reproach** as followers of Jesus (Hebrews 13:13, 1 Peter 4:14).

ii. "The Lord's grace to him will remove disgrace and will promote the fear of God." (VanGemeren)

c. **I long for Your precepts; revive me in Your righteousness**: Again the psalmist prays for revival. The prayer comes from a heart that loves God's word (**Your precepts**), asking to be made alive in the **righteousness** of God.

F. Waw ו: Liberty comes from loving God's word.

"*This commences a new portion of the Psalm, in which each verse begins with the letter* Vau, *or* ו. *There are almost no words in Hebrew that begin with this letter, which is properly a conjunction, and hence in each of the verses in this section the beginning of the verse is in the original a conjunction* – vau." (Barnes, cited in Spurgeon)

1. (41-42) Receiving from God and defending against man.

Let Your mercies come also to me, O LORD–
Your salvation according to Your word.

So shall I have an answer for him who reproaches me,
For I trust in Your word.

a. **Let Your mercies come...Your salvation according to Your word**: Here the psalmist acknowledged that *mercy and salvation come from God to man through the word of God.* The word of God doesn't merely point us toward mercy and salvation, as if it were a self-help book. It actually brings mercy and salvation to us.

i. The psalmist rightly said **mercies**, in the plural. God's gracious mercy to us is so great that it can only be described in the plural, with mercy piled on top of mercy.

ii. "He desires *mercy* as well as teaching, for he was guilty as well as ignorant." (Spurgeon)

- He needed mercy, not only teaching.

- He needed many mercies, so the request is in the plural.

- He needed mercy from God more than from man, so the request is made to God.

iii. The ancient Hebrew word here translated **mercies** is *hesed*. For centuries it was translated with words like *mercy, kindness,* and *love.* But in 1927, a scholar named Nelson Glueck (among others) argued that the real idea behind *hesed* was "covenant loyalty" and not so much love or mercy. Many disagreed and there is no good reason for changing the long-held understanding of *hesed* and taking it as a word that mainly emphasizes covenant loyalty (see R. Laird Harris on *hesed* in *Theological Wordbook of the Old Testament*).

iv. "It must *come to me*; or I shall never come to it." (Bridges)

b. **So shall I have an answer for him who reproaches me, for I trust in Your word**: Trust in God's word provides an answer to those who reproach us. The disapproving voices we often hear can be answered by our abiding trust in the approval that we believers find in God.

i. When we believe who God is and what He has done for us in Jesus Christ, the disapproval of this world is answered.

2. (43-44) A prayer that the word of God would remain in the mouth of the psalmist.

And take not the word of truth utterly out of my mouth,
For I have hoped in Your ordinances.
So shall I keep Your law continually,
Forever and ever.

a. **Take not the word of truth utterly out of my mouth**: This request is rooted in the understanding that it is only by the goodness and grace of God that His word does dwell with us. Therefore the prayer comes that it may continue so.

    i. This is true for humanity in general; hypothetically, God might have created man yet never communicated with him by His word.

    ii. Yet it is also true for the individual who is awakened and attentive to God's word – because of the work of God in him – so it is wise and worthy to pray that it would remain so.

    iii. It is true most of all for those who proclaim the word of God. "He who has once preached the gospel from his heart is filled with horror at the idea of being put out of the ministry; he will crave to be allowed a little share in the holy testimony, and will reckon his silent Sabbaths to be days of banishment and punishment." (Spurgeon)

b. **For I have hoped in Your ordinances**: His past hope is the ground for his future expectation. He has **hoped** in the word of God (**ordinances**) in the past, and he has not been disappointed.

c. **So shall I keep Your law continually**: The psalmist wanted God's word to remain in his **mouth** so that he could keep God's law. This was to glorify God through obedience to His word, not for any self-serving purpose.

3. (45-48) Loving the word that brings liberty.

And I will walk at liberty,
For I seek Your precepts.
I will speak of Your testimonies also before kings,
And will not be ashamed.
And I will delight myself in Your commandments,
Which I love.
My hands also I will lift up to Your commandments,
Which I love,
And I will meditate on Your statutes.

a. **And I will walk at liberty**: Having just spoken of the obedience that comes from having God's word within, the psalmist now testifies that this obedience brings a life of **liberty**. Freedom comes through obedience and submission to God.

    i. It is proven in many lives, in both the positive and the negative: Obedience and the pursuit of God's word and wisdom lead to **liberty**. Disobedience, rejection of God's word, and reliance upon one's own wisdom lead to bondage.

ii. "Saints find no bondage in sanctity. The Spirit of holiness is a free spirit; he sets men at liberty and enables them to resist every effort to bring them under subjection. The way of holiness is not a track for slaves, but the King's highway for freemen." (Spurgeon)

b. **I will speak of Your testimonies also before kings, and will not be ashamed**: This is an example of the **liberty** just mentioned. To have the boldness and ability to speak freely of God and His great word before **kings** and the great men of this earth shows true **liberty**.

i. "This is part of his liberty; he is free from fear of the greatest, proudest, and most tyrannical of men." (Spurgeon)

c. **And I will delight myself in Your commandments**: That he set this in an **I will** statement shows that delighting in God's word is a choice, a matter of the will. The psalmist didn't wait for a feeling of delight to overcome him; he simply said, **I will delight myself in Your commandments**.

i. In verse 44, the psalmist proclaimed: *So shall I keep Your law continually*. In the verses following he lists at least three things that come from this life of obedience: **liberty**, confidence (**will not be ashamed**), and **delight**. These are blessings of the obedient life – blessings not earned by our obedience, but simply enjoyed by those of us who will keep His law continually.

d. **Which I love...which I love**: The strength and the depth of the psalmist's love for God's word are impressive. That love is manifested not only in the feeling of **delight**, but also in an act of honor (**My hands also I will lift up to Your commandments**), and time and energy spent with God's word (**I will meditate**).

i. We may say that all true love has these three components: feeling, the giving of honor, and the desire to spend time and energy in knowing the beloved. This is a good measure of our love for God's word.

ii. **My hands also I will lift up to Your commandments**: "A bold expression of yearning for God's revelation in Scripture." (Kidner)

iii. "O shame to Christians who feel so little affection to the *Gospel of Christ*, when we see such cordial, conscientious, and inviolate attachment in a Jew to the laws and ordinances of Moses, that did not afford a thousandth part of the privileges!" (Clarke)

iv. "Why then is the Bible read only – not *meditated on*? Because it is not *loved*. We do not go to it, as the hungry man to his food, as the miser to his treasure. The loss is incalculable." (Bridges)

G. Zayin ז: The power of God's word to comfort and strengthen.

1. (49-50) God's word brings comfort.

Remember the word to Your servant,
Upon which You have caused me to hope.
This *is* my comfort in my affliction,
For Your word has given me life.

a. **Remember the word to Your servant**: The psalmist understood that God could never forget His word. Speaking in the manner of men, this was a plea for God to fulfill the promises stated in His word. God wants His people to plead His stated promises back to Him in prayer.

i. "When we hear any promise in the word of God, let us turn it into a prayer. God's promises are his bonds. Sue him on his bond. He loves that we should wrestle with him by his promises." (Sibbes, cited in Spurgeon)

ii. Spurgeon said that he often carried with him a small book of God's promises (*Clarke's Precious Promises*), and he turned to specific promises to help him at needful times. "But God – let us speak with reverence – when he gives a promise, binds himself with cords of his own making. He binds himself down to such and such a course when he says that such and such a thing shall be. Hence, when you grasp the promise, you get a hold on God." (Spurgeon)

iii. **To Your servant**: "If God's word to us as his servants is so precious, what shall we say of his word to us as his sons?" (Spurgeon)

b. **Upon which You have caused me to hope**: Again the psalmist understood that his trust and **hope** in God's word should not be credited to his own spiritual greatness or genius. It came because God worked in him to **hope** in His word.

i. This also demonstrates that the word of God is *worthy* of such hope. "It is an irrevocable word. Man has to eat his words, sometimes, and unsay his say. He would perform his engagement, but he cannot. It is not that he is unfaithful, but that he is unable. Now this is never so with God. His word never returns to him void. Go, find ye the snowflakes winging their way like white doves back to heaven! Go, find the drops of rain rising upward like diamonds flung up from the hand of a mighty man to find a lodging-place in the cloud from which they fell! Until the snow and the rain return to heaven, and mock the ground which they promised to bless, the word of God shall never return to him void." (Spurgeon)

c. **This is my comfort in my affliction, for Your word has given me life**: When the psalmist recalled how faithfully and powerfully God's word had brought him **life** in the past, he then found **comfort** in his present **affliction**.

> i. "It would seem as though this section expressed the feelings of one in the midst of affliction. It does not sing the song of deliverance therefrom. The word is distinctly, 'This is my comfort in my affliction.'" (Morgan)

> ii. In this stanza there is no specific prayer for help. Instead, there are "…statements by the writer that he trusts what God has written in his law and will continue to love it and obey its teachings. It is a way of acknowledging that suffering is common to human beings." (Boice)

> iii. In the midst of **affliction**, the psalmist proclaims his comfort: **this is my comfort**. "The worldling clutches his money-bag, and says, 'this is my comfort'; the spendthrift points to his gaiety and shouts, 'this is my comfort'; the drunkard lifts his glass and sings, 'this is my comfort'; but the man whose hope comes from God feels the life-giving power of the word of the Lord, and he testifies, 'this is my comfort.'" (Spurgeon)

> iv. **My comfort…my affliction**: In the midst of an **affliction** suited to the individual, the believer can also enjoy a **comfort** specifically suited to him. It is **my** affliction, and it is **my** comfort.

d. **Your word has given me life**: All should remember (especially preachers) that the word of God *gives* **life**; the preacher does not give it life. It isn't as if the poor, dead word of God lay lifeless until the wonderful preacher came and breathed life into it. Instead, the word of God gives life – especially to dead preachers.

2. (51-52) God's word adds strength to comfort.

The proud have me in great derision,
***Yet* I do not turn aside from Your law.**
I remembered Your judgments of old, O Lord,
And have comforted myself.

a. **The proud have me in great derision**: In this section as well as the previous, the idea is that the psalmist is mocked and reproached for his love and trust in God's word. These **proud** mockers look at the psalmist and his dedication to the word of God, and they hold him **in great derision**.

> i. And so it has ever been: those who love and trust God's word – especially with the depth and passion reflected by the psalmist in this mighty psalm –are mocked by **the proud** who want nothing to do with God and His word.

b. **Yet I do not turn aside from Your law**: We almost sense a note of *defiance* in the psalmist. No matter how great the **derision** that comes from the **proud**, he will hold faithful to God and His word.

i. Great harm has been done to the cause of God when believers find themselves unable to endure this **great derision**, and they begin to down-grade their view of God's word and its inerrant character. Hoping to appease or impress the **proud**, they lead themselves and others to trust and love God's word less. Such ones should instead find their strength and comfort in these very passages and declare, "**Yet I do not turn aside from Your law.**"

ii. "Christian! Be satisfied with the approbation of your God. Has he not adopted you by his Spirit, sealed you for his kingdom? And is not this 'honour that cometh from God only' enough – far more than enough – to counterbalance the *derision of the proud*?" (Bridges)

c. **I remembered Your judgments of old, O Lord, and have comforted myself**: When challenged to lessen his confidence and trust in God's word by the **proud** mockers, the psalmist wisely responded by *increasing* his confidence in God's word! Therein he **comforted** himself.

i. The **proud** who hold the simple believer in **great derision** enjoy the applause and honor of some in this world; but they can never know the comfort that the psalmist wrote of here.

ii. There was specific comfort in remembering **Your judgments of old, O Lord**. In a similar way, we are comforted and strengthened in hope as we remember how God has dealt with men and circumstances in the past. "The grinning of the proud will not trouble us when we remember how the Lord dealt with their predecessors in bygone periods; he destroyed them at the deluge, he confounded them at Babel, he drowned them at the Red Sea, he drove them out of Canaan: he has in all ages bared his arm against the haughty, and broken them as potters' vessels." (Spurgeon)

iii. "When we see no present display of the divine power it is wise to fall back upon the records of former ages, since they are just as available as if the transactions were of yesterday, seeing the Lord is always the same." (Spurgeon)

3. (53-56) Describing the comfort and strength the word of God brings.

Indignation has taken hold of me
Because of the wicked, who forsake Your law.
Your statutes have been my songs
In the house of my pilgrimage.

I remember Your name in the night, O LORD,
And I keep Your law.
This has become mine,
Because I kept Your precepts.

a. **Indignation has taken hold of me**: When the psalmist thought of the **wicked** – perhaps the proud who held him and others who trusted in God's word in great derision – it made him indignant. He recognized their great sin: **who forsake Your law.**

i. Those who deny or depreciate God's word do just this – they **forsake** the word of God. Worse yet, they often lead others to do the same. Jesus graphically described the penalty for those who lead others astray (Luke 17:1-2).

b. **Your statutes have been my songs in the house of my pilgrimage**: God's word (**Your statutes**) makes him sing with joy and confidence. Those who know the power of singing God's word have great comfort **in the house of** their **pilgrimage**.

i. Even as Paul and Silas could sing in the midst of suffering (Acts 16:25), so could the psalmist. Even as a pilgrim, not yet home and afflicted, he could sing unto his God.

ii. "A pilgrim is a person who is travelling through one country to another.... We are hurrying through this world as through a foreign land. We are in this country, not as residents, but only as visitors, who take this country en route for glory." (Spurgeon)

iii. "Since our songs are so very different from those of the proud, we may expect to join a very different choir at the last, and sing in a place far removed from their abode." (Spurgeon)

c. **I remember Your name in the night, O LORD**: This is true both literally and figuratively. In the dark of night when fears and anxieties often rush in upon us, the psalmist finds comfort in the **name** of the LORD, revealed to him by God's word. Yet this comfort is also real in the figurative **night** that believers may face.

i. The words following – **And I keep Your law** – remind us that the remembrance of God **in the night** made for an obedient life with God in the daytime. "The good effect of hours thus secretly passed in holy exercises, will appear openly in our lives and conversations." (Horne)

ii. "If we have no memory for the name of Jehovah we are not likely to remember his commandments: if we do not think of him secretly we shall not obey him openly." (Spurgeon)

d. **This has become mine**: This is a glorious, triumphant statement from the psalmist. The power, goodness, comfort, and strength of God's word are not only ideas or theories to him. By faith – faith that has come by God's word (Romans 10:17) – he can rightly say, **This has become mine**!

> i. "…'this' being the cheer and comfort so tellingly described in Psalm 119:54f. Although obedience does not earn these blessings, it turns us around to receive them." (Kidner)

> ii. "We are not rewarded for our works, but there is a reward *in* them." (Spurgeon)

e. **Because I kept Your precepts**: The psalmist enjoys this triumph not only because he knows the word of God, but also because he obeys them (**I kept Your precepts**). It isn't that the psalmist claims perfect obedience (as shown in verses 57-58 following), but a life generally lived in faithfulness to the word of God.

H. Heth ח: Hurrying to God with all my heart.

1. (57-58) Loyalty proclaimed and mercy requested.

You are **my portion, O** L**ORD**;
I have said that I would keep Your words.
I entreated Your favor with *my* **whole heart;**
Be merciful to me according to Your word.

a. **You are my portion, O** L**ORD**: These are the words of a *satisfied soul*. The psalmist is satisfied with the **portion** received, and that portion is the L**ORD** Himself.

> i. Spurgeon observed that this was "…a broken sentence. The translators have mended it by insertions, but perhaps it had been better to have left it alone, and then it would have appeared as an exclamation, – 'My portion, O Lord!'"

> ii. "The psalmist is saying that, like the Levites, he wants his portion of divine blessing to be God himself since nothing is better and nothing will ever fully satisfy his or anyone else's heart but God himself. To possess God is truly to have everything." (Boice)

> iii. We understand this in the broader context of this psalm. The L**ORD** Himself is satisfaction to the psalmist *because God has come to him through His word.* It isn't as if the word of God is in one place, and the psalmist must go to another place for experience of and satisfaction in God. He can say, "**You are my portion, O** L**ORD**, and I receive that **portion** as You meet me in Your word and I live it out."

iv. Thomas Brooks – quoted in Spurgeon – said that we could answer every temptation with the reply, "The Lord is my portion." If He truly is our portion, we don't need to look for satisfaction in fleshly pursuits.

v. "He is an exceedingly covetous fellow to whom God is not sufficient; and he is an exceeding fool to whom the world is sufficient. For God is an inexhaustible treasury of all riches, sufficing innumerable men; while the world has mere trifles and fascinations to offer, and leads the soul into deep and sorrowful poverty." (Thomas Le Blanc, cited in Spurgeon)

b. **I have said that I would keep Your words**: This promise would be an empty vow without the empowering of God in our lives. When we have a close connection with God and receive and enjoy Him as our **portion**, we also receive strength to **keep His words**.

i. "But if we take the Lord as our *portion*, we must take him as our king.... Here is the Christian complete – taking *the Lord* as his portion, and his *word* as his rule." (Bridges)

ii. He was public in this statement of his intentions. "*I have said*; I have not only purposed it in my own heart, but have professed and owned it before others, and I do not repent of it." (Poole)

c. **I entreated Your favor with my whole heart; be merciful to me according to Your word**: Here the psalmist understood both the *urgency* to seek and please God, and the *inability* to completely do so.

i. The words translated **Your favor** are literally, "Your *face*." To enjoy the face of God is to experience His favor. The psalmist here declares that he has sought the face of God.

ii. He sought the face of God with a sense of *urgency*, reflected in the words **entreated** and **whole heart**. The psalmist understood how important it was to seek the favor of God and to please Him with his life.

iii. He sought the face of God with a sense of *inability*, shown in the request **be merciful to me**. No matter how diligently the psalmist would seek after God and seek to please Him, he would always remain in need of mercy.

d. **Be merciful to me according to Your word**: This is a blessed and glorious apparent contradiction. The request for mercy is not based on it being a right, or that he deserves it. The psalmist speaks as one who expects mercy **according to** the promise of God's word.

i. While we have no *natural* right to mercy, there is a *spiritual* right to mercy for all who ask according to His promise.

2. (59-60) A life directed toward God's word.

I thought about my ways,
And turned my feet to Your testimonies.
I made haste, and did not delay
To keep Your commandments.

a. **I thought about my ways, and turned my feet to Your testimonies**: Time spent in God's word has given the psalmist sober reflection about his **ways**. This gave the insight necessary to turn in the right direction.

i. "While studying the word he was led to study his own life, and this caused a mighty revolution. He came to the word, and then he came to himself, and this made him arise and go to his father." (Spurgeon)

ii. "Blaise Pascal, the brilliant French philosopher and devout Christian, loved Psalm 119. He is another person who had memorized it, and he called verse 59 'the turning point of man's character and destiny.' He meant that it is vital for every person to consider his or her ways, understand that our ways are destructive and will lead us to destruction, and then make an about-face and determine to go in God's ways instead." (Boice)

iii. **I thought about my ways**: "How many, on the other hand, seem to pass through the world into eternity without a serious *thought on their ways!* Multitudes live for the world – forget God and die! This is their history." (Bridges)

b. **I made haste, and did not delay to keep Your commandments**: Once on the right path (with the **feet** having been **turned**), the psalmist can now speed his way in the course of obedience.

i. It is dangerous to make haste on a wrong path; it is glorious to make **haste** on the right way. We can also say that making **haste** to God is a sign of revival. When God is moving in power, people make haste to get right with him.

ii. "Speed in repentance and speed in obedience are two excellent things. We are too often in haste to sin; O that we may be in a greater hurry to obey." (Spurgeon)

iii. **Did not delay**: "The original word, which we translate *delayed not*, is amazingly emphatical.... I did not stand *what-what-whating*; or, as we used to express the same sentiment, *shilly-shallying* with myself: I was *determined*, and so set out. The *Hebrew* word, as well as the

English, strongly marks indecision of mind, positive action being suspended, because the mind is so unfixed as not to be able to make a choice." (Clarke)

iv. "*Delay* is the word used of Lot as he 'lingered', reluctant to leave Sodom [Genesis 19:16]." (Kidner)

3. (61-62) Faithfulness to God's word in adversity.

The cords of the wicked have bound me,
***But* I have not forgotten Your law.**
At midnight I will rise to give thanks to You,
Because of Your righteous judgments.

a. **The cords of the wicked have bound me, but I have not forgotten Your law**: The psalmist was attacked and afflicted by adversaries; but they could not make him forget or forsake the law of God.

b. **At midnight I will rise to give thanks to You**: The heart and the mind of the psalmist are so filled with **thanks** and appreciation toward God that he finds his sleep interrupted by these high thoughts.

i. **I will rise**: "The Psalmist observed posture; he did not lie in bed and praise. There is not much in the position of the body, but there is something, and that something is to be observed whenever it is helpful to devotion and expressive of our diligence or humility." (Spurgeon)

ii. Thomas Manton (cited in Spurgeon) listed several notable lessons to be drawn from the psalmist's midnight devotion:

- His devotion was earnest and passionate; the daylight hours did not give him enough time to thank God.

- His devotion to God was sincere, shown by its secrecy. He was willing to thank God when no one else could see him or be impressed by his devotion.

- He regarded time as precious; he even used the hours normally given to sleep for devotion to God.

- He regarded devotion to God as more important than natural refreshment. He was willing to sacrifice a legitimate thing (sleep) for the pursuit of God.

- He showed great reverence to God even in secret devotion, by rising up to praise Him. Praise requires something of both soul and body.

4. (63-64) Friendship with those who are friends of God's word.

I *am* a companion of all who fear You,
And of those who keep Your precepts.
The earth, O LORD, is full of Your mercy;
Teach me Your statutes.

a. **I am a companion of all who fear You**: The psalmist enjoyed the special fellowship present among those who honor and hold God's word, **of those who keep Your precepts**.

i. This wonderful companionship is the testimony of countless Christians, who experience warm fellowship across the lines of race, class, nationality, and education.

ii. "These then are the Lord's people; and union with him is in fact union with them.... To meet the Christian in ordinary courtesy, *not in unity of heart*, is a sign of an unspiritual walk with God." (Bridges)

iii. "If then we are not ashamed to confess ourselves Christians, let us not shrink from walking in fellowship with Christians. Even if they should exhibit some repulsive features of character, they bear the image of him, whom we profess to love." (Bridges)

b. **The earth, O LORD, is full of Your mercy**: Having experienced this broad companionship, the psalmist felt the goodness of God filling the **earth**. This experience of God's **mercy** increased his desire for knowledge and obedience (**teach me Your statutes**).

i. We see again the course of a never-ending cycle. The pursuit of God in and through His word leads to satisfaction and blessing. That satisfaction and blessing leads to a deeper pursuit, leading to even more satisfaction and blessing.

ii. When one lives in this glorious cycle, it feels as if the whole **earth** is **full** of the **mercy** of God. It is a glorious, blessed life with the experience of mercy all around.

I. Teth 𝕭: God's word brings benefit from a time of affliction.

1. (65-66) A prayer of praise and petition.

You have dealt well with Your servant,
O LORD, according to Your word.
Teach me good judgment and knowledge,
For I believe Your commandments.

a. **You have dealt well with Your servant, O LORD, according to Your word**: This section begins with a note of *gratitude*. The psalmist finds himself thankful for God's good dealing toward him, and that blessings have come **according to** His **word**.

i. We don't think about it enough, but it is wonderfully true that **You have dealt well with Your servant, O LORD**. Think of all the ways God has dealt well with us. He chose us, He called us, He drew us to Himself. He rescued us, He declared us righteous, He forgave us, He put His Spirit within us, He adopted us into His family. He loves us, He makes us kings and priests and co-workers with Him, and He rewards all our work for Him.

ii. **According to Your word** implies that the psalmist not only knew the promises of God and pled them in prayer (as in verse 49); he also *received* the promises by faith and experienced them.

iii. This *should* be the life experience of every child of God. We know that God has **deal well** with us, and we know that it has been **according to** His **word**.

iv. "When we are thus reaping the fruitful discipline of our Father's school (Hebrews 12:11), must we not put a fresh seal to our testimony – *Thou hast dealt well with thy servant, O Lord?* But why should we delay our acknowledgment till we come out of our trial? Ought we not to give it even in the midst of our 'heaviness?'" (Bridges)

b. **Teach me good judgment and knowledge**: This prayer for *wisdom* comes from a blessed life. Having received this well-dealing from God, the psalmist understood the need to live in **good judgment and knowledge**. The blessings were given to him for wise and obedient living to the glory of God.

i. **Good judgment**: "…Hebrew, *the goodness of taste*, an experimental sense and relish of divine things." (Poole)

ii. "*Judgment*, here, is literally 'taste', not in our sense of artistic judgment, but of spiritual discrimination: 'for the ear tests words as the palate tastes food' (Job 34:3). *Cf.* Hebrews 5:14." (Kidner)

iii. We far too easily forget our great need to learn **good judgment and knowledge**, and are far too ready to trust our own heart and conscience. "The faculty of conscience partakes, with every other power of man, of the injury of the fall; and therefore, with all its intelligence, honesty, and power, it is liable to misconception.... Conscience, therefore, must not be trusted without the light of the word of God; and most important is the prayer – *Teach me good judgment and knowledge.*" (Bridges)

iv. "No school, but the school of Christ – no teaching, but the teaching of the Spirit – can ever give this *good judgment and knowledge.*" (Bridges)

c. **For I believe Your commandments**: He wanted God to **teach** him because he really did **believe** the commands and words of God. If we really do believe His word, then we should want Him to teach us to live wisely and obediently.

2. (67-68) The goodness of God seen even in correction.

Before I was afflicted I went astray,
But now I keep Your word.
You *are* good, and do good;
Teach me Your statutes.

a. **Before I was afflicted I went astray, but now I keep Your word**: The psalmist speaks here of lessons learned the hard way. There was a time when he was far more likely to go **astray** from God's word and the wise life revealed in it. Yet, under a season of affliction, he was now devoted to the word of God.

i. This principle has been demonstrated in nearly everyone who has pursued God. This is one reason why God appoints affliction for His people (1 Thessalonians 3:3).

ii. "Often our trials act as a thorn hedge to keep us in the good pasture, but our prosperity is a gap through which we go astray." (Spurgeon)

iii. Bridges relates an old church prayer: *In all time of our wealth – Good Lord, deliver us!* "A time of wealth is indeed a time of special need. It is hard to restrain the flesh, when so many are the baits for its indulgence." (Bridges)

iv. "As the scourging and beating of the garment with a stick beateth out the moths and dust, so do afflictions [beat out] corruptions from the heart." (Trapp)

v. "Many have been humbled under affliction, and taught to know themselves and humble themselves before God, that probably without this could never have been saved; after this, they have been serious and faithful. *Affliction* sanctified is a great blessing; unsanctified, it is an additional curse." (Clarke)

vi. "We gain solace here by remembering what the Bible says even of Jesus, 'Although he was a son, he learned obedience from what he suffered' (Hebrews 5:8)." (Boice)

b. **You are good, and do good; teach me Your statutes**: This important and precious line follows the recognition of affliction and the good it has done in life. The psalmist did not become bitter or resentful toward God for the affliction that brought him to greater obedience.

i. Despite the affliction – which we should regard as genuine – he proclaimed, "**You are good, and do good**." In fact, he even wanted *more* instruction from God, saying "**Teach me Your statutes**." This is said with the implicit understanding that this teaching might require more affliction; yet it was the psalmist's desire. This shows how confident he was in the goodness of God.

ii. "Affliction is not the most frequently mentioned matter.... The most prominent word in these verses is 'good.' This is the *teth* stanza. *Teth* is the first letter of the Hebrew word 'good' (*tov*), so it was a natural thought for the composer of the psalm to use 'good' at the beginning of these verses." (Boice)

iii. In the most basic sense, this is praise for who God *is* (**You are good**), and praise for what God *does* (**and do good**). These are always two wonderful reasons for praise.

3. (69-70) Delight in God's law despite attacks from adversaries.

The proud have forged a lie against me,
But **I will keep Your precepts with** *my* **whole heart.**
Their heart is as fat as grease,
But **I delight in Your law.**

a. **The proud have forged a lie against me**: In reading of the godly and humble character of the psalmist, it is almost shocking to hear that he has enemies who carefully **forged a lie against** him. Yet he explains how this is possible: they are **the proud**, who are no doubt convicted in conscience and spiteful of his humble, obedient, teachable life before God.

i. "If the Lord *does us good*, we must expect Satan to do us evil...he readily puts it into the hearts of his children to *forge lies against* the children of God!" (Bridges)

ii. "To such slanders and calumnies, a good life is the best answer. When a friend once told Plato, what scandalous stories his enemies had propagated concerning him, – I will live so, replied the great Philosopher, that nobody shall believe them." (Horne)

b. **But I will keep Your precepts with my whole heart**: The lies of the proud did not distract or overly discourage the psalmist. Instead, he dedicated himself to greater obedience and honor of God, pledging to obey Him with his **whole heart**.

i. "If the mud which is thrown at us does not blind our eyes or bruise our integrity it will do us little harm. If we keep the precepts, the precepts will keep us in the day of [insults] and slander." (Spurgeon)

c. **Their heart is as fat as grease, but I delight in Your law**: Their **fat** heart was not good for their physical or spiritual health. It meant that their hearts were dull, insensitive, and drowning in luxury and excess. In contrast, the psalmist found **delight** in the word of God.

> i. "The tremendous blow of almighty justice has benumbed his heart…. 'seared with a hot iron' (1 Timothy 4:2), and therefore without tenderness; 'past feeling' (Ephesians 4:19); unsoftened by the power of the word." (Bridges)

> ii. "There is and always ought to be a vivid contrast between the believer and the sensualist, and that contrast is as much seen in the affections of the heart as in the actions of the life: *their* heart is as fat as grease, and our heart is delighted with the law of the Lord." (Spurgeon)

> iii. "As if he should say, My heart is a lean heart, a hungry heart, my soul loveth and rejoiceth in thy word. I have nothing else to fill it but thy word, and the comforts I have from it; but their hearts are fat hearts; fat with the world, fat with lust; they hate the word. As a full stomach loatheth meat and cannot digest it; so wicked men hate the word, it will not go down with them, it will not gratify their lusts." (William Fenner, cited in Spurgeon)

4. (71-72) Appreciation for the goodness of God even in seasons of affliction.

It is **good for me that I have been afflicted,**
That I may learn Your statutes.
The law of Your mouth *is* **better to me**
Than thousands of *coins of* **gold and silver.**

a. **It is good for me that I have been afflicted, that I may learn Your statutes**: The psalmist repeats the idea from earlier in this section (verse 67). This repetition is an effective way to communicate emphasis. Affliction, brought under the wisdom and guidance of God's word, did genuine **good** in his life.

> i. "I, for my part, owe more, I think, to the anvil and to the hammer, to the fire and to the file, than to anything else. I bless the Lord for the correctives of his providence by which, if he has blessed me on the one hand with sweets, he has blessed me on the other hand with bitters." (Spurgeon)

> ii. "'I never' – said Luther – 'knew the meaning of God's word, until I came into affliction. I have always found it one of my best schoolmasters.'" (Bridges)

> iii. Yet we must guard against the misunderstanding that seasons of affliction automatically make one better or godlier. Sadly, there are

many who are *worse* from their affliction – because they fail to turn to God's word for wisdom and life-guidance in such times. The worst affliction of all is a wasted affliction, wasted because we did not turn to God and gained nothing from it.

iv. This also shows how valuable the learning of God's word was to the psalmist. It was entirely worth it for him to endure affliction, if only he could **learn** the **statutes** of God in the process. This made a time of painful affliction worthwhile.

v. "Very little is to be learned without affliction. If we would be scholars we must be sufferers...God's commands are best read by eyes wet with tears." (Spurgeon)

vi. "By affliction God separates the sin which he hates from the soul which he loves." (John Mason, cited in Spurgeon)

b. **The law of Your mouth is better to me than thousands of coins of gold and silver**: This is a logical extension of the thought in the previous verse. If the psalmist understands that even trouble can be good if it teaches him the word of God – if it is more valuable than his comfort – then it is also possible to say that it is more valuable than riches.

i. This great estimation of the word of God came from a life that had known affliction. It was love and appreciation from the field of battle, not the palaces of ease and comfort.

ii. "Herbert Lockyer recounts a story concerning the largest Bible in the world, a Hebrew manuscript weighing 320 pounds in the Vatican library. Long ago a group of Italian Jews asked to see this Bible and when they had seen it they told their friends in Venice about it. As a result a syndicate of Russian Jews tried to buy it, offering the church the weight of the book in gold. Julius the Second was Pope at that time, and he refused the offer, even though the value of such a large amount of gold was enormous.... Today we pay little to possess multiple copies of God's Word. But do we value it? In many cases, I am afraid not." (Boice)

iii. "Who can say this? Who *prefers* the law of his God, the Christ that bought him, and the heaven to which he hopes to go, when he can live no longer upon earth, *to thousands of gold and silver*? Yea, how many are there who, like Judas, *sell their Saviour* even for *thirty* pieces of silver? Hear this, ye lovers of the world and of money!" (Clarke)

iv. "The word of God must be nearer to us than our friends, dearer to us than our lives, sweeter to us than our liberty, and pleasanter to us than all earthly comforts." (John Mason, cited in Spurgeon)

J. Yod ׳: Confidence in the Creator and His Word.

The yod *stanza represents the small Hebrew letter Jesus referred to as a "jot" in Matthew 5:18: Till heaven and earth pass away, one jot or one tittle will by no means pass from the law till all is fulfilled.*

1. (73) Surrendering to the word of the Creator.

Your hands have made me and fashioned me;
Give me understanding, that I may learn Your commandments.

a. **Your hands have made me**: Here the psalmist proclaimed God as Creator, and understood certain obligations to God because he was **fashioned** by the hands of God.

i. **Fashioned me**: "The reference to God forming him is a deliberate echo of Genesis 2, which says God 'formed man from the dust of the ground' (Genesis 2:7)." (Boice)

ii. The modern age, with its widespread denial of a Creator God, has a much lower sense of obligation to God as Creator. Despite the deeply seated rejection of God as Creator, man's obligation to his Maker remains. The psalmist understood what many today forget or deny.

iii. To say that God is our Creator is to recognize:

- That we are obligated to Him as the One who gives us life.
- That we respect Him as One who is greater and smarter than we are.
- That He, as our designer, knows what is best for us.
- That since our beginning is connected to the invisible world, so our end will be also.

iv. "The consideration, that God made us, is here urged as an argument why he should not forsake and reject us, since every artist hath a value for his own work, proportioned to its excellence. It is, at the same time, and acknowledgement of the service we owe him, founded on the relation which a creature beareth to his Creator." (Horne)

v. "If God had roughly made us, and had not also elaborately fashioned us, this argument would lose much of its force; but surely from the delicate art and marvellous skill which the Lord has shown in the formation of the human body, we may infer that he is prepared to take equal pains with the soul till it shall perfectly bear his image." (Spurgeon)

vi. **Your hands**: "'Oh look upon the wounds of thine hands, and forget not the work of thine hands,' as Queen Elizabeth prayed." (Trapp)

b. **Give me understanding**: In his thoughts of God as Creator, the psalmist prayed for **understanding**. He recognized that this was something often misunderstood, and one could ask for and expect help in **understanding** both how God created us and what our obligations are to our Maker.

i. We gain much **understanding** by considering God as Creator, and especially as the Creator of man. "Every part of creation bears the impress of God. Man – man alone – bears his image, his likeness. Everywhere we see his track – his footsteps. Here we behold his face." (Bridges)

c. **That I may learn Your commandments**: The understanding of God and man as Creator and creature should lead to this humble relationship in which man admits his need to **learn**: to learn God's word (**commandments**) and receive His word as *commands* from a wise, loving, and righteous Creator.

2. (74) The common gladness of those who fear God.

Those who fear You will be glad when they see me,
Because I have hoped in Your word.

a. **Those who fear You will be glad when they see me**: The psalmist considered that his righteous life would be an encouragement to others who also feared God. This was an additional reason to hear and obey God.

i. "When a man of God obtains grace for himself he becomes a blessing to others.... There are professors whose presence scatters sadness, and the godly quietly steal out of their company: may this never be the case with us." (Spurgeon)

ii. "They who 'fear God' are naturally 'glad when they see' and converse with one like themselves; but more especially so, when it is one whose faith and patience have carried him through troubles, and rendered him victorious over temptations; one who hath 'hoped in God's word,' and hath not been disappointed." (Horne)

b. **Because I have hoped in Your word**: His life could give encouragement and gladness to other righteous people **because** his hope and attention were put upon the **word** of God. Without this hope, his righteous life would be impossible.

3. (75-77) Comfort from God's word in a time of affliction.

I know, O Lord, that Your judgments *are* right,
And *that* in faithfulness You have afflicted me.
Let, I pray, Your merciful kindness be for my comfort,
According to Your word to Your servant.

Let Your tender mercies come to me, that I may live;
For Your law *is* my delight.

> a. **Your judgments are right...in faithfulness You have afflicted me**: His attention upon God's word has given the psalmist a wise and godly perspective even in seasons of suffering. He can proclaim the rightness of God's **judgments** even when *he* is afflicted.

> > i. It is one thing to say, "God has the right to do with me as He pleases." It is a greater thing to say that His **judgments are right, and that in faithfulness You have afflicted me**.

> > ii. This was the place Job eventually came to through his long and desperate struggle through the Book of Job. He came to **know** that the **judgments** of the LORD were **right**, and even understood God's **faithfulness** in affliction. Eli, David, and the Shunammite mother had similar moments of understanding.

> > > • Job could say in his affliction, *Blessed be the name of the LORD* (Job 1:21).

> > > • Eli could say in his affliction, *It is the LORD. Let Him do what seems good to Him* (1 Samuel 3:18).

> > > • David could say in his affliction, *Let him alone, and let him curse, for so the LORD has ordered him* (2 Samuel 16:11).

> > > • The Shunammite mother could say in her affliction, *It is well* (2 Kings 4:26).

> b. **Let, I pray, Your merciful kindness be for my comfort, according to Your word**: The psalmist prayed on solid ground, asking on the basis of promises made in God's **word**. With such promises, he asked for **merciful kindness** in his affliction.

> > i. **According to Your word**: "Our prayers are according to the mind of God when they are according to the word of God." (Spurgeon)

> > ii. "Lord, these promises were given to be made good to some, and why not to me? I hunger; I need; I thirst; I wait. Here is thy hand-writing in thy word.... I am resolved to be as importunate [persistent to the point of annoyance] till I have obtained, and as thankful afterwards, as by thy grace I shall be enabled.... Thy promises are the discoveries of thy purposes, and vouchsafed [graciously given] as materials for our prayers; and in my supplications I am resolved every day to present and tender them back to thee." (Prayer of Monica, the mother of Augustine; cited in Bridges)

c. **Your word to Your servant**: The psalmist rightly received the word of God as something *personal* to himself. It was not only a word to mankind in general, or even the covenant people; it was something personal to the psalmist himself (**Your servant**).

d. **Let Your tender mercies come to me, that I may live; for Your law is my delight**: The psalmist prayed with the understanding that God's **tender mercies** came to him through the word (**law**) of God. By staying close to God's word and letting it fill his life, he also received God's **tender mercies**.

> i. "The mercies of God are 'tender mercies,' they are the mercies of a father to his children, nay, tender as the compassion of a mother over the son of her womb. They 'come unto' us, when we are not able to go to them." (Horne)

> ii. Without the gift of these **tender mercies**, we find ourselves lost and discouraged. "All the candles in the world, in the absence of the sun, can never make the day. The whole earth, in its brightest visions of fancy, destitute of the Lord's love, can never cheer nor revive the soul." (Bridges)

> iii. "Yet we have no just apprehension of these *tender mercies*, unless they *come unto us*. In the midst of the wide distribution, let me claim my interest. *Let them come unto me*." (Bridges)

4. (78-80) The contrast between the proud and those who fear God.

> Let the proud be ashamed,
> For they treated me wrongfully with falsehood;
> *But* I will meditate on Your precepts.
> Let those who fear You turn to me,
> Those who know Your testimonies.
> Let my heart be blameless regarding Your statutes,
> That I may not be ashamed.

a. **Let the proud be ashamed**: The psalmist said this not only out of a sense of God's righteousness, but also out of a sense of being personally wronged. These **proud** ones had **treated** him **wrongfully with falsehood**; therefore they should be put to shame.

> i. "Shame is for the proud, for it is a shameful thing to be proud. Shame is not for the holy, for there is nothing in holiness to be ashamed of." (Spurgeon)

> ii. If the proud ones who opposed the psalmist knew he was praying against them, they had good reason to be afraid. David's prayers made failure and doom for Ahithophel. Hezekiah's prayer meant failure and doom for the Assyrian army. The fasting of Esther and the Jews

brought failure and doom for Haman. God knows how to defend His own who cry to Him.

iii. Yet even the prayer that **the proud be ashamed** is a prayer for their good. It is as the prayer of Asaph: *Fill their faces with shame, that they may seek Your name, O LORD* (Psalm 83:16).

b. **But I will meditate on Your precepts**: In contrast to the **proud** who loved lies, the psalmist loved and meditated on God's word.

i. "He would study the law of God and not the law of retaliation. The proud are not worth a thought. The worst injury they can do us is to take us away from our devotions; let us baffle them by keeping all the closer to our God when they are most malicious in their onslaughts." (Spurgeon)

ii. **I will meditate**: "Truths lie hid in the heart without efficacy or power, till improved by deep, serious, and pressing thoughts.... A sudden carrying a candle through a room, giveth us not so full a survey of the object, as when you stand a while beholding it. A steady contemplation is a great advantage." (Thomas Manton, cited in Spurgeon)

c. **Let those who fear You turn to me**: The psalmist recognized the presence of proud enemies, but he did not believe that all were against himself or God. There were others who feared God, and he could find companionship with them. They had much in common – they both were those who knew God's word (**Those who know Your testimonies**).

i. **Those who fear...those who know**: "David has two descriptions for the saints, they are God-fearing and God-knowing. They possess both devotion and instruction; they have both the spirit and the science of true religion." (Spurgeon)

ii. **Turn to me**: "As the believer finds trouble from the world, he prays that he may find help from the Lord's people.... It is painful therefore to see Christians often walking aloof from each other, and suffering coldness, distance, differences and distrust to divide them from their brethren." (Bridges)

iii. "Either, 1. Turn their eyes to me as a spectacle of God's wonderful mercy; or rather, 2. Turn their hearts and affections to me, which have been alienated from me." (Poole)

d. **Let my heart be blameless regarding Your statutes**: As the psalmist compared himself with the **proud** who spoke lies, he still recognized his need for greater obedience to God. He asked God, and depended on Him, for an obedient (**blameless**) heart and life.

i. The New Testament has many examples of hearts that were not **blameless**: Judas, Ananias and Sapphira, Alexander, and Demas (Matthew 26:14-16; Acts 5:1-11; 1 Timothy 1:20; 2 Timothy 4:10). Such examples should make us pray according to Psalm 139:23: *Search me, O God, and know my heart.*

ii. "Examine your settled judgment, your deliberate choice, your outgoing affections, your habitual, allowed practice; apply to every detection of unsoundness the blood of Christ, as the sovereign remedy for the diseases of 'a deceitful and desperately wicked heart.'" (Bridges)

iii. "Let it be *perfect* – all given up to thee, and all possessed by thee." (Clarke)

e. **That I may not be ashamed**: This is a valid desire. The psalmist wanted a life lived **unashamed**. The desire was for a sense of no inward shame because he was right with God, and had no public shame in the eyes of others. His obedient life (**Let my heart be blameless regarding Your statutes**) would lead to this unashamed life.

i. In this section we are taught by the repetition of the plea, "**Let….**" Taken together, these make for a healthy life with God.

- Let me be comforted by Your kindness.
- Let me live by Your mercies.
- Let me be vindicated by God.
- Let me be in the presence of those who fear You.
- Let my heart be blameless.

K. Kaph ‎כ‎: Fainting from affliction, revived by God's word.

"Some writers…pointed out that for the ancients there was often significance in the shape of the Hebrew letters. Such is the case here. This is the kaph stanza. Kaph is a curved letter, similar to a half circle, and it was often thought of as a hand held out to receive some gift or blessing…. He holds out his hand toward God as a suppliant." (Boice)

1. (81-82) Seeking comfort in the word of God.

My soul faints for Your salvation,
But I hope in Your word.
My eyes fail *from searching* Your word,
Saying, "When will You comfort me?"

a. **My soul faints for Your salvation**: The psalmist gives a sense of *desperation*. His soul aches for God, so much that it **faints** in waiting for the salvation he needs. Yet he has **hope in** God's **word**.

i. **Faints** has the idea of "coming to the end." (Kidner) It is same verb in a slightly different form is used in verse 87: *They almost made an end of me.* Fainting is a loss of strength; a collapse. Here the psalmist felt that his **soul** was so weak, so empty of strength, that it was unable to stand.

ii. This place of *desperate* yet *not despairing* is known to the followers of God. The Apostle Paul related something of this in 2 Corinthians 4:8-9: *We are hard pressed on every side, yet not crushed; we are perplexed, but not in despair; persecuted, but not forsaken; struck down, but not destroyed….* In it all, Paul could say, *…we have the same spirit of faith* (2 Corinthians 4:13).

iii. **Your salvation**: What he wanted was *God's* salvation. "He wished for no deliverance but that which came from God, his one desire was for '*thy* salvation.' But for that divine deliverance he was eager to the last degree." (Spurgeon)

b. **But I hope in Your word**: In contrast to the sense of weakness and failing, the psalmist found **hope** and strength in God's word. 1 Thessalonians speaks of the endurance (patience) of hope (1:3), and refers to the hope of salvation as a protecting helmet (5:8).

i. "Saul, under protracted trial, resorted to the devil for relief (1 Samuel 28:6-7)…. Even a good man, under a few hours' trial, murmurs against God – nay, even defends his murmuring (Jonah 4:7-9). How did this man behave? When his *soul was fainting, his hope in the word* kept him from sinking." (Bridges)

ii. **I hope in Your word**: "Beloved, let none of us give way to despair. No doubt Satan will tell us that it is humble to despair, but, it is not so. The pride of despair is truly terrible. I believe that, when a man altogether doubts the power of God to save him, and gives himself up to sin because he thinks he cannot be saved, so far from there being any humility in it, it is the prouder action that depraved flesh and blood can perform. Man, how darest thou say that there is no hope for thee?" (Spurgeon)

c. **My eyes fail from searching Your word**: This indicates how diligently the psalmist read and studied God's word. *He studied so hard that his eyes hurt.* One reason he loved God's word so much was because he studied it so intently. God's word yields its treasures to us in proportion to our **searching** it.

d. **Saying, "When will You comfort me?"** This was *why* the psalmist searched so diligently. It was to find **comfort** in his present distress.

Personal need continues to be a greater motivation for diligent study than theological curiosity.

i. "While the promised salvation is delayed, the afflicted soul thinketh every day a year, and looketh toward heaven for the accomplishment of God's word." (Horne)

ii. In his sermon titled *God's Time for Comforting*, Spurgeon sought to give some practical answers to the question, **"When will You comfort me?"**

- Comfort will come when we put away unbelief.
- Comfort will come when we are finished complaining.
- Comfort will come when we put away the sin that we tolerate.
- Comfort will come when we fulfill the duties we have neglected.

iii. When we reach out to God in obedient faith, His comfort is always available. The pain may continue, but God's comfort is there.

2. (83-84) Appreciating weakness and trusting God and His word.

For I have become like a wineskin in smoke,
***Yet* I do not forget Your statutes.**
How many *are* the days of Your servant?
When will You execute judgment on those who persecute me?

a. **I have become like a wineskin in smoke**: The psalmist felt weak, as if he were a fragile **wineskin** that had turned dry and had become black with **smoke**. His soul and spiritual life felt *dry*.

i. **A wineskin in smoke** was "…useless, shriveled, and unattractive because of being blackened with soot." (VanGermen) We don't know if the psalmist said this about his inward condition, his outward condition, or both.

ii. "My natural moisture is dried and burnt up; I am withered, and deformed, and despised, and my case grows worse and worse every day." (Poole)

iii. Though this illustration speaks about the difficult nature of the psalmist's trial, it also speaks to the character of the trial: "Our trials are smoke, but not fire; they are very uncomfortable, but they do not consume us." (Spurgeon)

b. **Yet I do not forget Your statutes**: Despite his sense of weakness, he was determined to **not forget** God's **statutes**. Weakness would not make him **forget** God's word.

i. John Trapp quoted a martyr of the Christian faith: "No trouble must pull us from the love of the truth. You may pull my tongue out of my head, but not my faith out of my heart."

c. **How many are the days of Your servant? When will You execute judgment on those who persecute me?** Here the sense of weakness led the psalmist to despair that God would **execute judgment** against those who persecuted him.

i. Verse 84 is one of the few verses in the psalm that *does not* specifically mention God's word. The context leads us to feel that personal weakness and a sense of injustice have led the psalmist to such distraction and despair that he has lost focus on God's word.

ii. "This stanza has a great deal to say about the psalmist's enemies, as if at this point his thoughts were nearly monopolized by them." (Boice) Yet at the end of the stanza, his thoughts are once again on God and His word.

iii. "To complain *of* God is dishonourable unbelief. To complain to God is the mark of his 'elect, which cry day and night unto him, though he bears long with them' (Luke 18:7)." (Bridges)

3. (85 86) A cry for help when attacked and persecuted.

The proud have dug pits for me,
Which *is* not according to Your law.
All Your commandments *are* faithful;
They persecute me wrongfully;
Help me!

a. **The proud have dug pits for me, which is not according to Your law**: The traps set for the psalmist were in fact directly against the **law** of God. Exodus 21:33-34 gives the principle that a man is responsible for damage when he digs a pit.

i. The idea is that they hunted him as if he were a wild animal. "The manner of taking wild beasts was by 'digging pits,' and covering them over with turf, upon which when the beast trod, he fell into the pit, and was there confined and taken." (Horne)

ii. "Neither the men nor their pits were according to the divine law: they were cruel and crafty deceivers, and their pits were contrary to the Levitical law, and contrary to the command which bids us love our neighbour." (Spurgeon)

b. **All Your commandments are faithful; they persecute me wrongfully**: The psalmist found faithfulness and refuge in the **commandments** of God;

this was strong contrast to the persecution he found from his enemies. In such times, he prayed the logical prayer: **Help me!**

i. "Many a time have these words been groaned out by troubled saints, for they are such as suit a thousand conditions of need, pain, distress, weakness, and sin. '*Help,* Lord,' will be a fitting prayer for youth and age, for labour and suffering, for life and death. No other help is sufficient, but God's help is all-sufficient and we cast ourselves upon it without fear." (Spurgeon)

4. (87-88) Revived by God unto obedience.

They almost made an end of me on earth,
But I did not forsake Your precepts.
Revive me according to Your lovingkindness,
So that I may keep the testimony of Your mouth.

a. **They almost made an end of me on earth, but I did not forsake Your precepts**: The point is emphasized through repetition. *Nothing* would make the psalmist **forsake** God's word. He would cling to it in good times and in bad times.

i. There are many things that may cause a person to **forsake** the word of God in one way or another.

• Sinful compromise.

• Intellectual arrogance.

• Mocking and persecution.

• Coldness of heart.

• Worldly distractions.

• Love of material things.

• Chosen or allowed busyness.

ii. Here, the psalmist was *almost dead* (**they almost made an end of me on earth**), yet he would not **forsake** the word of God.

iii. There is gold in that word "**almost**." It reminds us that though our foes (especially our spiritual adversaries) may press for our complete destruction, God will preserve us. He allows us to be attacked, yet at the same time He sets a limit to the success of the attackers. **Almost** is a word of God's gracious protection.

b. **Revive me according to Your lovingkindness**: The psalmist looked to God for new life, for *revival*. Yet he knew that this was not deserved, even by someone as in love with God's word as he was. Instead, he prayed

Revive me according to Your lovingkindness, not according to what he deserved or had earned.

> i. "If we are revived in our own personal piety we shall be out of reach of our assailants. Our best protection from tempters and persecutors is more life." (Spurgeon)

> ii. The psalmist spoke freely about his great love for God and His word. Yet his trust was in the goodness and grace and **lovingkindness** of God, not in his own love for God and His word.

c. **So that I may keep the testimony of Your mouth**: Here the psalmist understood the *purpose* of a revived spirit within him. It wasn't merely to enjoy a season of spiritual excitement; it was for a more faithful, obedient walk with God.

> i. Many people look to revival as merely a time of heightened spiritual excitement that has little purpose other than giving people a sense of blessing and thrills. This mistaken idea of revival actually *hinders* the work of true revival.

> ii. This revived life was also given for the sake of steadfastness to the **testimony of** God's **mouth**. "[Spiritual] life is absolutely essential to steadfastness in the truth. Whenever I hear of churches and ministers departing from the faith, I know that piety is at [a] low ebb among them. It is proposed that we should argue with them: it is of no avail to argue with dead people. It is proposed that we should bring out another book of Christian evidences: it is small benefit to provide glasses for those who have no eyes. What is wanted is more spiritual life; for as the truth quickens men, they love the quickening word, but dead men care little about that which is to them a dead letter." (Spurgeon)

d. **The testimony of Your mouth**: The psalmist rightly understood that the word of God actually came from the **mouth** of God. God used human authors, and those human authors expressed their personality through the inspired writings, yet God so directed those human authors that what they wrote could accurately be called words from the **mouth** of God.

> i. If the Bible gives us words from the **mouth** of God, we can confidently say that the Bible is *infallible*; that is, that in its original, autograph documents (of which we have extremely reliable copies), it is absolutely without error.

> ii. Since the **mouth** communicates *words*, we also insist that the *words* of the Bible are infallible, and not merely the *ideas*. "To me there is no explanation of those words except that which involves verbal and

infallible inspiration. The testimony of God's mouth must be given in words: God's heart has thoughts, but God's mouth has words; and words from the omniscient and true God must be infallible." (Spurgeon)

L. Lamed ל: Saved by the word settled in heaven.

1. (89-91) A faithful God and His settled word.

Forever, O Lord,
Your word is settled in heaven.
Your faithfulness *endures* to all generations;
You established the earth, and it abides.
They continue this day according to Your ordinances,
For all *are* Your servants.

a. **Forever, O Lord, Your word is settled in heaven**: The psalmist here meditated on the *unchanging nature* of God's word. Because it **is settled in heaven**, it will not change on earth.

i. The word **is settled in heaven**, not merely settled in the heart or mind of the psalmist. It is *objectively* **settled in heaven**, whether the psalmist or anyone else believes it to be or not to be. If someone were to say to the psalmist, "That's your opinion – that is good for you," he would object most strongly that God's word **is settled in heaven** quite apart from any opinion of man.

ii. It's not settled at Tübingen. It's not settled at Harvard. It's not settled at Heidelberg. It's not settled at Oxford. It's not settled at Paris. There is quite a debate at the seminaries these days! We care not for any of that when we know, **Forever, O Lord, Your word is settled in heaven.**

iii. "If I can prove *a word* to have been spoken by God, I must no more question it than his own Being. It may seem to fail on earth; but *it is for ever settled in heaven*." (Bridges)

iv. "After tossing about on a sea of trouble the Psalmist here leaps to shore and stands upon a rock. Jehovah's word is not fickle nor uncertain; it is settled, determined, fixed, sure, immovable. Man's teachings change so often that there is never time for them to be settled; but the Lord's word is from of old the same, and will remain unchanged eternally." (Spurgeon)

v. "Sentiments fluctuate so constantly in this nineteenth century that I suppose we shall soon require to have barometers to show us the variations of doctrine as well as the prospects of the weather. We shall have to consult quarterly reviews, to see what style of religious thought is predominant, and then we shall have to accommodate our sermons to the dictum of the last wise man who has chosen to make a special fool of himself. As for myself, I shall continue to be unfashionable, and abide where I am. 'Sticking in the mud,' says somebody. 'Standing on the Rock,' say I." (Spurgeon)

b. **Settled in heaven**: The psalmist also declared his belief that the word of God was exactly that – not the words of man, but the very words of God. He believed that the Scriptures come from **heaven** and not earth, from the LORD and not man.

i. The psalmist believed what the Apostle Paul wrote hundreds of years later in 2 Timothy 3:16: *All Scripture is given by inspiration of God, and is profitable for doctrine, for reproof, for correction, for instruction in righteousness.*

ii. This means something more than saying that God inspired the men who wrote Scripture, though we believe that He did; God also inspired the very words they wrote. We notice it doesn't say, "All Scripture writers are inspired by God," even though that is true. Yet that statement doesn't go far enough. *The words they wrote were breathed by God*, **Your word is settled in heaven**.

iii. It isn't that God breathed into the human authors. That is true, but not what Paul wrote in 2 Timothy 3:16. He says that from **heaven**, God breathed out of them His holy word.

iv. We remember what Jesus said in Matthew 5:18, *...one jot or one tittle will by no means pass from the law till all is fulfilled.* The *jot* refers to *yod* (י), the smallest letter in the Hebrew alphabet; it looks like half a letter. The *tittle* is a small mark in a Hebrew letter, somewhat like the crossing of a "t" or the tail on a "y."

- The difference between *bet* (ב) and *kaf* (כ) is a *tittle*.
- The difference between *dalet* (ד) and *resh* (ר) is a *tittle*.
- The difference between *vav* (ו) and *zayin* (ז) is a *tittle*.

v. These are small, tiny, almost insignificant differences – yet Jesus said that even these smallest differences would not pass away from God's word. He said that heaven and earth would sooner pass away than a *yod* or a tittle from the word of God. Truly, **Your word is settled in heaven**.

vi. Every preacher should *especially* be able to say, **Your word is settled in heaven**. Charles Spurgeon knew of some preachers who could *not* say that. "They say that they are thinking out their doctrines. I would be greatly sorry to have to think out the road to heaven without the guiding star of heaven's grace or the map of the word. Not gospel-preachers but gospel-makers these men aspire to be, and their message comes forth, not as the gospel of the grace of God, but as the gospel of the imagination of men; a gospel concocted in their own kitchen, not taught them by the Holy Spirit. It is the reverse of being 'settled in heaven,' it is not even settled in the mind of its inventor."

c. **Your faithfulness endures to all generations**: The psalmist believed that the **settled** word of God was a demonstration of the **faithfulness** of God, and that **faithfulness** extends across **all generations**.

i. We recognize the truth of this when we look at **generations** past. We trace the line of the amazing faithfulness of God to each generation, despite the worst impulses and works of man.

ii. We recognize the truth of this when we consider **generations** present and future. The present and future often look gloomy; we wonder where the great men and women of God are who were seen in previous generations. Yet we should not fear; **Your faithfulness endures to all generations**.

iii. We recognize the truth of this when we consider how God has preserved His word through the **generations**. There are many great works of ancient literature that are lost; one author or another makes mention of them, but we have no text that has survived to our day. The Bible not only survives; it thrives.

iv. "Throughout much of this time, the Bible was an object of extreme hatred by many in authority. They tried to stamp it out, but the text survived. In the early days of the church, Celsus, Prophyry, and Lucien tried to destroy it by their arguments. Later the emperors Diocletian and Julian tried to destroy it by force. In some periods of history it was a capital offense to possess a copy of the Bible. Yet the text survived." (Boice)

d. **You established the earth, and it abides. They continue this day according to Your ordinances**: The word of God itself (**Your ordinances**) is what established the earth and caused it to abide. The earth and all of creation began with a word from God (Genesis 1); it is no surprise that they are also sustained and endure **according to** the word of God.

i. This gives new understanding to two wonderful statements of Scripture:

- *The grass withers, the flower fades, but the word of our God stands forever* (Isaiah 40:8).

- *Heaven and earth will pass away, but My words will by no means pass away* (Matthew 24:35).

ii. These passages put the word of God *outside the created world* and indicate that the word of God is more permanent and enduring than creation itself. Since the created world came into being by God's word and is sustained by His word, this makes perfect sense.

iii. "He establishes the world and it abideth. Let us be confident then. Whenever God means to break his word and change his ordinances we may expect to find this earth go steaming into the sun, or else it will rush far off into space, nobody knows where. But while it keeps its place, what have you and I to worry about? Is it not the sign that the Lord will keep us also?" (Spurgeon)

e. **For all are Your servants**: The psalmist looked at the created order and understood that all creation ultimately serves God and His purpose. The **earth**, which He **established** and which **abides**, obeys His word.

i. "There is constancy and order in all of creation, reflecting the 'faithfulness' of the Lord." (VanGemeren)

ii. "A striking feature of these verses is the coupling of God's creative, world-sustaining word with His law for man. Both are the product of the same ordering mind; and not only men but 'all things' are His 'servants'." (Kidner)

2. (92-93) The sustaining power of God's word.

Unless Your law *had been* my delight,
I would then have perished in my affliction.
I will never forget Your precepts,
For by them You have given me life.

a. **Unless Your law had been my delight**: The psalmist rejoiced that the word of God had been his **delight**. Reading and studying and meditating on God's word were not burdensome; they were a **delight**.

i. We can speculate that one reason this was so was because *God met him in His word*. When we have fellowship with God in and through His word, it makes our time in His law delightful.

b. **I would then have perished in my affliction**: The psalmist knew that without his relationship with God and His word, he would not have been sustained in his season of **affliction**.

i. Again, it should be stressed that this **delight** goes beyond mere Bible knowledge. It is the relationship with God in and through His word that gives strength and spiritual nourishment.

ii. "What got him through his afflictions was his lifelong habit of reading, marking, learning, meditating upon, spiritually digesting, and above all obeying God's Law." (Boice)

iii. " *'Thy law...my delights...in mine affliction.'* I happened to be standing in a grocer's shop one day in a large manufacturing town in the west of Scotland, when a poor, old, frail widow came in to make a few purchases. There never was, perhaps, in that town a more severe time of distress. Nearly every loom was stopped. Decent and respectable tradesmen who had seen better days, were obliged to subsist on public charity. So much money per day (but a trifle at most) was allowed to the really poor and deserving. The poor widow had received her daily pittance, and she had now come into the shop of the grocer to lay it out to the best advantage. She had but a few coppers in her withered hands. Carefully did she expend her little stock – a pennyworth of this and the other necessary of life nearly exhausted all she had. She came to the last penny, and with a singular expression of heroic contentment and cheerful resignation on her wrinkled face, she said, '*Now* I must buy oil with this, that I may see to read my Bible during these long dark nights, for it is my only comfort now when every other comfort has gone *away.*'" (Alexander Wallace, cited in Spurgeon)

c. **I will never forget Your precepts, for by them You have given me life**: The psalmist remembered the *life-giving* power and character of God's word. It was this **life** that strengthened him in the season of **affliction**.

i. God's word brings **life** because it *is* alive. "The Bible is alive, it speaks to me; it has feet, it runs after me; it has hands, it lays hold of me. The Bible is not antique or modern. It is eternal." (Luther, cited in Boice)

3. (94-95) Safety in seeking God's word.

I *am* Yours, save me;
For I have sought Your precepts.
The wicked wait for me to destroy me,
***But* I will consider Your testimonies.**

a. **I am Yours, save me**: This speaks of the wonderful relationship between the psalmist and His God, flowing from the word of God.

• He recognized that God was his God.

• He recognized that salvation was not in Himself.

- He recognized that God hears and answers prayer.
- He recognized that God would indeed save him.

> i. "We are the Lord's by creation, election, redemption, surrender, and acceptance; and hence our firm hope and assured belief that he will save us. A man will surely save his own child: Lord, save *me*." (Spurgeon)

> ii. "But what a powerful plea for mercy may we draw from the Lord's interest in us! Will not a man be careful of his children, his treasure, his jewels? 'Such am I. Thy sovereign love hath bought me – made me *thine – I am thine; save me*'." (Bridges)

b. **For I have sought Your precepts**: The basis of this confidence was a relationship built upon the word of God (**Your precepts**). This was not a relationship built upon feelings or subjective experiences, but upon the solid foundation of God's word.

> i. "But then let it be remembered, that no man can say to God with good conscience, 'I am thine,' unless he can also go on, and say, 'I have sought thy precepts.'" (Horne)

c. **The wicked wait for me to destroy me, but I will consider Your testimonies**: The psalmist speaks of his enemies in an almost causal way. While they do their worst against him – they **wait for** him **to destroy** him – he will not panic, but find refuge in the word of God.

> i. "If the enemy cannot cause us to withdraw our thoughts from holy study, or our feet from holy walking, or our hearts from holy aspirations, he has met with poor success in his assaults." (Spurgeon)

4. (96) The perfection of God's word.

I have seen the consummation of all perfection,
***But* Your commandment *is* exceedingly broad.**

a. **I have seen the consummation of all perfection**: The psalmist considered the excellent things he had seen in this world. Perhaps he thought of the things of great natural beauty…the small things of intricate creation…the beauty of human love and care. Yet, all these things have a **consummation** – in the sense of a limit or a barrier. The best things of this world only go so far.

> i. "He has considered all the perfections of things other than Jehovah Himself, that is, of created things; and has discovered their limits." (Morgan)

ii. "Of 'all perfection' in this world, whether of beauty, wit, learning, pleasure, honour, or riches, experience will soon show us the 'end.' But where is the end or boundary of the word of God?" (Horne)

b. **But Your commandment is exceedingly broad**: Despite all the great and beautiful things of this world, something is greater still – the **commandment** of God, His revealed word to us. His word is not limited as the things, even the great things, of this earth are.

- His word is before creation.

- His word is the sustainer of creation.

- His word will endure beyond all creation.

    i. "He has found that stretching out beyond them, and enwrapping them all is the commandment of God." (Morgan)

    ii. "This verse could well be a summary of Ecclesiastes, where every earthly enterprise has its day and comes to nothing, and where only in God and His commandments do we get beyond these frustrating limits." (Kidner)

    iii. "*Broad*, or *large*, both for extent and for continuance; it is useful to all persons in all times and conditions, and for all purposes to inform, direct, quicken, comfort, sanctify, and save men; it is of everlasting truth and efficacy; it will never deceive or forsake those who trust it, as all worldly things will, but will make men happy both here and for ever." (Poole)

    iv. Strangely, many today think that the Bible is *narrow*. They think of themselves as **exceedingly broad**-minded people; yet they show little tolerance for those who disagree with *them*. God's word is indeed **exceedingly broad**, and it will make us broad-minded, broad-hearted, and tolerant in the best sense, if we read and obey it. God's word will prevent us from being tyrants over others and will teach us to tolerate and love others even when their lives and thinking are decidedly against God and His word.

    v. This **broad** place is a firm and safe foundation for us. "Give me the plenary, verbal theory of biblical inspiration with all its difficulties, rather than the doubt. I accept the difficulties and I humbly wait for their solution. But while I wait, I am standing on rock." (J.C. Ryle, Anglican Bishop cited in Boice)

M. Mem מ: Loving the sweetness of God's word.

"This is a pure song of praise. It contains no single petition, but is just one glad outpouring of the heart." (Morgan)

1. (97) The love of God's word expressed through meditation.

Oh, how I love Your law!
It *is* my meditation all the day.

a. **Oh, how I love Your law**: Twice before in this psalm, the writer has declared his love for the word of God (verses 47-48). Yet here, the phrasing is more passionate. His devotion to God and His word has built a love-relationship between the psalmist and God's word.

i. It isn't "I used to love Your law," or "One day I will love Your law." He describes how he feels about the word of God *right now*. He also speaks for himself; the psalmist isn't saying how others should feel, but about how *he* feels.

ii. We also notice that he says, "**Oh, how I love Your law!**" The word **how** describes a comparison; the psalmist loves the word of God *more than* other things. "It is a word of admiration, or a note of comparison; so is it taken in divers other places...it noteth a kind of excess or excellency, even such as cannot be well expressed. The prophet seemeth to speak with a kind of sighing, as being so ravished with love towards the law of God, that he was even sick of love." (Thomas Stoughton, cited in Spurgeon)

iii. "The Order of the Divine mind, embodied in the Divine Law, is beautiful.... It is the language of a man ravished by moral beauty. If we cannot at all share his experience, we shall be the losers." (C.S. Lewis from *Reflections on the Psalms*, cited in Boice)

iv. The superficial Christian may read and understand and even, in an outward sense, obey the word of God. But only the spiritual man *loves* it; he lives as if he could not live without the word of God. To the superficial Christian it is a duty to satisfy the conscience; to the believer it is food and medicine, light and comfort – the word of God is life.

v. If you desire to, you can increase your love for God's word. You can't *make* yourself love something or someone; but you *can* cultivate love toward someone or something.

- Give it your time; set it before you constantly.
- Give it your attention and care; *look after* the word of God (**it is my meditation all the day**).
- Give it a truly *listening* ear.
- Give it your honor and your obedience.

- Give it your appreciation; value it for all the good it has done for you and be thankful for all that good.

- Give it your dependence and trust; let it care for you.

- Give it your praise; speak highly of it before others.

vi. When we truly love someone, we don't wish to *change* him. "You cannot bend the Bible to your mind; how much better it would be for you to bend your mind to the Bible, and to say, 'O how I love thy law, – the doctrines of it, the precepts of it, the promise of it, the ordinances it enjoins upon me, the warnings it sets before me, the exhortations it gives me!' Love the whole Bible from the beginning of Genesis to the end of Revelation, and be prepared even to die rather than to give up half a verse of it." (Spurgeon)

vii. "I beseech you to let your Bibles be everything to you. Carry this matchless treasure with you continually, and read it, and read it, and read it again and again. Turn to its pages by day and by night. Let its narratives mingle with your dreams; let its precepts color your lives; let its promises cheer your darkness, let its divine illumination make glad your life. As you love God, love this Book which is the Book of God, and the God of books, as it has rightly been called." (Spurgeon)

b. **It is my meditation all the day**: Because the psalmist loved God's word, it was natural and expected that he would think about it often. A lover finds it easy to think about, to meditate upon, the one he loves.

i. "*My meditations*; the matter of my constant and most diligent study…" (Poole)

ii. "He meditated in God's word because he loved it, and then loved it the more because he meditated in it." (Spurgeon)

iii. When we love the Bible, we find much to meditate on.

- The Bible is a letter from our distant Father.

- The Bible is a picture of our best and most faithful Friend.

- The Bible is the certificate of our adoption into the family of God.

- The Bible is the declaration of our liberty, our freedom from slavery.

- The Bible is the description of our heavenly inheritance.

- The Bible is the evidence of our nobility, for we are made kings and priests by God.

- The Bible is the instruction manual for wise and blessed living.

- The Bible is both a statement of our account, and a checkbook for what belongs to us by the promises of God.

- The Bible is a telescope where we see the heavenly city that is our destination.

2. (98-100) God's word gives great wisdom.

You, through Your commandments, make me wiser than my enemies;
For they *are* ever with me.
I have more understanding than all my teachers,
For Your testimonies *are* my meditation.
I understand more than the ancients,
Because I keep Your precepts.

a. **You, through Your commandments, make me wiser than my enemies**: The psalmist had many enemies, some of them evil and some proud. Perhaps the proud ones boasted that they were **wiser** or more educated than the writer of the psalm. Yet the writer was confident that God's word had given him greater wisdom.

i. The psalmist is wiser and has more understanding than his enemies (verse 98), his teachers (verse 99), and the ancients (verse 100). "The comparison is not a prideful assertion of superiority, but a form of exultation in the Lord himself, whose wisdom is more direct and superior." (VanGemeren)

b. **For they are ever with me**: The psalmist was real about the abiding presence of his enemies. They were with him **ever**, and he had to gain enough spiritual strength and enough strength of character to survive and even thrive with them **with** him.

i. "Neither grace received, nor experience attained, nor engagements regarded, will secure me for one moment without continual teaching from thyself." (Bridges)

c. **I have more understanding than all my teachers, for Your testimonies are my meditation**: Here the psalmist explained why he was **wiser than** his enemies. He even had more **understanding** than **all** his **teachers** (who, we hope were not the same as his previously mentioned **enemies**) because of his serious study and **meditation** on God's word.

i. This verse teaches us that it is vitally important to have **understanding**, even great **understanding**. We know this because of the value the psalmist places on having **more understanding**.

ii. This verse teaches us that it is not wrong or bad to have **teachers**, because the psalmist indeed had (either now or in the past) **teachers** who taught him about life and God's word. This verse is *not* a renunciation of those teachers.

iii. This verse teaches us that our **understanding** of God's word and ways is not limited to what we receive from our **teachers**. We can learn from our own study and **meditation**; teachers are often helpful but not absolutely necessary. **Understanding** is necessary; **teachers** may or may not be.

iv. This verse teaches us that this **understanding** does not come easily; true **meditation** involves some element of work. It requires the ability to stay focused and the necessary tools for Biblical understanding and analysis.

v. This principle has been proven in the lives of God's servants again and again. The Bible tells us of men who were not educated by the world's standards (such as the disciples, as in Acts 4:13) yet they had great **understanding** and were effective in serving God.

vi. This principle has also been proven in the lives of God's servants since Bible times. Notable examples of men greatly used without the accepted educational credentials of their day include Charles Spurgeon, D.L. Moody, William Carey, D. Martyn Lloyd-Jones, and Hudson Taylor.

vii. God has also used many who were greatly educated. Moses, Daniel, and Paul are all Biblical examples. Augustine, Martin Luther, and Billy Graham are just a few historical examples. It's just as wrong to think that formal education *disqualifies* someone for effective service as it is to think that it automatically qualifies someone for effective service.

viii. "We may hear the wisest teachers and remain fools, but if we meditate upon the sacred word we must become wise. There is more wisdom in the testimonies of the Lord than in all the teachings of men if they were all gathered into one vast library. The one book outweighs all the rest." (Spurgeon)

ix. "It is no reflection upon my teachers, but rather an honour to them, for me to improve so as to excel them, and no longer to need them." (Matthew Henry, cited in Spurgeon)

d. **I understand more than the ancients, because I keep your precepts**: The psalmist was even more bold than just saying that God's word had given him an education greater than his **teachers**. Now he says "**I understand more than the ancients**."

i. "He understands more than the aged, that is, the direct keeping of the Divine precepts is of more value than the advice of others, even though they have had long experience." (Morgan)

ii. This is particularly meaningful when we realize how highly regarded the wisdom of **the ancients** was in that day and culture. In the modern world it is all too common to disregard the wisdom and understanding of the ancients, but not in the psalmist's time.

iii. This also tells us that while we should in general respect the understanding and wisdom of **the ancients** (which the psalmist surely did, in general), we *are not slaves to their wisdom and understanding.* Our rule for faith and doctrine and living is the Bible itself, not the understanding or interpretation of it from even the great men of history.

iv. "The ancients are held in high repute, but what did they all know compared with that which we perceive in the divine precepts? 'The old is better' says one: but the oldest of all is the best of all, and what is that but the word of the Ancient of days." (Spurgeon)

v. James Montgomery Boice told a story about the life of Harry Ironside, the pastor, author, and Bible commentator. Ironside went to visit a man near death, who was suffering from tuberculosis. The man was almost dead and could barely speak. As Ironside spoke to him he asked, "Young man, you are trying to preach Christ, are you not?" Ironside said that he was, and the man replied: "Well, sit down a little, and let us talk together about the Word of God." Then the man opened his Bible and spoke with Ironside until his strength was gone; he shared insights from the Bible that Ironside had not appreciated or even seen before. Ironside was stunned, and he asked the man: "Where did you get these things? Can you tell me where I can find a book that will open them up to me? Did you get them in seminary or college?" The old man replied: "My dear young man, I learned these things on my knees on the mud floor of a little sod cottage in the north of Ireland. There with my open Bible before me, I used to kneel for hours at a time and ask the Spirit of God to reveal Christ to my soul and to open the Word to my heart. He taught me more on my knees on that mud floor than I ever could have learned in all the seminaries or colleges in the world."

3. (101-102) The word of God keeps one from evil.

I have restrained my feet from every evil way,
That I may keep Your word.

I have not departed from Your judgments,
For You Yourself have taught me.

> a. **I have restrained my feet from every evil way, that I may keep Your word**: The psalmist understood that restraining himself from evil would also help him understand God's word better. He could better **keep** God's word by staying away from **every evil way**.
>
>> i. "There is no treasuring up the holy word unless there is a casting out of all unholiness: if we keep the good word we must let go the evil." (Spurgeon)
>
> b. **I have not departed from Your judgments, for You Yourself have taught me**: The personal connection the psalmist had with God through His word *encouraged* a faithful walk.
>
>> i. This also demonstrates that God can teach the believer through His word in a direct sense – **You Yourself have taught me**. This does not mean that *everything* one comes to through self-study is correct or from God, and it does not eliminate the need for Bible teachers. Yet it does fulfill what Jesus later said in John 16:13: ...*when He, the Spirit of truth, has come, He will guide you into all truth*.
>
>> ii. **You Yourself have taught me**: "The word *thou* [**You**] is emphatic. Here is the guarantor of biblical truth, and the One who alone opens the disciple's eyes to see it." (Kidner)

4. (103-104) The sweet understanding from the word of God.

How sweet are Your words to my taste,
***Sweeter* than honey to my mouth!**
Through Your precepts I get understanding;
Therefore I hate every false way.

> a. **How sweet are Your words to my taste**: The psalmist felt the word of God was as pleasant to him as **sweet** things – even **sweeter than honey**! Time spent in God's word was not an unpleasant duty; it was a **sweet** experience to be thankful for.
>
>> i. **How sweet**: "He expresses the fact of their sweetness, but as he cannot express the degree of their sweetness he cries, '*How* sweet!'" (Spurgeon)
>
>> ii. "The study and obedience of thy words yields me more satisfaction and delight than any worldly men find in their sensual pleasures." (Poole)
>
>> iii. The psalmist had very little of God's word – perhaps just the five books of Moses and a few books more. We have so much more riches

and sweetness in the word of God than he did; yet most of us seem to value it less.

iv. The Bible is filled with passage after passage that anyone with spiritual sensitivity would find **sweet**. Passages like Psalm 23:1-3, Psalm 8:1, John 3:16, Romans 8:28, or Revelation 22:20 are just a sample. "If you can't find anything beautiful or sweet in these verses, your taste bids are terribly dulled and your eyes horribly glazed by the tawdry glitz of our culture." (Boice)

v. "For what argument could ever persuade us that honey is bitter, at the moment we are tasting its sweetness?" (Bridges)

vi. "If the word of God be not very sweet to me, have I an appetite? Solomon says, 'The full soul loatheth a honeycomb; but to the hungry soul every bitter thing is sweet' [Proverbs 27:7]. Ah, when a soul is full of itself, and of the world, and of the pleasures of sin, I do not wonder that it sees no sweetness in Christ, for it has no appetite!" (Spurgeon)

vi. "It is a blessed sign of grace in the heart when God's words are sweet to us as a whole, – when we love the truth, not cast into a system or a shape, but as we find it in God's word. I believe that no man who has yet lived has ever proposed a system of theology which comprises all the truth of God's word. If such a system had been possible, the discovery of it would have been made for us by God himself: – certainly it would if it had been desirable and useful for our profit and holiness. But it has not pleased God to give us a body of divinity; let us receive it as he has given it, each truth in its own proportion, – each doctrine in harmony with its fellow, – each precept carefully carried out into practice, and each promise to be believed, and by-and-by received. Let the truth, and the whole truth, be sweet to our taste." (Spurgeon)

b. **Through Your precepts I get understanding; therefore I hate every false way**: The **understanding** gained by the psalmist gave him *discernment* and the power to persevere and **hate every false way**.

i. Notably, the psalmist began this section with love; he ends it with **hate**. "The Christian life is not all sweetness.... It has its sweet moments, and there is incomparable beauty in God. But we still live in a sour, ugly world, and it is equally important to learn to hate evil as well as love the good." (Boice)

N. Nun **נ**: Never-ending confidence in God's word.

1. (105) The illuminating guidance of God's word.

Your word *is* a lamp to my feet
And a light to my path.

a. **Your word is a lamp to my feet**: The psalmist walked the road of life, the **word** of God made his steps clear. He would not know where to step without the guidance of God's word.

i. It is possible to walk the path of life without knowing where our steps will fall. We don't know if our foot will step on good ground or dangerous ground; we are not self-aware. God's **word** can be a **lamp** to our feet.

ii. Simply said, the Bible should help us walk the way God wants us to walk. Think of all the different words we use to clarify walking: stroll, saunter, amble, trudge, plod, dawdle, hike, tramp, tromp, slog, stomp, march, stride, sashay, glide, troop, patrol, wander, ramble, tread, prowl, promenade, roam, traipse, mosey, and perambulate. The different words show that there are many different ways to walk, and each of them *says* something.

iii. How are Christians to walk?

- Worthy (Ephesians 4:1).
- Uprightly (Isaiah 57:2).
- In the light (1 John 1:7).
- Humbly (Micah 6:8).

None of these are possible without the word of God lighting our way.

iv. The picture of a **lamp** says something. "Thus is our passage in a dark and perilous way irradiated by the *lamp and light of the word*. But except *the lamp* be lighted – except the teaching of the Spirit accompany *the word*, all is darkness – thick darkness. Let us not be content to read *the word* without obtaining some *light* from it in our understanding." (Bridges)

b. **A light to my path**: The word of God not only showed the psalmist where his feet stepped, but also the **path** he should remain upon. It showed him the next few steps to take.

i. We need the Bible to teach us right from wrong. We certainly do have some inner sense of this in our conscience; but our conscience can be weak, ignorant, or damaged. The word of God is higher even than our conscience, and it teaches our conscience.

ii. "This is not convenient guidance for one's career, but truth for moral choices; see, for example, the kind of 'snare' and 'straying' that are implied in 119:110." (Kidner)

iii. "One of the most practical benefits of Holy Writ is guidance in the acts of daily life." (Spurgeon)

c. **Your word is a lamp...and a light**: These pictures show us that the word of God is **light** and brings **light**; it doesn't make things darker or harder to understand. It is a **light** book, not a dark book.

i. "This stanza emphasizes the clarity of Scripture, the attribute of the Bible that meant so much to the Protestant Reformers, who also called it perspicuity. What they meant by clarity of perspicuity is that the Bible is basically comprehensible to any open-minded person who reads it." (Boice)

ii. Not all parts of Scripture are equally clear or easy to understand; it is helpful to have wisdom from others in what they have seen in the Scriptures. Yet at its core, the Bible can be understood, and Christians *do* understand it. Think of all the common ground Christians, even of greatly different denominations, have together:

- The truth of a Triune God.
- The truth of the full deity and full humanity of Jesus.
- The truth of our sin.
- The truth of Jesus' death for us to save us from sin and death.
- The work of the Holy Spirit in leading us to faith.
- The establishment of the church, the community of believers.
- The return of Jesus Christ.
- The resurrection of the dead.

Taken together, these are a lot! In general, Christians *do* agree in their understanding of the Bible.

iii. This doesn't mean that someone's opinion on the meaning of a Bible passage is just as good as everyone else's opinion. It is really just the opposite; the Bible is clear enough to be understood, and this means that some so-called understandings are wrong.

2. (106-108) Trusting the life-giving power of God's word.

I have sworn and confirmed
That I will keep Your righteous judgments.
I am afflicted very much;

Revive me, O Lord, according to Your word.
Accept, I pray, the freewill offerings of my mouth, O Lord,
And teach me Your judgments.

a. **I have sworn and confirmed that I will keep Your righteous judgments**: The psalmist showed a *determination of life* to obey the word of God. It was a double-decision, both **sworn and confirmed**.

i. **I have sworn and confirmed**: Bridges tells of a man named Pearce, who read a book titled *Rise and Progress of Religion*. From it, he decided that he would live a more dedicated and obedient life. He wrote out a covenant with God, and in a very serious and solemn way, he even signed it with his own blood. It wasn't long until he started failing in his commitment to the covenant – first in small ways and then more and more. This plunged him into deep distress, almost to total despair. Then he considered that the arrangement he had made with God was actually legalistic and pharisaical, especially in the way that it relied on the power of his own vows and resolutions. So he took the covenant to the top of his house, tore it into small pieces, and threw it to the wind. He did not feel himself free from the promises themselves, only now he was of a mind to not rely on himself or his own vows, but only on the blood of Jesus Christ and the indwelling power of His Spirit. This led to a much better result, and he was close to the source of comfort and restoration when he did fail.

b. **I am afflicted very much; revive me, O Lord, according to Your word**: His determination to be obedient came from a season of affliction, not comfort and ease. Despite his many problems and pains, he looked to God's word for a reviving of life, and for this to happen **according to** His **word**.

i. "The faithful servants of God may be 'afflicted'; they may be 'very much' and grieviously afflicted: but let them consider, that, by afflictions, their corruptions are purged away, their faith is tried, their patience is perfected, their brethren are edified, and their Master is glorified." (Horne)

c. **Accept, I pray, the freewill offerings of my mouth**: The psalmist presented these words to the Lord as if they were a sacrifice brought to an altar. They were **freewill offerings** meant to show his love and devotion to God.

i. "God's revenues are not derived from forced taxation, but from freewill donation. There can be no acceptance where there is no willingness; there is no work of free grace where there is no fruit of free will." (Spurgeon)

d. **And teach me Your judgments**: It is very easy for us to have a sinful confidence in our own judgment – to simply "follow my heart." Yet Spurgeon wrote well: "These repeated cries for teaching show the humility of the man of God, and also discover to us our own need of similar instruction. Our judgment needs educating till it knows, agrees with, and acts upon, the judgments of the Lord."

3. (109-110) Trusting God's word despite danger.

My life *is* continually in my hand,
Yet I do not forget Your law.
The wicked have laid a snare for me,
Yet I have not strayed from Your precepts.

a. **My life is continually in my hand, yet I do not forget Your law**: The psalmist's life was often in danger, yet his connection to the word of God stayed strong.

b. **The wicked have laid a snare for me, yet I have not strayed from Your precepts**: The dangers came from determined enemies, who were **wicked** people. Yet he would not forsake the **precepts** of God.

i. "From this verse let us learn to be on our guard, for we, too, have enemies both crafty and wicked. Hunters set their traps in the animals' usual runs, and our worst snares are laid in our own ways. By keeping to the ways of the Lord we shall escape the snares of our adversaries, for his ways are safe and free from treachery." (Spurgeon)

ii. "Whenever we find the psalms talking about danger, we usually think of physical danger.... But the psalms also speak of spiritual dangers like falling into sin or forgetting God." (Boice)

4. (111-112) An enduring commitment to God and His word.

Your testimonies I have taken as a heritage forever,
For they *are* the rejoicing of my heart.
I have inclined my heart to perform Your statutes
Forever, to the very end.

a. **Your testimonies I have taken as a heritage forever, for they are the rejoicing of my heart**: The psalmist rejoiced in God's word with a deep heart-felt joy. Therefore, the **testimonies** became his **heritage forever**.

i. "What is the psalmist's spiritual heritage, that is, what is he looking toward and working for? Some heavenly reward? A word of praise from God? Surprisingly, he says that his heritage is what he has been speaking about all along: God's Word itself." (Boice)

ii. How do the **testimonies** of God belong to us? "How did he claim an interest in them? Not by purchase, or by merit, it was his *heritage*.... Man looks at his *heritage*. 'This land – this estate – or this kingdom is mine.' The child of God looks round on the universe – on both worlds – on God himself with his infinite perfections – and says, 'All things are mine.' My title is more sure than to any earthly *heritage*." (Bridges)

iii. "I take possession of my *heritage*, I live on it, I live in it, it is my treasure, my portion. If a man is known by his *heritage*, let me be known by mine." (Bridges)

iv. "*Thy testimonies have I taken as a heritage.* To these he was *heir*; he had *inherited* them from his fathers, and he was determined to leave them to his *family* for ever. If a man can leave nothing to his child but a *Bible*, in that he bequeaths him the greatest treasure in the universe." (Clarke)

b. **I have inclined my heart to perform Your statutes forever, to the very end**: The theme is once again emphasized. The psalmist would never forsake God's word – never stop reading, learning, meditating, and especially obeying it.

i. "Observe where he begins his work – not with the eye – the ear – the tongue – but with *the heart*." (Bridges)

ii. "The whole movement ends with a declaration which must be read in the light of the opening affirmation, and the following experience and need. It is that of complete abandonment to the will of God...even unto the end." (Morgan)

iii. The believer feels that every step is dangerous; this is why he cried out for the lamp to his feet and the light to his path. With every step dangerous, how can he ever hope to endure **forever, to the very end**? He can, because the same God who lights and sustains him for one step can do it for every step, **to the very end**.

O. Samek ס: Held up and supported by the word of God.

The fifteenth letter, Samek, denotes a prop *or* pillar, *and this agrees well with the subject matter of the strophe, in which God is twice implored to uphold his servant (119:116,117).* (Neal and Littledale, cited in Spurgeon)

1. (113-114) Protection found in the word of God.

I hate the double-minded,
But I love Your law.
You *are* my hiding place and my shield;
I hope in Your word.

a. **I hate the double-minded, but I love Your law**: The psalmist knew the frustration of dealing with those who were **double-minded**. They were uncertain and uncommitted in their lives. In contrast, the **law** of God is sure and certain.

> i. "*Double-minded* is akin to the word in Elijah's taunt at those who hobbled 'first on one leg and then on the other' (1 Kings 18:21, Jerusalem Bible)." (Kidner)

> ii. "Double-minded people are people who know about God but are not fully determined to worship and serve him only. They are those who want both God and the world. They want the benefits of true religion, but they want their sin too.... The Psalmist hates this double-mindedness; he also hates it in himself." (Boice)

> iii. **But I love Your law**: "When we love the law it becomes a law of love, and we cling to it with our whole heart." (Spurgeon)

b. **You are my hiding place and my shield; I hope in Your word**: The God the psalmist knew so well through His word became a refuge in troubled times. The **hope** he had in the **word** of God was not initiated by mere academic or intellectual knowledge; it was founded on a relationship with and security in God Himself (**my hiding place and my shield**).

> i. A good hiding place has strength, height, concealment, and reliability. Jesus is our *safe-room* or *panic-room*.

> ii. "There is a time in which I may be called to *suffer in secret*; then thou *hidest me*. There may be a time in which thou callest me to *fight*; then thou art my *Shield* and *Protector*." (Clarke)

> iii. "This is an experiential verse, and it testifies to that which the writer knew of his own personal knowledge: he could not fight with his own thoughts, or escape from them, till he flew to his God, and then he found deliverance. Observe that he does not speak of God's word as being his double defence, but he ascribes that to God himself." (Spurgeon)

2. (115) A word to the wicked.

Depart from me, you evildoers,
For I will keep the commandments of my God!

a. **Depart from me, you evildoers**: In a rare departure in his ongoing conversation with God about His word, the psalmist here addressed the **evildoers** that brought him such trouble. He knew that the best remedy was to put space between him and these **evildoers**, so he boldly told them, **"Depart from me."**

i. The psalmist was careful in the choosing of his friends. As it has been said, "Show me your friends, and I will show you your future."

ii. "Every man will insensibly contract the good or bad qualities of the company which he keeps; and should, therefore, be careful to keep such as will make him wiser and better, and fit him for the goodly fellowship of saints and angels." (Horne)

iii. "Not that we would indulge morose or ascetic seclusion. We are expressly enjoined to courtesy and kindness (1 Peter 3:8); to that wise and considerate 'walk towards them that are without' (Colossians 4:5), which 'adorns the doctrine of God our Saviour' (Titus 2:10), and indeed in some instances has been more powerful even than the word itself (Compare 1 Peter 3:1,2), to 'win souls to Christ.' But when they would tempt us to a devious or backsliding step – when our connexion with them entices us to a single act of conformity to their standard, dishonourable to God, and inconsistent with our profession – then we must take a bold and unflinching stand." (Bridges)

b. **For I will keep the commandments of my God**: This is *why* he wanted space between him and the **evildoers**. He was committed to obedience, to keeping the **commandments** of God.

i. The second line of this verse very much connects with the first line. "Since he found it hard to keep the commandments in the company of the ungodly, he gave them their marching orders. He *must* keep the commandments, but he did not need to keep their company." (Spurgeon)

ii. Jesus demonstrated the same spirit when He steadfastly resisted the devil while being tempted in the wilderness (Matthew 4). He told the devil to go away (Matthew 4:10) and repeatedly relied on the word of God (Matthew 4:4,7,10).

iii. "The word *God* only occurs in this one place in all this lengthened Psalm, and then it is attended by the personal word '*my*' – 'my God.'" (Spurgeon)

3. (116-117) Held up and supported by the word of God.

Uphold me according to Your word, that I may live;
And do not let me be ashamed of my hope.
Hold me up, and I shall be safe,
And I shall observe Your statutes continually.

a. **Uphold me according to Your word, that I may live**: The psalmist knew that he could not stand before his enemies without God holding him up. Without this continual support from God, he could not **live** – either physically or spiritually.

i. His idea was that this support (**Uphold me**) would come **according to** God's **word**. It would be *consistent* with God's word and *find its source* in God's word.

ii. "In the Middle Ages, under the monastic order of the Benedictines, when a novice's period of preparation was ended and he was ready to become attached to the monastery for life, there was an induction ceremony in which, with outstretched arms, the novice recited Psalm 119:116 three times.... The community repeated the words and then sang the Gloria Patri, which was a way of acknowledging that the commitments of the monastic life could only be sustained by God, to whom all glory belongs." (Boice)

b. **Do not let me be ashamed of my hope**: The psalmist could pray this because he had his **hope** properly set. It was set upon God and His word (verses 43, 49, 74, 81, and 114). When our **hope** is so set, we can ask God to protect and vindicate us.

c. **Hold me up, and I shall be safe, and I shall observe Your statutes continually**: This is the second request in this brief section for support from God, and especially through His word. In receiving this support and security, the psalmist would use it for further obedience to God.

i. This constant dependence upon God – the constant prayer, "**Hold me up, and I shall be safe**" – will in fact keep one safe.

4. (118-120) The righteous judgment of God.

You reject all those who stray from Your statutes,
For their deceit *is* falsehood.
You put away all the wicked of the earth *like* dross;
Therefore I love Your testimonies.
My flesh trembles for fear of You,
And I am afraid of Your judgments.

a. **You reject all those who stray from Your statutes**: The psalmist here speaks of the righteous judgment of God. He uses His word (**statutes**) as a measuring line for His judgment, rejecting **all those who stray** from His word and the principles revealed therein.

b. **You put away all the wicked of the earth like dross**: In His judgments, God has a purifying purpose and effect. He will cleanse the **earth** from the **wicked**, treating them as impurities that need to be scraped away.

i. **Dross**: "The scum that forms on the top when a precious metal is being refined, is discarded by the metalsmith (cf. Isaiah 1:22; Jeremiah 6:28-30; Ezekiel 22:18-19)." (VanGemeren)

ii. **Like dross**: Sin is really very much **like dross**.

- **Dross** takes away from the shine and glory of metal; it makes it dull.

- **Dross** is deceptive; it is not silver, but seems like it; it is not gold but seems like it.

- **Dross** is not made better by the fire.

- **Dross** is worthless. It has no value, no purpose.

- **Dross** is actually damaging to metal, because it can lead to rust. Metal with dross in it will be eaten away.

c. **Therefore I love Your testimonies**: The consideration of these righteous judgments made the psalmist praise God even more. He praised God and His word (**Your testimonies**) as righteous measures of judgment.

i. **Therefore I love Your testimonies**: "...because they take out the precious from the vile, and make men the same within as without." (Trapp)

d. **My flesh trembles for fear of You, and I am afraid of Your judgments**: As the psalmist considered the righteous judgments of God, he looked to his own life and understood that it was not entirely righteous. This sense of trembling **fear** would make him run to God for His atoning, covering sacrifice.

i. The psalmist didn't celebrate over the judgment on the wicked; it made him tremble in holy fear himself.

ii. "The presence of God is so real for the psalmist that he responds to his God in spirit and body. His life of obedience is lived in the presence of the living God, whereas the wicked act as if God does not see or care." (VanGemeren)

iii. "His best servants are not exempted from an awful dread, upon such occasions; scenes of this kind, shown in vision to the prophets, cause their flesh to quiver, and all their bones to shake." (Horne)

iv. "It is only as we tremble before the exalted and holy God that we will ever see the world and its distorted values to be the empty things they are. If we do not tremble before God, the world's system will seem wonderful to us and consume us pleasantly." (Boice)

P. Ayin ע: The servant seeks the word.

1. (121-122) A prayer for protection from the proud.

I have done justice and righteousness;
Do not leave me to my oppressors.
Be surety for Your servant for good;
Do not let the proud oppress me.

a. **I have done justice and righteousness**: As in other sections of this psalm, this is not a claim to sinless perfection. The psalmist is expressing confidence in the general **righteousness** of his life. The psalmist knew his life and the lives of his **oppressors**; he knew that his life was dedicated to God and theirs was not.

i. "Nor is this kind of pleading to be censured as self-righteous: when we are dealing with God as to our shortcomings, we use a very different tone from that with which we face the censures of our fellow-men; when they are in the question, and we are guiltless towards them, we are justified in pleading our innocence." (Spurgeon)

ii. This confidence in his spiritual condition and his separation from those who *didn't* follow God is notable. The psalmist *knew* that his life was different from those who did not follow God. The difference was in more than theology; it was in life.

iii. Horne saw in these words something that Jesus could claim: "The Son of David might use the words in their full and absolute sense, and plead for a glorious resurrection, on the foot of his having performed a perfect obedience to the law."

b. **Be surety for Your servant for good**: The psalmist asked God to defend and stand up for him. It was only through God defending him that he could avoid the oppression of the proud.

i. "Take up my interests and weave them with thine own, and stand for me. As my Master, undertake thy servants' cause, and represent me before the faces of haughty men till they see what an august ally I have in the Lord my God." (Spurgeon)

ii. This provides evidence that his previous claim to **justice and righteousness** was not in an absolute sense. If he felt completely just and righteous before God, he would not have pleaded for God to stand as a **surety** for him – but he did. "Though upright before man, he ever felt himself a sinner before God." (Bridges)

iii. The psalmist cried out to God as Job did: *Now put down a pledge for me with Yourself* (Job 17:3). The psalmist prayed that God would be to him what Jesus is to His people – a surety of the covenant (Hebrews 7:22).

iv. "…as Judah in the place of Benjamin – 'I will be surety of him: of mine hand shalt thou require him.' (Genesis 43:9)" (Bridges)

v. "We should have been crushed beneath our proud adversary the devil if our Lord Jesus had not stood between us and the accuser, and become a surety for us." (Spurgeon)

c. **Do not let the proud oppress me:** Verse 22 is another rare verse in this psalm that does not mention the word of God in some way.

i. "According to the Masoretes, verse 122 is the only verse in the psalm that does not mention the Word of God. We have seen that verse 84 also seems not to mention it; verses 90, 121, and 132 may be examples too." (Boice)

ii. "The fact that the Bible is not mentioned here, in verse 122, may be an indication of the depth of mental anguish to which the psalmist fell as a result of the oppression he had endured from wicked men. For a moment his eyes seem to be off the Bible and on his fierce oppressors instead." (Boice)

2. (123-125) The servant of God seeks salvation in His statutes.

My eyes fail *from seeking* Your salvation
And Your righteous word.
Deal with Your servant according to Your mercy,
And teach me Your statutes.
I *am* Your servant;
Give me understanding,
That I may know Your testimonies.

a. **My eyes fail from seeking Your salvation and Your righteous word:** This was another indication of how committed the psalmist was to the **word** of God, and how much he valued the **salvation** he found from it.

i. "He looked to God alone, he looked eagerly, he looked long, he looked till his eyes ached. The mercy is, that if our eyes fail, God does not fail, nor do *his* eyes fail." (Spurgeon)

ii. This waiting expectation shows us that *faith* came before *experience*. The psalmist was willing to have faith until the experience came. He would wait for God's salvation, and wait as long as it took.

b. **Deal with Your servant according to Your mercy, and teach me Your statutes:** The psalmist understood that when God teaches His people, it is evidence of His **mercy**. He has no inherent obligation to teach us; yet out of the merciful impulse of His heart, He does so.

c. **I am Your servant; give me understanding**: For the third time in four verses, the psalmist calls himself a **servant** of God. He understood that this meant he had obligations to God, and that God – as his Master – had obligations to him. Therefore he could ask for **understanding**.

> i. "I have voluntarily hired myself unto thee, chosen the things that please thee, and taken hold of the covenant.... Now, this is all the wages I crave of thee, 'Give me understanding.'" (Trapp)

> ii. "We may expect a master to teach his own servant the meaning of his own orders." (Spurgeon)

d. **Give me understanding, that I may know Your testimonies**: The psalmist wanted **understanding** – not so much to know the future or some hidden secrets of his soul or that of someone else's, but so that he would **know** the **testimonies** of God better.

> i. He believed that the word of God could be understood, with the help of God Himself.

> ii. He believed that **understanding** God's word was of great importance, because it would lead him into other wisdom and understanding of life.

> iii. "It is remarkable that the psalmist does not pray for understanding through acquiring knowledge, but begs of the Lord first that he may have the gracious gift of understanding, and then may obtain the desired instruction." (Spurgeon)

3. (126) A plea for God to act.

It is **time for *You* to act, O** LORD,
For **they have regarded Your law as void.**

a. **It is time for You to act, O** LORD: We admire the holy boldness of the psalmist. It almost seems rude for a man to tell God, **It is time for You to act**. Yet many who walk with God understand the desperate plea of the psalmist perfectly. He is so needy and dependent on God that it is good and right to make his request so boldly.

> i. "The psalmist speaketh not as prescribing God a time, but as reminding him of his own glory and of his people's necessity." (Trapp)

> ii. It is true that we don't know the ways of God's timing; many times, we have been wrong on this point. We have thought God must act *now*, when in His wisdom and glory He worked *later*. Yet all we can do

is pray by what we can see; and when we see conditions as the psalmist saw, it is good for us to say, **It is time for You to act, O Lord.**

iii. "We might expect the writer to have said that God should act now because if he delays it will be too late; he will be crushed by his oppressors.... Here, instead of pleading his own desperate condition, he calls on God to act because God's 'law is being broken'." (Boice)

b. **For they have regarded Your law as void**: Prompting the bold plea was the observation that many disregarded the word and **law** of God. In such times – when every man does what is right in his own eyes (Judges 21:25) – it is proper for the people of God to plead for Him to **act**.

i. "The 'law' of God is 'made void' by those who deny its authority, or its obligation; by those who render it of none effect, through their traditions or their lives." (Horne)

ii. "To persist in *making void the law* after so magnificent an exhibition of Almighty *working* – must it not expose the transgressors to reap the fruit of their own obstinacy, and to prepare to meet him as their Judge, whom they refuse to receive as their Saviour?" (Bridges)

4. (127-128) The word of God is precious and right.

Therefore I love Your commandments
More than gold, yes, than fine gold!
Therefore all *Your* precepts *concerning* all *things*
I consider *to be* right;
I hate every false way.

a. **Therefore I love Your commandments more than gold**: Though others regarded the word of God as void, the psalmist decided to love His **commandments** all the more in response. He valued them **more than gold** – even more **than fine gold**.

i. The psalmist remembered what kind of men considered the word of God as *void*. When he considered the monstrous men who had been enemies of God's word – men in our own age like Stalin, Hitler, Mao – he knew that the word of God was lovely.

ii. "I like them better because they slight them, and prize that way the more they persecute. I kindle myself from their coldness." (Trapp)

iii. "...*above solid gold*; gold separated from the dross, perfectly *refined*." (Clarke)

iv. "Should I not *love* [**Your commandments**]? Can *gold, yea, fine gold,* offer to me blessings such as these? Can it heal my broken heart? Can it give relief to my wounded spirit? Has it any peace or prospect of comfort for me on my death bed?" (Bridges)

b. **Therefore all Your precepts concerning all things I consider to be right**: With great confidence, the psalmist proclaimed the inerrancy of God's word. It was **right**, not wrong; and it was right **concerning all things**.

- When the Bible gives us history, it is **right** and true; the events actually happened as described.

- When the Bible gives us poetry, it is **right** and true; the feeling and experiences were real for the writer and ring true to human experience.

- When the Bible gives us prophecy, it is **right** and true; the events described will or have already come to pass, just as it is written.

- When the Bible gives us instruction, it is **right** and true; it truly does tell us the will of God and the best way of life.

- When the Bible tells us of God, it is **right** and true; it reveals to us what the nature and heart and mind of God are, as much as we can comprehend.

c. **I hate every false way**: Because the psalmist loved and trusted the word of God so much, he naturally hated **every false way**. He could not love the truth without also hating lies.

i. As Jesus said, *No one can serve two masters; for either he will hate the one and love the other, or else he will be loyal to the one and despise the other* (Matthew 6:24).

ii. "We cannot love the right path without hating the wrong ones.... Are you willing to hate what God hates? If not, you will never learn to love God truly, and you will certainly never walk in the way that brings true blessing." (Boice)

iii. And significantly, he hated **every false way**, not just some of them. "If Satan get a grip of thee by any one sin, is it not enough to carry thee to damnation? As the butcher carries the beast to the slaughter, sometime bound by all the four feet, and sometime by one only; so it is with Satan. Though thou be not a slave to all sin; if thou be a slave to one, the grip he hath of thee, by that one sinful affection, is sufficient to captive thee." (William Cowper, cited in Spurgeon)

Q. Pe פ: Steps directed by God's wonderful word.

1. (129) Obeying the wonderful testimonies of God.

Your testimonies are wonderful;
Therefore my soul keeps them.

a. **Your testimonies are wonderful**: The psalmist again declared his wonder and pleasure in the word of God. It was a continuing source of fascination to him.

i. "The word 'wonderful' is equivalent to our use of the word miraculous. These testimonies are supernatural, superhuman." (Morgan)

ii. The **testimonies** are supernatural in their nature, being free from error. They are supernatural in their effects, as they instruct, elevate, strengthen, and comfort the soul.

iii. "Jesus the eternal Word is called Wonderful, and all the uttered words of God are wonderful in their degree. Those who know them best wonder at them most. It is wonderful that God should have borne testimony at all to sinful men, and more wonderful still that his testimony should be of such a character, so clear, so full, so gracious, so mighty." (Spurgeon)

iv. "There is a height, length, depth, and breadth in thy word and testimonies that are truly astonishing; and on this account my soul loves them, and I deeply study them. The more I study, the more light and salvation I obtain." (Clarke)

v. "Let us not enter into the *testimonies*, as a dry task, or an ordinary study; but let us concentrate our minds, our faith, humility, and prayer, in a more devoted contemplation of them." (Bridges)

b. **Therefore my soul keeps them**: The enduring, abiding delight he had in the word of God prompted greater obedience. This was obedience in more than outward action; it was obedience in **soul**.

i. "Holy admiration of the *testimonies* will kindle spiritual devotedness to them – *Therefore doth my soul keep them*." (Bridges)

2. (130-131) Receiving the light-giving word.

The entrance of Your words gives light;
It gives understanding to the simple.
I opened my mouth and panted,
For I longed for Your commandments.

a. **The entrance of Your words gives light**: The psalmist repeated a previous idea, that God's word brought **light** to him. His **words** made things more clear, not less. When the word came in, **light** and clarity came in.

i. "The Hebrew word for 'entrance' is *pethach*. Depending on whether it is pronounced with a short or a long *e* it can mean either 'door' (with a short *e*) or 'revelation' (with a long *e*).... Martin Luther thought it had to do with revelation; so his translation read, '*Wenn dein Wort offenbar wird* ('When your word is revealed')." (Boice)

ii. "The explanation for this double meaning is that in the early days of the formation of the Hebrew language the Jews were bedouins, who lived in tents. The only opening in the tent was the flap of skin that was the door. So when the door was opened, light came into the tent, illuminating everything inside." (Boice)

iii. "It is painful to remember how much light may be shining around us on every side, without finding an *entrance* into the heart." (Bridges)

iv. "The word finds no entrance into some minds because they are blocked up with self-conceit, or prejudice, or indifference; but where due attention is given, divine illumination must surely follow upon knowledge of the mind of God." (Spurgeon)

b. **It gives understanding to the simple**: The word of God is so clear and **light**-giving that even **the simple** find **understanding**. It does not take great intellect or mental powers to benefit from God's word.

i. "It is a most striking instance of Divine condescension, that this word – so *wonderful* in its high and heavenly mysteries – should yet open a path so plain, that the most unlearned may find and walk in it." (Bridges)

ii. "So astonishing is the power of this heavenly light, that from any one page of this holy book, a child, or even [the simple], under heavenly teaching, may draw more instruction than the most acute philosopher could ever attain from any other fountain of light!" (Bridges)

iii. "These simple-hearted ones are frequently despised, and their simplicity has another meaning infused into it, so as to be made the theme of ridicule; but what matters it? Those whom the world dubs as fools are among the truly wise if they are taught of God." (Spurgeon)

- This is a *blessing* for **the simple**; God does not forget them. He has not made salvation or growth in godliness primarily a matter of the intellect.

- This is a *promise* for **the simple**; they can approach God's word with confidence, expecting God to give them **understanding**.

- This is a *responsibility* for **the simple**; they cannot make excuses for their average (or lower) intellect or mental powers. They are still responsible to seek God in His word.

c. **I opened my mouth and panted, for I longed for Your commandments**: Because the word of God is **light**-giving and clear (clear enough for the **simple**), the psalmist desired God's word like a thirsty animal pants for water.

> i. He may be panting because he is thirsty, or he may be panting gasping for air; but panting always denotes *desire*.

> ii. "A metaphor taken from an animal exhausted in the chase. He runs, open-mouthed, to take in the cooling air; the heart beating high, and the muscular force nearly expended through fatigue. The psalmist sought for salvation, as he would run from a ferocious beast for his life. Nothing can show his earnestness in a stronger point of view." (Clarke)

> iii. **I longed for Your commandments**: "This cannot mean anything else than that he longed to know them, longed to keep them, longed to teach them, longed to bring all around him into obedience to them. Many religious people long after the promises, and they do well; but they must not forget to have an equal longing for the commandments." (Spurgeon)

> iv. Yet longing that is not acted upon is more *wishing* than longing. As Spurgeon observed, true longing will show itself in *action*: "Never rest content with mere longings. He that really longs is not content to long."

3. (132-135) Four requests rooted in the word of God.

Look upon me and be merciful to me,
As Your custom *is* toward those who love Your name.
Direct my steps by Your word,
And let no iniquity have dominion over me.
Redeem me from the oppression of man,
That I may keep Your precepts.
Make Your face shine upon Your servant,
And teach me Your statutes.

a. **Look upon me and be merciful to me**: This first request is really two: asking God to **look** and then to **be merciful**. The psalmist had reason to believe God would answer, knowing that this was God's **custom...toward those who love Your name**.

> i. It is wonderful to think that God has a **custom**, a pattern of action, **toward those who love** His **name**. That **custom** is to **look upon** them (giving them His attention) and to **be merciful** to them. This promise is a solid ground for trusting, bold prayer in a time of need.

ii. **Look...be merciful**: Yet God's **look** – the turning of His attention – would be a curse and not a blessing unless it was accompanied by His mercy. If we have the first, we desire the second.

iii. "Lord! Since our looks to thee are often so slight, so cold, so distant, that no impression is made upon our hearts; do thou condescend continually to *look upon us* with mercy and power." (Bridges)

iv. "Brethren, there is great virtue in our looking to Christ: it is the way of salvation. What virtue, then, must there be in Christ's love-gaze upon us!" (Spurgeon)

v. **Those who love Your name**: To love the name of God means to…

- Love the *person* of God.
- Love the *character* of God.
- Love the *revelation* of God.
- Love the *glory* of God.

b. **Direct my steps by Your word**: The second request shows what he wanted to do with the mercy received from God. He wanted to take that mercy and use it to walk rightly before God. One part of this was to **let no iniquity have dominion over** him.

i. Many today want to **direct** their **steps** by something else, *anything* else other than the word of God.

- "Direct my steps by my feelings."
- "Direct my steps by my lusts."
- "Direct my steps by my friends."
- "Direct my steps by my parents."
- "Direct my steps by my circumstances."
- "Direct my steps by my fate."
- "Direct my steps by my comfort."

ii. The idea of the Hebrew here, according to Spurgeon, is "*Make my steps firm in thy word.*" We can walk forward in life with confidence as we find direction in God's word.

iii. "The psalmist would be kept from all vacillation, hesitation, or wandering; but he wants, when he is right, to be firmly right, to be distinctly, decidedly right, so he pleads, 'Make my steps firm.' Oh, how we often stagger along! We do what is right, but we quiver and shake while we are doing it." (Spurgeon)

iv. The psalmist was wise to understand that sin can **have dominion over** a man, even a man or woman who has a strong spiritual life. The Apostle Paul recognized the same danger: *All things are lawful for me, but all things are not helpful. All things are lawful for me, but I will not be brought under the power of any* (1 Corinthians 6:12).

v. Sin, unchecked, will attempt to gain and hold dominion in my life. First it may be in a small or seemingly insignificant area, but that dominion will grow in size and strength until my spiritual life is seriously compromised.

vi. "I had rather be a prisoner to man all my life than be in bondage to sin one day. He says not, Let not this and the other man rule over me; but '*let* not *sin* have dominion over me.' Well said!" (Michael Bruce, cited in Spurgeon)

vii. Yet when our **steps** are directed by the **word** of God, we will avoid being under the dominion of sin, and we can be freed from whatever level of dominion sin may have gained.

viii. In a New Testament context, this prayer has even greater grounds for confidence. "But let us mark, how fully is this prayer warranted by the special promise of the Gospel – '*Sin shall not have dominion over you; for ye are not under the law, but under grace*' (Romans 6:14, with 12)." (Bridges)

ix. "Brethren, *we can* overcome sin in the power of the Lord…. Sin is strong, but grace is stronger. Satan is wise, but God is all-wise. The Lord is on our side." (Spurgeon)

c. **Redeem me from the oppression of man**: The third request recognizes that there are dangers beyond the potential dominion of sin in the psalmist's spiritual life. There are also dangers from **the oppression of man**, from those who would oppose and oppress.

i. Notably, the psalmist asked for this so **that I may keep Your precepts**. He didn't just want liberty from man's oppression so he could serve himself, but so that he could properly obey God.

d. **Make Your face shine upon Your servant**: The fourth request is for an experience of the grace and goodness of God. To know the **face** of God shining upon you is to be at peace with God and to know He is at peace with you.

4. (136) Sorrow that others do not keep the law of God.

Rivers of water run down from my eyes,
Because *men* do not keep Your law.

a. **Rivers of water run down from my eyes**: This is a good example of poetic hyperbole in the psalms. Though there were not literal **rivers of water** coming down the face of the psalmist, he spoke truly according to the literary style of poetry. There is not the slightest problem in understanding his meaning.

> i. "The idiom 'streams [lit., "irrigation canals," see Psalm 1:3] of tears' is a hyperbole for deep sorrow and anguish of soul." (VanGemeren)

> ii. "Tears show compassion, and compassion wins others far more effectively than belligerent arguments and certainly more effectively than anger." (Boice)

b. **Because men do not keep Your law**: The psalmist here did not sorrow over his own troubles, but over the sins of others and the consequences those sins would bring. As Jesus grieved over Jerusalem (Matthew 23:37-39) and over the hard hearts of the religious leaders (Mark 3:5), so the psalmist grieved here.

> i. "It grieveth me greatly to see thy law violated, and the transgressors thereof so careless of their own eternal good." (Trapp)

> ii. "…plentiful and perpetual tears, witnesses of my deep sorrow for God's dishonour and displeasure, and for the miseries which sinners bring upon themselves." (Poole)

> iii. "The want of this spirit is ever a feature of hardness and pride – a painful blot upon the profession of the gospel.… The same yearning sympathy forms the life, the pulse, and the strength of Missionary exertion, and has ever distinguished those honoured servants of God who have devoted their time, their health, their talent, their all." (Bridges)

> iv. "The experience of this verse indicates a great advance upon anything we have had before: the Psalm and the Psalmist are both growing. That man is a ripe believer who sorrows because of the sins of others." (Spurgeon)

R. Tsadde **צ**: The purity and truth of God's word.

"The initial letter with which every verse commences sounds like the Hebrew word for righteousness: *our keynote is righteousness."* (Spurgeon)

1. (137-138) The righteousness of God and His word.

Righteous *are* You, O LORD,
And upright *are* Your judgments.
Your testimonies, *which* You have commanded,
***Are* righteous and very faithful.**

a. **Righteous are You, O LORD, and upright are Your judgments**: The psalmist understood that the **righteous** character of God was displayed in His word (**Your judgments**). In this the word of God is an accurate revelation of God, not only of His thoughts but also of His very character.

> i. We might say that God's written word is an *incomplete* display of His character and nature; that is, there is *more* to God than what we can receive from His word. But what we do have in His word is *accurate* and properly displays to us who He is.

> ii. We might say that the God who actually exists is not *different than* His written revelation to us. He is *greater than* what can be comprehended through His written word, but He is not *different from* what is revealed to us through that word.

> iii. "The strophe begins on an affirmation of the Lord's righteousness... and ends on an affirmation of his word. In between the psalmist laments his troubles." (VanGemeren)

b. **Your testimonies, which You have commanded, are righteous and very faithful**: For emphasis, the psalmist repeats the idea from the previous verse. The written word of God reflects both His **righteous** character and the fact that He is **very faithful**.

> i. "The force of this expression is much feebler than that of the original, which literally may be rendered, '*Thou* hast commanded righteousness, thy testimonies, and truth exceedingly.' So the Septuagint hath it. Righteousness and truth were his testimonies; the testimonies were one with his righteousness and truth." (Stephen, cited in Spurgeon)

> ii. God's words are especially helpful for establishing that He is **very faithful**. We often judge a person's faithfulness by seeing if their words and their actions match. Along with other believers through the centuries, the psalmist could say that the words of God and the actions of God were and are consistent, and show Him to be **very faithful**.

> iii. "Trust in the reliability of God's word is directly proportionate to one's trust in the Lord himself." (VanGemeren)

> iv. "The Bible mirrors the character of God. Anyone who cares about knowing what is righteous and wants to act righteously should study the Bible." (Boice)

2. (139-140) Zeal and love for God's word.

My zeal has consumed me,
Because my enemies have forgotten Your words.

Your word *is* very pure;
Therefore Your servant loves it.

a. **My zeal has consumed me, because my enemies have forgotten Your words**: The more the **enemies** of the psalmist rejected the word of God, the more he was determined to be zealous for those words. He would make sure that *he* honored the word of God even if others did not.

i. **Zeal** implies energy and action. The appreciation of the psalmist for the word of God was not passive. The living and active word of God brought forth a living and active response from the psalmist.

ii. "Thus we see every man is eaten up with some kind of zeal. The drunkard is consumed with drunkenness, the whore-monger is spent with his whoredom, the heretic is eaten with heresies. Oh, how ought this to make us ashamed, who are so little eaten, spent, and consumed with the zeal of the word!... Oh, what a benefit it is to be eaten up with the love and zeal of a good thing!" (Greenham, cited in Spurgeon)

iii. "Such was [the psalmist's] high estimation of *the testimonies of his God*, that his spirits were *consumed* with vehement grief in witnessing their neglect. He could bear that *his enemies* should *forget him*; but his *zeal* could not endure, that they should *forget the words of his God*." (Bridges)

iv. This brings to mind the passage remembered by the disciples when Jesus cleansed the temple courts of the merchants and moneychangers at the beginning of His ministry (John 2:13-17). At that time, the disciples remembered the line from Psalm 69:9: *Zeal for Your house has eaten Me up*. This line carries much the same thought, and also reflects the kind of zeal that Jesus had when He cleared the temple courts. *They* had forgotten His words.

v. "*They have forgotten thy words*, i.e. despise and disobey them; which in Scripture use is oft called a forgetting of them, as the remembering of them is oft put for loving and practicing them." (Poole)

b. **Your word is very pure, therefore Your servant loves it**: The psalmist understood and appreciated the *purity* of God's word. In its original autograph writings it is *perfectly* **pure**, being absolutely inspired by God. In addition, the copies we have of those original writings are also **pure**, being extremely reliable copies.

i. **Pure**: "...in the original, 'tried, refined, purified, like gold in the furnace,' absolutely perfect, without the dross of vanity and fallibility, which runs through human writings. The more we try the promises, the surer we shall find them." (Horne)

ii. "In the word of God there is no admixture of error or sin. It is pure in its sense, pure in its language, pure in its spirit, pure in its influence, and all this to the very highest *degree* – '*very* pure'." (Spurgeon)

iii. For the Hebrew Scriptures, the quality of the text was preserved by the diligent practices of the professional scribes. According to researchers (such as Josh McDowell in *Evidence that Demands a Verdict*), they practiced the following in the preparation and copying of manuscripts:

- The parchment was made only from the skin of clean animals. It had to be prepared by a Jew only, and the skins were fastened together by strings taken from clean animals.

- Each column had to have no less than 48 and no more than 60 lines. The entire parchment had to be lined before writing began.

- The ink had to be of no other color than black, and it had to be prepared according to a special recipe.

- No word and no letter could be written from memory; the scribe had to have an authentic copy before him, and he had to read and pronounce out loud each word before writing it.

- He was required to reverently wipe his pen each time before writing the word for "God" (*Elohim*) and wash his whole body before writing the word used in place of "Jehovah" [LORD in the New King James Version) so as not to contaminate the Holy Name.

- Strict rules were given concerning forms of the letters, spaces between letters, words, and sections, the use of the pen, the color of the parchment, and so forth.

- The revision of a roll had to be made within 30 days after the work was finished; otherwise it was worthless. *One mistake on a sheet condemned the entire sheet; if three mistakes were found in any larger section, the entire manuscript was condemned.*

- Every word and every letter was counted, and *if a letter had been omitted, or an extra letter inserted, or if any letter touched one another, the manuscript was condemned and destroyed.*

iv. The manuscript evidence for the accuracy of the Hebrew text is established. Until 1947, the oldest Hebrew manuscripts were from about AD 900. In 1947, the discovery of the Dead Sea Scrolls revealed manuscripts from 150-200 BC. In comparing the manuscripts, almost 1000 years apart, there were remarkably few differences. This proved that the diligent practices of the professional scribes had accurately preserved the text of the Hebrew Scriptures.

v. Regarding the Greek Scriptures, there is a similarly astonishing rate of accuracy. Because of the vast number and quality of ancient Greek manuscripts, and the existence of relatively early copies, scholars often say that the error rate is between 0.5% and 2%.

vi. "New Testament specialist Daniel Wallace notes that although there are about 300,000 individual variations of the text of the New Testament, this number is very misleading. Most of the differences are completely inconsequential – spelling errors, inverted phrases and the like. A side by side comparison between the two main text families (the Majority Text and the modern critical text) shows agreement a full 98% of the time." (Greg Koukl)

vii. Of the remaining differences, virtually all yield to vigorous textual criticism. According to Geisler and Nix in their book *A General Introduction to the Bible*, this means that our New Testament is 99.5% textually pure. In the entire New Testament text of 20,000 lines, only 40 lines are in doubt. These lines concern about 400 words, and none of the questioned lines or words affect any significant doctrine of the Christian faith.

viii. Indeed! **Your word is very pure, therefore Your servant loves it**. This is true for both the original autographs and the extremely reliable copies we have of the Hebrew and Greek Scriptures. "*Therefore*; because of that exact purity and holiness of it…ungodly men either despise or hate it." (Poole)

c. **Your word is very pure, therefore your servant loves it**: The Bible gives us almost unending reasons to love the word of God and the God who gave it to us.

- It is the word of the LORD (Genesis 15:1).
- It is the word of God (Luke 8:11).
- It is the word of the kingdom (Matthew 13:19).
- It is the word of salvation (Acts 13:26).
- It is the word of grace (Acts 14:3).
- It is the word of the gospel (Acts 15:7).
- It is the word of faith (Romans 10:8).
- It is the word of the cross (1 Corinthians 1:18).
- It is the word of reconciliation (2 Corinthians 5:19).

- It is the word of truth (2 Corinthians 6:7).
- It is the word of life (Philippians 2:16).
- It is the word of Christ (Colossians 3:16).
- It is the word of His power (Hebrews 1:3).

3. (141-142) Holding fast to the true word.

I *am* small and despised,
Yet I do not forget Your precepts.
Your righteousness *is* an everlasting righteousness,
And Your law *is* truth.

a. **I am small and despised, yet I do not forget Your precepts**: The psalmist felt himself insignificant, both in his own estimate (**small**) and in the estimation of others (**despised**). Yet he found comfort and strength in remembering the word of God.

i. We think of individuals who have been small and despised – a young man like David (1 Samuel 16:10-13) and an older man like Paul (2 Corinthians 11). Yet they found courage in God, and they understood God by His word.

ii. It also shows us that the psalmist would not neglect God's word when he was depressed or downcast. **Small and despised** does not feel good; yet he still remembered the word of God when he felt this way. It is common to run away from exactly what we need when we feel **small and despised**.

b. **Your righteousness is an everlasting righteousness, and Your law is truth**: The psalmist confidently stated the **everlasting** character of God's **righteousness**; He is righteous and will not change. Connected to that, he proclaimed that this unchanging God has given us a word (**Your law**) that **is truth**.

i. **Your righteousness is an everlasting righteousness**: "This is the joy and glory of the saints, that what God is he always will be, and his mode of procedure towards the sons of men is immutable. Having kept his promise, and dealt out justice among his people, he will do so world without end." (Spurgeon)

ii. **Your law is truth**: We remember the conversation between Jesus and Pontius Pilate. Jesus said, "*For this cause I was born, and for this cause I have come into the world, that I should bear witness to the truth. Everyone who is of the truth hears My voice.*" Pilate's cynical reply was, "*What is truth?*" (John 18:37-38). For Pilate, soldiers and armies were truth; Rome was truth; Caesar was truth; and political power was truth. Yet Jesus knew what truth was, while Pilate was still seeking. Jesus knew, **Your law is truth**.

iii. This is especially meaningful in a day when *relativism* has a strong hold in the everyday thinking of people. It is common for people today to think there is no such thing as "real" truth; there is only *your* truth and *my* truth and *their* truth. Western society used to believe that truth was that which corresponded to reality (what is really there); now truth is often held to be what makes sense or is helpful to me individually.

iv. The late Christian philosopher Francis Schaeffer used to promote the idea of "true truth." His concept was that the Biblical message is *true* fundamentally, apart from how one receives it or how it works in one's life.

4. (143-144) God's word gives life in times of trouble.

Trouble and anguish have overtaken me,
***Yet* Your commandments *are* my delights.**
The righteousness of Your testimonies *is* everlasting;
Give me understanding, and I shall live.

a. **Trouble and anguish have overtaken me, yet Your commandments are my delights**: Despite the difficulties of his life, the psalmist still found *delight* in God's word. His appreciation of God and His word was not only valid in good times, but also in **trouble and anguish**.

i. "When we are most sorely afflicted, and cannot see the reason for the dispensation, we may fall back upon this most sure and certain fact, that God is righteous, and his dealings with us are righteous too. It should be our glory to sing this brave confession when all things around us appear to suggest the contrary. This is the richest adoration." (Spurgeon)

ii. "Years ago there were Christians who used to put the promises of God to the test and when they received what was promised would write 'T' and 'P' in their Bible next to the promise. The letters stood for 'tried and proven,' exactly what the psalmist says he found to be true in his experience." (Boice)

b. **The righteousness of Your testimonies is everlasting; give me understanding, and I shall live**: We might think that what the psalmist needed to **live** was deliverance from his **trouble and anguish**. He found **understanding** the word of God more important.

i. One reason he found this to be so was because he understood that **the righteousness of** God's word **is everlasting**. He knew the eternal character of the word of God, and it made that word all the more important and relevant to him.

ii. "When all other laws and sentences, though engraven in brass or marble, shall decay and determine, Thy law lasteth for ever, and so shall they that observe it." (Trapp)

S. Qoph ק: Praying to the God of the Bible.

1. (145-147) Crying out to God with hope in His word.

I cry out with *my* whole heart;
Hear me, O LORD!
I will keep Your statutes.
I cry out to You;
Save me, and I will keep Your testimonies.
I rise before the dawning of the morning,
And cry for help;
I hope in Your word.

a. **I cry out with my whole heart.... I will keep Your statutes**: The psalmist pleaded with God, crying out before Him. In his pleading, he wanted to **keep** the word of God. This was not merely a cry for help or deliverance or forgiveness; this was a cry for *obedience*.

i. "Yet these verses are not really about the psalmist's enemies, as bad as they were. They are about the writer's prayer life and how he learned to use God's word when praying." (Boice)

ii. "The whole soul of the psalmist was engaged in this good work. He whose *whole heart* cries to God will never rise from the throne of grace without a blessing." (Clarke)

iii. "There may be no beauty of elocution about such prayers, no length of expression, no depth of doctrine, nor accuracy of diction; but if the whole heart be in them they will find their way to the heart of God." (Spurgeon)

iv. "God looks not at the elegancy of your prayers, to see how neat they are; nor yet at the geometry of your prayers, to see how long they are; nor yet at the arithmetic of your prayers, to see how many they are; nor yet at the music of your prayers, nor yet at the sweetness of your voice, nor yet at the logic of your prayers; but at the sincerity of your prayers, how hearty they are." (Brooks, cited in Spurgeon)

b. **I cry out to You; save me, and I will keep Your testimonies**: For emphasis, the idea is repeated from the previous verse. The psalmist passionately cried out to God for the wisdom and strength and ability to obey God. This is a prayer that pleases God.

i. **I cry out** means that the prayer was *vocal*. "Men find it very helpful to use their voices in prayer; it is difficult long to maintain the intensity of devotion unless we hear ourselves speak; hence [the psalmist] at length broke through his silence, arose from his quiet meditations, and began crying with voice as well as heart unto the Lord his God." (Spurgeon)

c. **I rise before the dawning of the morning, and cry for help; I hope in Your word**: The psalmist passionately depended on God and His word, but that did not eliminate the participation of the psalmist in any way. He still woke early to seek God, in prayer (**cry for help**) that was helped by God's word (**I hope in Your word**).

i. "So long as *the duty only* of prayer is known, we shall be content with our set seasons. But when *the privilege* is felt, we shall be early at work, following it closely morning and night." (Bridges)

ii. "The word furnished his hope, and his hope his prayer." (Trapp)

iii. We use prayer in our study of the word of God; this is essential. Yet we also use the word of God in our prayers. In prayer, the word of God shows us:

- The nature and heart of the God we pray to.
- What we have received from God, and what we should thank Him for.
- His greatness, informing and expanding our praise.
- His moral will, directing us to pray that we can do it.
- His promises to His people, which we claim by faith.
- Substance for our prayers, as we pray-read the Scriptures.

iv. "He who is diligent in prayer will never be destitute of hope. Observe that as the early bird gets the worm, so the early prayer is soon refreshed with hope." (Spurgeon)

2. (148-149) Diligently seeking the word that brings life.

My eyes are awake through the *night* watches,
That I may meditate on Your word.
Hear my voice according to Your lovingkindness;
O Lord, revive me according to Your justice.

a. **My eyes are awake through the night watches, that I may meditate on Your word**: The psalmist not only woke early to seek God (as in the previous verse), he also stayed awake **through the night** to think about God and His **word**.

i. Jesus sometimes prayed early in the morning (Mark 1:35). On some occasions Jesus prayed all night (Luke 6:12).

ii. Boice defines **meditate**: "Internalizing the Bible's teaching to such an extent that the truths discovered in the Bible become part of how we think, so that we think differently and then also function differently as a result."

b. **Hear my voice according to Your lovingkindness; O LORD, revive me according to Your justice**: The psalmist asked for God to **hear** him **according to** the goodness and mercy (**lovingkindness**) of God; he also asked God to **revive** him **according** to the **justice** of God. Both are reasons to pray and to have confidence in our pleading.

i. We can pray **according to Your lovingkindness**: "Lord, I know that I don't deserve to be heard by You. Yet I believe that You are rich in grace and mercy. Please, according to Your generous and kind love, hear my prayer."

ii. Spurgeon on **lovingkindness** (*hesed*): "Lovingkindness is one of the sweetest words in our language. Kindness has much in it that is most precious, but lovingkindness is doubly dear; it is the cream of kindness."

iii. We can pray **according to Your justice**: "Lord, I know that my sins are righteously forgiven because of what Jesus did on the cross. I know that You have forgiven me **according to Your justice**, and as one so forgiven I pray. I also know that You, **according to Your justice**, see the righteousness of my cause with those who are against me. Because of these, please bring me new life."

iv. **Revive me according to Your justice**: Though revival from God is never deserved, it can still be asked for **according** to the justice of God. It can be prayed for based on the justice-satisfying work of Jesus Christ. It can also be prayed for with an eye to honoring the justice of God on earth, especially when wickedness abounds.

3. (150-151) Near and far.

They draw near who follow after wickedness;
They are far from Your law.
You *are* near, O LORD,
And all Your commandments *are* truth.

a. **They draw near who follow after wickedness**: The psalmist could sense that the wicked who opposed him were coming closer and becoming more of a threat to him.

b. **They are far from Your law**: Though they came closer to the psalmist, they were **far** from God's word.

> i. "Before these men could become persecutors of [the psalmist] they were obliged to get away from the restraints of God's law. They could not hate a saint and yet love the law." (Spurgeon)

c. **You are near, O LORD**: Though the wicked were both near to the psalmist and far from God's word, the psalmist knew that God was **near**. God had come near to the psalmist, and one way was through the word of God itself.

> i. "Note the realism of the double statement, *They draw near...but thou art near*. The threat is not glossed over; it is put in perspective by a bigger fact." (Kidner)

d. **And all Your commandments are truth**: Because God came **near** to the psalmist, he could see clearly that **all** God's **commandments are truth**. He understood that God's word was truly inspired and infallible.

4. (152) Confidence in the eternal word.

Concerning Your testimonies,
I have known of old that You have founded them forever.

a. **I have known of old**: The psalmist had an **old** relationship with the word of God. The great love and appreciation he had with the Scriptures was not a youthful surge of infatuation; it was the deep, settled love with roots made deep by time.

b. **You have founded them forever**: His long love and appreciation for the Scriptures led him to understand that they were *eternal* (**founded... forever**). The more he studied and meditated upon them, the more he understood their divine origin.

> i. "We are satisfied with the truth which is old as the hills and as fixed as the great mountains. Let 'cultured intellects' invent another god, more gentle and effeminate than the God of Abraham; we are well content to worship Jehovah, who is eternally the same." (Spurgeon)

> ii. This was his testimony to answered prayer. This whole passage shows us:

> • How he prayed (*with my whole heart*, verse 145).

- What he prayed for (*save me, and I will keep Your testimonies*, verse 146).

- When he prayed (*before the dawning of the morning*, verse 147).

- How long he prayed (*through the night watches*, verse 148).

- The grounds of his request (*according to Your lovingkindness... according to Your justice*, verse 149).

- How God answered his prayer (*You are near, O LORD*, verse 150).

- His testimony to answered prayer (*Your testimonies... You have founded them forever*, verse 152).

T. Resh ר: Revival according to the word of God.

1. (153-154) In hard times, a plea for new life from God's word.

Consider my affliction and deliver me,
For I do not forget Your law.
Plead my cause and redeem me;
Revive me according to Your word.

a. **Consider my affliction and deliver me**: We are reminded that the psalmist's life was not lived in an ivory tower or a secluded place where all he did was study the Scriptures all day long. He lived a real life, interacting with people (some of whom became his enemies or opponents). He lived a life that experienced **affliction**.

> i. "Yet there is no impatience: he does not ask for hasty action, but for consideration. In effect he cries – 'Look into my grief, and see whether I do not need to be delivered. From my sorrowful condition judge as to the proper method and time for my rescue.'" (Spurgeon)

b. **For I do not forget Your law**: In the lives of some, **affliction** drives them away from God and His word. For the psalmist, such troubled times drove him closer to God and His word.

c. **Plead my cause and redeem me**: The psalmist looked for help and salvation *outside of himself*. This reinforces the idea that his previous claims to righteousness were not absolute, and were made comparing himself to other men, ungodly men. He knew that he needed God to **plead** his **cause**; he knew he needed God to **redeem** him.

> i. **Plead my cause** uses language from the courtroom. The psalmist asked God to defend him as a lawyer might. "The verb 'defend' [**plead**] (*ribah*) as well as the noun 'cause' (*rib*) represent a technical legal jargon (Psalm 35:1; 43:1; 74:22), often used by the prophets as God's covenant prosecutors (cf. Hosea 4:1). (VanGemeren)

ii. "But you say, – 'How do I know that he speaks for me?' Yet if not for you, then for whom does he speak? Who needs an advocate more than you? He pleads nothing favorable *of you*; but much, very much, *for you*. For he pleads the merit of his own blood." (Bridges)

d. **Revive me according to Your word**: This thought is repeated from previous passages in this psalm (verse 25, 107). The psalmist wanted to be made alive, and to have that life brought to him **according to** God's **word**.

i. The word of God is a *source* of revival. If we will read the word of God and do what it tells us to do – in prayer, in repentance, in dedication, and in pursing God with the whole heart – it will be a source of personal and corporate revival.

ii. Revival itself is **according to** God's **word**. The concept of revival (both personal and corporate) is Biblical. A genuine revival will honor and promote God's word.

iii. However, there may be a false or pseudo revival which is *not* **according to Your word**. It is fair to assess purported words of revival according to the measure, "Is this **according to** God's **word**?"

iv. "What a mighty plea is this – 'according to thy word.' No gun in all our arsenals can match it." (Spurgeon)

2. (155-156) The wicked are far from a close salvation.

Salvation *is* far from the wicked,
For they do not seek Your statutes.
Great *are* Your tender mercies, O LORD;
Revive me according to Your judgments.

a. **Salvation is far from the wicked**: The psalmist understood that the wicked would not be saved, even as Paul later stated (Galatians 5:19-21). Yet he also understood that their wickedness was rooted in their refusal to seek God through His word (**they do not seek Your statutes**).

i. "By their perseverance in evil they have almost put themselves out of the pale of hope. They talk about being saved, but they cannot have known anything of it or they would not remain wicked." (Spurgeon)

ii. "They have no one to *consider their affliction* – no one to *deliver them* – no one to *plead their cause*. Indeed, all the misery that an immortal soul is capable of enduring throughout eternity is included in this sentence – *Salvation is far from the wicked*." (Bridges)

iii. **Salvation is far from the wicked**: "How can it be otherwise? When as God is neither in their heads (Psalm 10:4), nor hearts (Psalm 14:1), nor words (Psalm 12:4), nor ways (Titus 1:16), can these have part or portion in his salvation?" (Trapp)

iv. "The Lord is almighty to pardon; but he will not use it for thee an impenitent sinner. Thou hast not a friend on the bench, not an attribute in all God's name will speak for thee. Mercy itself will sit and vote with the rest of its fellow-attributes for thy damnation." (Gurnall, cited in Spurgeon)

v. **They do not seek Your statutes**: "And they who *do not seek, shall not find.*" (Clarke)

b. **Great are Your tender mercies, O LORD**: Though the wicked are far from **salvation** and far from God's word, the **tender mercies** of God are close to all who will seek them. In a paradoxical way, though the salvation of God is **far** from them, God is not far because of His **tender mercies**.

i. We can measure the greatness of this mercy:

- By the infinite debt that it blots out (Isaiah 1:18; 43:22-25).
- By the eternal ruin from which it saves (Psalm 86:13).
- By the heavenly crown to which it raises (Revelation 1:5-6).

ii. "The other epithet he gives them is, that they are 'tender' mercies; because the Lord is easy to be entreated; for he is slow unto wrath, but ready to show mercy." (Cowper, cited in Spurgeon)

c. **Revive me according to Your judgments**: This is the same thought repeated from verse 154. The psalmist is emphasizing in the two verses that God's word is both a source and a measure of revival.

3. (157-158) Keeping to God's word despite persecution.

Many *are* my persecutors and my enemies,
***Yet* I do not turn from Your testimonies.**
I see the treacherous, and am disgusted,
Because they do not keep Your word.

a. **Many are my persecutors and my enemies**: The psalmist lived life in the real world, not sheltered in a constant Scripture-study environment. His trust in the word of God was forged in the real world, a world full of **persecutors** and **enemies**.

i. "Persecution, to the false professor, is an occasion of apostasy (Matthew 13:20-21); to the faithful servant of Christ, it is the trial of his faith (1 Peter 1:6-7), the source of his richest consolations (Matthew 5:10-12, Acts 13:50-52, 1 Peter 4:12-16), the guard of his profession (Matthew 10:16, Philippians 2:14-16), and the strength of his perseverance (Acts 20:22-24)." (Bridges)

b. **Yet I do not turn from Your testimonies**: The presence of so many **persecutors** and **enemies** did not make the psalmist despair or doubt the love of God for him. He didn't have the expectation that a godly life was a problem-free life. Instead, he was determined to keep turned to and focused on the word of God.

> i. "So long as they cannot drive or draw us into a spiritual decline our foes have done us no great harm, and they have accomplished nothing by their malice. If we do not decline they are defeated. If they cannot make us sin they have missed their mark. Faithfulness to the truth is victory over our enemies." (Spurgeon)

c. **I see the treacherous and am disgusted, because they do not keep Your word**: It wasn't that the psalmist expected godly behavior from the ungodly – something that Paul warned about (1 Corinthians 5:9-13). He felt **disgusted** because God and His word were being disgraced, even if it came from the disgraceful.

> i. "I was sorry to see such sinners. I was sick of them, disgusted with them, I could not endure them. I found no pleasure in them, they were a sad sight to me, however fine their clothing or witty their chattering. Even when they were most mirthful a sight of them made my heart heavy; I could not tolerate either them or their doings." (Spurgeon)

> ii. This sensitivity toward sin and passion for the glory of God is entirely characteristic of the *revival* that the psalmist prays for repeatedly in this section.

> iii. "A fellowship with the joys of angels over repenting sinners (Luke 15:10) will be accompanied with bitterness of godly sorrow over the hardness and impenitency of those, who *keep not the word of God.*" (Bridges)

4. (159-160) Revived by the completely true and lasting word.

Consider how I love Your precepts;
Revive me, O LORD, according to Your lovingkindness.
The entirety of Your word *is* truth,
And every one of Your righteous judgments *endures* forever.

a. **Consider how I love Your precepts; revive me, O LORD, according to Your lovingkindness**: The psalmist asked God to look at his love for His word, but then asked for revival on the basis of God's **lovingkindness** instead of on his own merit.

i. "A second time he asks for consideration. As he said before, 'Consider mine affliction,' so now he says, 'Consider mine affection.' He loved the precepts of God – loved them unspeakably – loved them so as to be grieved with those who did not love them." (Spurgeon)

b. **Revive me, O LORD, according to Your lovingkindness**: An idea stated before (verse 88) is here repeated. Revival is never deserved or earned, but given from the **lovingkindness** of God.

i. "The consciousness of need is revealed in the thrice repeated, 'Quicken [**Revive**] me.' He feels the weakening of his very life under the pressure of circumstances." (Morgan)

c. **The entirety of Your word is truth, and every one of Your righteous judgments endures forever**: The psalmist again declares the infallible character of the word of God. The *entire* word is true, not merely portions or individual concepts from the word. Not only is it true; it is *eternally* true.

i. "The Scriptures are as true in Genesis as in Revelation, and the five books of Moses are as inspired as the four Gospels.... There is not one single mistake either in the word of God or in the providential dealings of God. Neither in the book of revelation nor of providence will there be any need to put a single note of errata. The Lord has nothing to regret or to retract, nothing to amend or to reverse." (Spurgeon)

U. Shin ‎ש‎: In awe of God's word.

"*The qoph stanza was almost entirely a prayer. In these stanzas the petitions tend to drop away – stanza twenty-one (the sin/shin stanza) has no explicit prayers at all – and in their place comes a quiet, obedient waiting for God.*" (Boice)

1. (161-162) The treasure of God's awe-inspiring word.

**Princes persecute me without a cause,
But my heart stands in awe of Your word.
I rejoice at Your word
As one who finds great treasure.**

a. **Princes persecute me without a cause**: In the real-life world of the psalmist, he even interacted with **princes** – rulers among men, who persecuted him **without a cause**.

i. Those who believe that David was the anonymous psalmist of this great psalm know that David was indeed persecuted by princes (Saul and his associates) **without a cause**.

ii. "It was well that the sufferer could truthfully assert that this persecution was without cause. He had not broken their laws, he had not injured them, he had not even desired to see them injured, he had not been an advocate of rebellion or anarchy, he had neither openly nor secretly opposed their power, and therefore, while this made their oppression the more inexcusable, it took away a part of its sting, and helped the brave-hearted servant of God to bear up." (Spurgeon)

iii. "This division is remarkable in that it is one of the only two which contain no petition [the other was *Mem*, 97-104]. That fact is the more remarkable because its opening sentence shows that the singer is still conscious of the circumstances of trial." (Morgan)

b. **But my heart stands in awe of Your word**: Difficult trials – even persecution by those in authority – would not make the psalmist lose his **awe** of God's **word**. He did not have a *conditional* appreciation of the word of God; he loved it in good times and bad.

i. "He might have been overcome by awe of the princes had it not been that a greater fear drove out the less, and he was swayed by awe of God's word. How little do crowns and sceptres become in the judgment of that man who perceives a more majestic royalty in the commands of his God." (Spurgeon)

ii. Bridges says that some great Jewish Scripture collections have on their frontispiece Jacob's statement of fear and astonishment connected with his vision of God at Bethel: *How awesome is this place! This is none other than the house of God, and this is the gate of heaven!* (Genesis 28:17).

c. **I rejoice at Your word as one who finds great treasure**: The psalmist loved God's word as some people love **treasure**. He knew it was precious and enriching to life. Yet the original Hebrew has **treasure** in the sense of *spoil* or *plunder* from battle.

i. **Rejoice at Your word**: "I will go to the length of saying that unless we do have deep awe of the word we shall never have high joy over it. Our rejoicing will be measured by our reverencing." (Spurgeon)

ii. "This appears to refer to such *spoil* as is acquired by *stripping the dead* in a field of battle, taking the rich garments of the slain chiefs; or it may refer to *plunder* in general. As God *opened his eyes* he *beheld wonders in his law*; and each discovery of this kind was like finding a prize." (Clarke)

iii. Sometimes spoil is fought for, and riches from God's word must be fought for. Other times spoil is found, and the riches from God's word are simply received.

• If riches from the Bible are like spoil from battle, the battle is over.

- If riches from the Bible are like spoil from battle, the enemy has less to fight with.

- If riches from the Bible are like spoil from battle, there is a sense of victory.

- If riches from the Bible are like spoil from battle, there is profit, pleasure, and honor.

2. (163-164) Continually praising the God of the word.

I hate and abhor lying,
***But* I love Your law.**
Seven times a day I praise You,
Because of Your righteous judgments.

a. **I hate and abhor lying, but I love Your law**: The hatred and love in this verse fit together perfectly. One who truly *loves* the pure truth of God will naturally **hate** lies.

i. "If we keep clear of all lying, our song will be the more acceptable because it comes out of pure lips. If we never flatter men we shall be in the better condition for honouring the Lord." (Spurgeon)

b. **Seven times a day I praise You, because of Your righteous judgments**: The goodness and the glory of God's word (**Your righteous judgments**) prompted **praise** from the psalmist. This praise was constant and continual (**seven times a day**).

i. "...*seven times*; many times; that definite number being oft taken indefinitely, as Leviticus 26:28, and elsewhere." (Poole)

ii. It is good to make regular times for prayer, Bible reading, and reflection throughout the day; but it must be done without a legalistic spirit. "Young Christians indeed sometimes unwarily bring themselves into 'bondage,' in forcing their consciences to a frequency of set times for duty, interfering with present obligations, or pressing unduly upon the weaknesses of the flesh." (Bridges)

iii. "Do we praise God seven times a day? Do we praise him once in seven days?" (Spurgeon)

3. (165-166) The peace of obedience to God's word.

Great peace have those who love Your law,
And nothing causes them to stumble.
LORD, I hope for Your salvation,
And I do Your commandments.

a. **Great peace have those who love Your law, and nothing causes them to stumble**: The great love that the psalmist had for the law brought real benefits to his life. It brought him **great peace** and stability in life (**nothing causes them to stumble**).

> i. "*Shalom* is a large, embracing word for the good that comes to the one God favors." (Boice)

> ii. "Amidst the storms and tempests of the world, there is a perfect calm in the breasts of those, who not only do the will of God, but 'love' to do it." (Horne)

> iii. "They are at peace with God, by the blood of reconciliation; at peace with themselves, by the answer of a good conscience, and the subjection of those desires which war against the soul; at peace with all men, by the spirit of charity; and the whole creation is at peace with them, and all things work together for their good." (Horne)

> iv. "This verse does not promise peace to those who perfectly keep God's Law, for who can keep it? It promises peace to those who 'love' God's Law." (Boice)

> v. "In every age there have been Luthers and Latimers [Hugh Latimer, martyred in 1555], who have not only held fast their confidence, but whose peace has deepened with the roaring of the waves. The more they have been forsaken of men, the closer has been their communion with God." (Martin, cited in Spurgeon)

b. **I hope for Your salvation, and I do Your commandments**: The psalmist here displays the kind of active faith and trust that saves. He had faith in God for **salvation**; yet it was a faith that could also say, "**I do Your commandments**." This is the kind of living faith so strongly promoted in the Epistle of James.

> i. "This saying he borrowed from good old Jacob, Genesis 49:18." (Trapp)

> ii. This **hope** is very much like faith. "Faith is the exercise of the soul in a sense of need, in desire, and in trust. Faith goes to God on the ground of the promise; *hope* in the expectation of the thing promised. Thus *hope* implies the operation of faith." (Bridges)

4. (167-168) Keeping the word of God.

My soul keeps Your testimonies,
And I love them exceedingly.
I keep Your precepts and Your testimonies,
For all my ways *are* before You.

a. **My soul keeps Your testimonies, and I love them exceedingly**: The psalmist *kept* the word of God not only with his outward actions, but also with his **soul**. His love and conformity to the word of God was deeply rooted, not superficial.

i. "Indeed, the bias of the new nature to *keep the precepts* is as prevalent, as that of the old nature to break them." (Bridges)

b. **I keep Your precepts and Your testimonies, for all my ways are before You**: For the psalmist, the knowledge that **all my ways are before You** prompted obedience. He knew that the God who gave the word also observed his life. This is in contrast to the many who live as if God does not observe **all...ways** of a man.

i. "The Jews covered Christ's face, and then buffeted him: Mark 14:65. So does the hypocrite; he first says in his heart, God sees not, or at least forgets that he sees, and then he makes bold to sin against him." (Gurnall, cited in Spurgeon)

ii. **Your precepts...Your testimonies...before You**: "Note the reverence for God Himself, not for Scripture in isolation." (Kidner)

V. Tau ת: Sought by God and His Word.

"The psalmist is approaching the end of the Psalm, and his petitions gather force and fervency; he seems to break into the inner circle of divine fellowship, and to come even to the feet of the great God whose help he is imploring. This nearness creates the most lowly view of himself, and leads him to close the Psalm upon his face in deepest self-humiliation, begging to be sought out like a lost sheep." (Spurgeon)

1. (169-170) Deliverance according to God's word.

Let my cry come before You, O Lord;
Give me understanding according to Your word.
Let my supplication come before You;
Deliver me according to Your word.

a. **Let my cry come before You...give me understanding according to Your word**: The **cry** of the psalmist is an expression of *prayer*, a plea to gain **understanding according to Your word**. He wanted his thoughts to be transformed **according** to the word of God.

i. This is very much the same kind of thought the Apostle Paul expressed in Romans 12:2: *And do not be conformed to this world, but be transformed by the renewing of your mind, that you may prove what is that good and acceptable and perfect will of God.* The psalmist wanted his **understanding** of life and the world shaped – *transformed* – by the word of God.

ii. "Here the psalmist's cry for deliverance is *personified*; made an intelligent being, and sent up to the throne of grace to negotiate in his behalf." (Clarke)

iii. **Come before You**: "The verb *q-r-b* in the Hiphil is a technical term for the act of presenting an offering.... He has nothing left to present but a 'cry.'" (VanGemeren)

b. **Let my supplication come before You**: This is another reference to prayer by the psalmist, this time a prayer for deliverance **according to Your word**. He wanted deliverance, but wanted it only as it was consistent with God's revealed word and will. He did not want an unrighteous or unwise deliverance.

i. He also asked for this deliverance according to the *promises* of God's word. "It is beautiful to observe the oil of the Psalmist's faith feeding the flame of his supplication. Every petition is urged upon the warrant of a promise – *according to thy word*." (Bridges)

ii. "Many prayers hath he made to God in this Psalm: now in the end he prays for his prayers, that the Lord would let them come before him." (Cowper, cited in Spurgeon)

2. (171-172) Praising God and speaking of His word.

My lips shall utter praise,
For You teach me Your statutes.
My tongue shall speak of Your word,
For all Your commandments *are* righteousness.

a. **My lips shall utter praise.... My tongue shall speak of Your word**: The psalmist wanted his words (**lips.... tongue**) to both **praise** God and to **speak of** His **word**. He knew that often words are either wicked or vain or both. He was determined that others would hear him **praise** God, and **speak** of His **word**.

i. "In the two expressions, *pour forth* [**shall utter**] and *sing* [**shall speak**], there may be a hint of, respectively, the spontaneous personal and the corporate: the former word suggesting the bubbling up of a spring, and the latter (lit. 'my tongue will answer') the antiphonal praise of a choir." (Kidner)

b. **My lips shall utter praise, for You teach me Your statutes**: His **lips** could praise God because they had been taught His word. The psalmist's **lips** did not praise God by nature; he had to be *taught* God's truth, and taught from God Himself. Also, the word of God *informed* his praise; it was intelligent.

i. "And yet who of us are fit to *praise*, except those whom *God has taught?* The 'new song' ill accords with the old heart." (Bridges)

c. **For all Your commandments are righteous**: Knowing the purity and inerrancy of God's word made the psalmist want to **speak** of it to others. He was confident in his convictions.

i. "Then should we break through our sinful silence.... It is not only of God's works that we are to speak, but of his word." (Spurgeon)

3. (173-174) Longing for salvation and loving God's word.

Let Your hand become my help,
For I have chosen Your precepts.
I long for Your salvation, O LORD,
And Your law *is* my delight.

a. **Let Your hand become my help, for I have chosen Your precepts**: The psalmist felt he could boldly ask for God's **help**, because he had chosen to love and keep the word of God.

i. "The prayer reminds us of Peter walking on the sea and beginning to sink; he, too, cried, 'Lord, help me,' and the hand of his Master was stretched out for his rescue." (Spurgeon)

b. **I long for Your salvation...Your law is my delight**: These two expressions go together. Because God's **salvation** is from and according to His word (1 Peter 1:23), it was natural for him to **delight** in God's word as he longed for God's **salvation**.

i. **Salvation** "...hath long been the object of the hopes, the desires, and the 'longing' expectation of the faithful, from Adam to this hour; and will continue so to be, until He, who hath already visited us in great humility, shall come again in glorious majesty, to complete our redemption and take us to himself." (Horne)

4. (175-176) Depending on the word of the God who seeks us.

Let my soul live, and it shall praise You;
And let Your judgments help me.
I have gone astray like a lost sheep;
Seek Your servant,
For I do not forget Your commandments.

a. **Let my soul live, and it shall praise You; and let Your judgments help me**: The psalmist recognized that his **soul** needed both *life* from God and *guidance* from God's word. With this combination of life and guidance, he would build a healthy relationship with God.

i. "Verse 175, the next to the last verse, is a good biblical statement of what the Westminster Shorter Catechism calls 'the chief end of man,' namely, to glorify God and to enjoy him forever: 'Let me live that I may praise you.' But verse 176, the last verse, reminds us that this praise comes from poor, weak, lost, and straying sinners like ourselves." (Boice)

ii. The ending section of this great psalm emphasizes the psalmist's great need for God and his dependence upon Him. His love for and dedication to the word of God has not made him more spiritually *independent*, but more spiritually *dependent* upon God. What did the psalmist need?

- Understanding (verse 169).
- Deliverance (verse 170).
- Ability to worship God rightly (verses 171-172).
- Power to live an upright life (verses 173-174).
- Strength to persevere (verse 175).

iii. "The consciousness of need is revealed in each successive petition. Yet the song is never a wail of despair, because side by side with the sense of need, there is evident throughout a profound conviction of the sufficiency of the will of God." (Morgan)

b. **I have gone astray like a lost sheep**: This great psalm ends on a touching note. The psalmist remembered his own frailty and sinful tendencies (**astray like a lost sheep**), and therefore asked God to **seek** him.

i. "Here is, first, *a confession of imperfection and of helplessness*. It means really a continual imperfection and helplessness, for the Hebrew verb relates not only to the past, but to the present." (Spurgeon)

ii. "The author had not become self-righteous by his devotions, despite his reiterated claims to have obeyed the Bible's teachings." (Boice)

iii. "This verse is extremely emotional and full of tears, for truly we are all thus going astray, so that we must pray to be visited, sought, and carried over by the most godly Shepherd, the Lord Jesus Christ, who is God blessed forever. Amen." (Luther, cited in Boice)

iv. "He was not like a dog, that somehow or other can find its way back; but he was like a lost sheep, which goes further and further away from home; yet still he was a sheep, and the Lord's sheep, his property, and precious in his sight, and therefore he hoped to be sought in order to be restored." (Spurgeon)

c. **Seek Your servant, for I do not forget Your commandments**: We can surmise that *God sought His servant in His word*. God does **seek** after us in His word. His word tests us; it encourages us; it strengthens us; it rebukes us; it helps us; it teaches us; it gives us understanding; it protects us.

i. **Seek Your servant**: "A poor, lost, weak, sinful – yes, even unprofitable – servant (see Luke 17:10), but still a servant of God." (Boice)

ii. The psalmist describes a Romans 7:21 kind of experience: *I find then a law, that evil is present with me, the one who wills to do good.* "And the Psalmist had the same remedy at the early period, as had the apostle in the later times; for God's salvation is one. The psalmist's remedy was, 'Seek thy servant;' the apostle's, 'O wretched man that I am, who shall deliver me from the body of this death? I thank God through Jesus Christ our Lord.'" (Stephen, cited in Spurgeon)

iii. "The note of urgent need on which the psalm ends is proof enough that the love of Scripture, which has motivated the scribes of every age, need not harden into academic pride. This man would have taken his stance not with the self-congratulating Pharisee of the parable, but with the publican who stood afar off, but went home justified." (Kidner)

iv. The psalm ends on the reminder that the power and greatness of God's word does not rest only in its literary brilliance. Its greatness and glory is in the fact that God comes to us and seeks us in and through His word.

v. "I do not think that there could possibly be a more appropriate conclusion of such a Psalm as this, so full of the varied experience and the ever-changing frames and feelings even of a child of God, in the sunshine and the cloud, in the calm and in the storm, than this ever-clinging sense of his propensity to wander, and the expression of his utter inability to find his way back without the Lord's guiding hand to restore him." (Bouchier, cited in Spurgeon)

"As far as I have been able, as far as I have been aided by the Lord, I have treated throughout, and expounded, this great Psalm. A task which more able and learned expositors have performed, or will perform better; nevertheless, my services were not to be withheld from it on that account." (Augustine, cited in Spurgeon)

Psalm 120 – The Prayer and Journey of the Outsider

Psalm 120 is the first of a series of 15 psalms each with the title, **A Song of Ascents**. *The reason for this collection and arrangement is not precisely stated. Many different explanations have been given for these "degrees" or "steps" or "ascents":*

- The Stairs of the Temple Songs.
- The Step Songs.
- The Gradual Songs.
- The Progression Songs.
- The Procession from Babylon Songs.
- The Pilgrim Festival Songs.

James Montgomery Boice explained the first suggestion: "The Talmud says that the fifteen songs correspond to the fifteen steps between these courtyards (Middoth ii. 5; Succa 51b). Some have even supposed that the songs were sung by the Levites from these steps, though this is pure speculation."

Probably the best explanation is the last one listed, that these were songs for the people of God as they made the pilgrim journey to Jerusalem and the temple at the three appointed feasts (Passover, Pentecost, and Tabernacles).

1 Chronicles 13:6 uses this phrase to describe the bringing of the ark of the covenant into Jerusalem: to bring up from there the ark of God the LORD. *According to Charles Spurgeon (and many others), the word we translate* **ascents** *shares the same root with* to bring up *in 1 Chronicles 13:6. The same root word is used in the same context in 1 Chronicles 15:15.*

"We shall consider them as songs sung by those pilgrims who went up to Jerusalem to worship…. These songs of desire, and hope, and approach are appropriate for the pilgrims' use as they go up to worship." (G. Campbell Morgan) This being likely

so, then Jesus would have sung these songs on His many journeys to Jerusalem from Galilee.

"The author of these fifteen Psalms is not known; and most probably they were not the work of one person. They have been attributed to David, to Solomon, to Ezra, to Haggai, to Zechariah, and to Malachi, without any positive evidence. They are, however, excellent in their kind, and written with much elegance; containing strong and nervous sentiments of the most exalted piety, expressed with great felicity of language in a few words." (Adam Clarke)

A. The distress and destiny of liars who oppose.

1. (1-2) Distress and deliverance from deceitful tongues.

In my distress I cried to the LORD,
And He heard me.
Deliver my soul, O LORD, from lying lips
***And* from a deceitful tongue.**

> a. **In my distress I cried to the LORD**: The people of God often find themselves in **distress**. They have a refuge in their distress; they can do as the psalmist did when he **cried to the LORD**. They can share the singer's testimony, **and He heard me**.

> > i. **In my distress**: "Distress addeth wings to our devotions. Our Saviour, being in agony, prayed more earnestly, Luke 22:44. So do all his members, and especially when they lie under the lash of a lying tongue, as here." (Trapp)

> > ii. **I cried to the LORD**: "It is of little use to appeal to our fellows on the matter of slander, for the more we stir in it the more it spreads; it is of no avail to appeal to the honour of the slanderers, for they have none, and the most piteous demands for justice will only increase their malignity and encourage them to fresh insult." (Spurgeon)

> > iii. **And He heard me**: The psalmist remembered God's past faithfulness in his present need. "Devout hearts argue that what Jehovah has done once He will do again. Since His mercy endureth forever, He will not weary of bestowing, nor will former gifts exhaust His stores. Men say, 'I have given so often that I can give no more'; God says, 'I have given, therefore I will give.'" (Maclaren)

> > iv. "When we are slandered it is a joy that the Lord knows us, and cannot be made to doubt our uprightness. He will not hear the lie against us, but he will hear our prayer against the lie." (Spurgeon)

b. **Deliver my soul, O Lord, from lying lips**: The psalmist described the nature of his distress – evil words spoken against him from **lying lips** and **a deceitful tongue**.

> i. There was some comfort in this cry, knowing that the evil that was spoken against the singer *was not true*. It was spoken with **lying lips** and with a **deceitful tongue**.

> ii. The lies our soul needs deliverance from are not only the lies said *about* us, but also the lies said *to us* – lies about God, lies about man, lies about ourself, lies about life, identity, purpose, and happiness. From *these* lies, **deliver my soul, O Lord**.

2. (3-4) The destiny of the deceitful tongue.

What shall be given to you,
Or what shall be done to you,
You false tongue?
Sharp arrows of the warrior,
With coals of the broom tree!

a. **What shall be given to you**: The psalmist shifted from his prayer to God to speak to the **false tongue** of those who caused him distress. He warned those lying lips of their destiny, of **what shall be done to you**.

> i. In light of the judgment described in these verses, it is worth remembering that "…a false tongue is likened to a sharp razor, Psalm 52:2-4; to a sharp sword, Psalm 57:4; to sharp arrows, Proverbs 26:18-19." (Trapp)

b. **Sharp arrows of the warrior**: The **false tongue** of the singer's enemies would soon know **sharp arrows**. They had cast out lies like dangerous missiles, and now the **sharp arrows** of judgment would come against them.

> i. These are "…punishments justly inflicted on a tongue, the words of which have been keen and killing as arrows, and which, by its lies and calumnies, hath contributed to set the world on fire." (Horne)

> ii. Clarke suggested that the picture here is of *flaming arrows* or *fiery darts* (Ephesians 6:16): "*Fiery arrows, or arrows wrapped about with inflamed combustibles*, were formerly used in sieges to set the places on fire."

> iii. "The liar, wounding though his weapons are, will be destroyed with far more potent shafts than lies: God's *arrows* of truth and *coals* of judgment." (Kidner)

B. Living in a troubled place, longing for God's peace.

1. (5-6) The weariness of living with those who hate God's *shalom*.

Woe is me, that I dwell in Meshech,
That **I dwell among the tents of Kedar!**
My soul has dwelt too long
With one who hates peace.

a. **Woe is me, that I dwell in Meshech**: **Meshech** was a distant place, far from the land of Israel (Ezekiel 27:13, 32:26, 39:1). **Kedar** was a place associated with the nomadic tribes in the lands surrounding Israel (Isaiah 21:16-17, Jeremiah 49:28).

> i. "Meshech was the name of [a group of] barbarous tribes who, in the times of Sargon and Sennacherib inhabited the highlands to the east of Cilicia, and in later days retreated northwards to the neighbourhood of the Black Sea.... Kedar was one of the Bedouin tribes of the Arabian desert." (Maclaren)

> ii. "These two peoples were located so far apart geographically that they can only be taken here as 'a general term for the heathen.' No one person could have lived among both. They are examples of warlike tribes, among whom the singers of Psalm 120 had no true home." (Boice)

> iii. "The verbs 'dwell' (*garti*, 'sojourn') and 'live' (*sakanti*, 'tabernacle,' 'dwell') are significantly chosen. Even though the psalmist may have enjoyed a permanent residence, he felt as if he was no more than a sojourner among his contemporaries. He did not feel at home among an ungodly people." (VanGemeren)

b. **My soul has dwelt too long with one who hates peace**: The psalmist ached because he lived among the ungodly and was distant from Israel and its people. He longed for God's *shalom* (**peace**); his enemies, who had lying lips, hated God's *shalom*.

> i. This was a *good* discontentment. "Contentment in the place where deceit is practiced, and strife is loved, is base contentment. Men of faith must there find the distress which inspires the cry to God." (Morgan)

> ii. "The very society of such (be they ever so tame and civil) is tedious and unsavoury to a good soul; like the slime and filth that is congealed when many toads and other vermin join together." (Trapp)

> iii. God can work good even in the troubles of difficult company. "And remember, there is a compensation, in that the strict scrutiny of thy foes makes thee ever so much more watchful and prayerful, and drives thee oftener to the bosom of God." (Meyer)

> iv. This makes Psalm 120 a fitting start to the Songs of Ascents. As the pilgrim journey to Jerusalem began, the author was mindful of

the weariness endured living apart from the supportive community of God's people. The psalmist *needed* this trip to Jerusalem at feast time and *needed* the larger community of the people of God.

2. (7) The contrast between the singer and the community where he lives.

I *am for* peace;
But when I speak, they *are* for war.

a. **I am for peace**: He loved and longed for God's **peace**, His *shalom*.

i. **I am for peace**: "Properly, 'I am peace'; desirous of peace, peaceful, forbearing, in fact, peace itself." (Spurgeon)

ii. "The clause 'I am a man of peace' translates a nominal phrase: 'I peace.' In his whole being the psalmist longs for the establishment of peace." (VanGemeren)

iii. "Jesus was a man of peace…he lived to make peace 'by the blood of his cross;' he died to complete it." (Pierce, cited in Spurgeon)

b. **When I speak, they are for war**: The psalmist sought to speak words of peace and goodness, to represent and promote those values in our own community. Yet every time he did, the response was hostile, characteristic of those who **are for war**.

i. At least for a while, he needed better company – and he would find it among the pilgrims who came to Jerusalem and who shared in these *Songs of Ascents*.

ii. "So the psalm ends as with a long-drawn sigh. It inverts the usual order of similar psalms, in which the description of need is wont to precede the prayer for deliverance. It thus sets forth most pathetically the sense of discordance between a man and his environment, which urges the soul that feels it to seek a better home. So this is a true pilgrim psalm." (Maclaren)

Psalm 121 – The God Who Keeps and Helps

This is the second of the series of psalms which are titled **A Song of Ascents.** *As a song sung by travelers, this is particularly relevant for the trust placed in God through the journey.*

"David Livingstone, the famous missionary and explorer of the continent of Africa, read Psalm 121 and Psalm 135, which praises God for his sovereign rule over all things, as he worshiped with his father and sister before setting out for Africa in 1840. His mother-in-law, Mrs. Moffat, wrote him at Linyardi that Psalm 121 was always in her mind as she thought about and prayed for him." (James Montgomery Boice)

A. Help from the LORD, the Creator of all and helper of Israel.

1. (1-2) Help from Yahweh.

I will lift up my eyes to the hills—
From whence comes my help?
My help *comes* from the LORD,
Who made heaven and earth.

> a. **I will lift up my eyes to the hills**: The singer of this psalm looked **to the hills**, likely the distant **hills** of Jerusalem as he travelled toward the city to fulfill his pilgrimage.

> > i. "The singer is still far from the appointed place of worship, lifting his eyes toward the distant mountains. He is not far from Jehovah, however. In Jehovah's keeping, even though far from the center of external worship, the pilgrim realizes his safety." (Morgan)

> > ii. The point is wonderful. The singer understood that the group didn't need to arrive at Jerusalem before they came under God's protective care. He would watch over them on the journey. God is just as present in the journey as in the destination.

iii. There are two other suggestions of what was intended by this looking **up** to the **hills**, though they are less likely.

- Some suggest this was a consideration of the *high places* where idolaters set their altars (Numbers 22:41, Deuteronomy 33:29, 1 Kings 12:31).

- Some suggest this was an *anxious* look to the hills, looking for danger and threats from often-present robbers and gangs.

b. **My help comes from the LORD**: The traveller looked to Jerusalem as his goal, yet his trust was not in that city itself. **Help** would come from the God **who made heaven and earth**. The Creator would be his helper.

i. "The sole source of 'help' comes from Yahweh, who, as Creator, has unlimited power." (VanGemeren)

ii. "What he is telling us is that his gaze did not stop when he looked upward to the hills but that he looked beyond them to God, who made the mountains." (Boice)

iii. "The City of God, and the Temple, are to be desired and delighted in; the mountains upon which they rest are to be remembered. But not from them does help come to distressed souls; it comes from Jehovah." (Morgan)

2. (3-4) The help God brings.

He will not allow your foot to be moved;
He who keeps you will not slumber.
Behold, He who keeps Israel
Shall neither slumber nor sleep.

a. **He will not allow your foot to be moved**: God would help His people by establishing them in a firm place, allowing them to stand and not allowing their **foot to be moved**.

i. "The foundation, God's infinite power and goodness, on which thou standest, cannot be moved; and whilst thou standest on this basis, thy foot cannot be moved." (Clarke)

ii. "Our feet shall move in progress, but they shall not be moved to their overthrow." (Spurgeon)

iii. For the Christian, this reminds us of the principles found in Ephesians 6:11 and 13 – that the believer is to find a place to *stand*, and this can only be done by looking to the Lord and trusting the One who **will not allow your foot to be moved**.

iv. The standing of the believer in Jesus is impressive.

- We stand in grace (Romans 5:2).
- We stand in the gospel (1 Corinthians 15:1).
- We stand in courage and strength (1 Corinthians 16:13).
- We stand in faith (2 Corinthians 1:24).
- We stand in Christian liberty (Galatians 5:1).
- We stand in Christian unity (Philippians 1:27).
- We stand in the Lord (Philippians 4:1).
- The goal: We will stand perfect and complete in the will of God (Colossians 4:12).

b. **He who keeps you**: This is the first of six times in this short psalm that the Hebrew word *shamar* (translated **keeps** and **preserve**) is used. The theme is that God will watch over His people as a watchman watches over the city or the party of travelers.

> i. "This psalmist is so absorbed in the thought of his Keeper that he barely names his dangers. With happy assurance of protection, he says over and over again the one word which is his amulet against foes and fears. Six times in these few verses does the thought recur that Jehovah is the Keeper of Israel or of the single soul." (Maclaren)

> ii. "The Divine Being represents himself as a *watchman*, who takes care of the city and its inhabitants during the night-watches; and who is never overtaken with slumbering or sleepiness." (Clarke)

c. **He who keeps you will not slumber**: When we look to the LORD, we have confidence in the fact that God does not sleep. The idea is repeated in verse 4 for emphasis. God's watchful eye is always open, looking with love and care upon His people.

> i. In his confrontation with the prophets of Baal on Mount Carmel, Elijah mocked the idol prophets when Baal did not respond, saying of Baal *perhaps he is sleeping and must be awakened* (1 Kings 18:27). We have the great comfort in knowing that **He who keeps Israel shall neither slumber nor sleep**.

> ii. This promise was especially meaningful for the pilgrims on their way to Jerusalem. "Their daily march and their nightly encampment will then be placed under the care of Jehovah, who will hold up their feet unwearied on the road and watch unslumbering over their repose." (Maclaren)

> iii. "A poor woman, as the Eastern story has it, came to the Sultan one day, and asked compensation for the loss of some property. 'How

did you lose it?' said the monarch. 'I fell asleep,' was the reply, 'and a robber entered my dwelling.' 'Why did you fall asleep?'.... 'I fell asleep because I believed that you were awake.' The Sultan was so much delighted with the answer of the woman, that he ordered her loss to be made up." (McMichael, cited in Spurgeon)

B. The care of the LORD for His people.

1. (5-6) The LORD brings relief from the sun.

The LORD is your keeper;
The LORD is your shade at your right hand.
The sun shall not strike you by day,
Nor the moon by night.

a. **The LORD is your shade at your right hand:** The brutal rays of the sun in the world of the Middle East could assault the traveler, such as the pilgrim on the way to one of Israel's feasts in Jerusalem. God promised care for the traveler, with a reference that goes back to the cloud by day that followed Israel in the wilderness from Egypt and shielded them from the sun.

i. Similar promises are made in other verses such as Isaiah 4:6 and 25:4. Psalm 91:1 is especially precious, with **shade** being the same word as "shadow": *He who dwells in the secret place of the Most High shall abide under the shadow of the Almighty.*

ii. **Your shade:** "...both to refresh thee and keep thee from the burning heat of the sun, as it is expressed in the next verse, and to protect thee by his power from all thine enemies; for which reason God is oft called a *shadow* in Scripture." (Poole)

b. **Nor the moon by night:** Any superstitious fears they may have had from the light of the moon were of no concern to those whom God protected. He would keep and preserve His people day and night.

i. "What the psalmist really means, though in figurative language, is that nothing either of the day or night can harm us if God is keeping guard. God is our covering against every calamity. He is our shade against the visible perils of the day as well as the hidden perils of the night." (Boice)

ii. "God has not made a new sun or a fresh moon for his chosen, they exist under the same outward circumstances as others, but the power to smite is in their case removed from temporal agencies; saints are enriched, and not injured, by the powers which govern the earth's condition." (Spurgeon)

iii. "But let the pope be the sun and the emperor the moon (as the canonists called them), yet the sun shall not smite the Church by day nor the moon by night. Luther was at the same time excommunicated by the pope and proscribed by the emperor; yet died he in his bed." (Trapp)

2. (7-8) God preserves His people.

The Lord shall preserve you from all evil;
He shall preserve your soul.
The Lord shall preserve your going out and your coming in
From this time forth, and even forevermore.

a. **The Lord shall preserve you from all evil**: The singer had great confidence in God's protecting power. **Evil** men may come and afflict the child of God, but the Lord **shall preserve your soul**.

i. "'All evil' will be averted from him who has Jehovah for his keeper; therefore, if any so called Evil comes, he may be sure that it is Good with a veil on." (Maclaren)

ii. "In the light of other scriptures, to be kept *from all evil* does not imply a cushioned life, but a well-armed one." (Kidner)

iii. **He shall preserve your soul**: "Our soul is kept from the dominion of sin, the infection of error, the crush of despondency, the puffing up of pride; kept from the world, the flesh and the devil; kept for holier and greater things; kept in the love of God; kept unto the eternal kingdom and glory." (Spurgeon)

iv. **The Lord shall preserve...He shall preserve.... The Lord shall preserve**: "Three times have we the phrase, 'Jehovah shall keep,' as if the sacred Trinity thus sealed the word to make it sure: ought not all our fears to be slain by such a threefold flight of arrows? What anxiety can survive this triple promise?" (Spurgeon)

b. **The Lord shall preserve your going out and your coming in**: The promise is comprehensive. God's people may trust in His preserving power for all of one's activity (**going out** and **coming in**) and at all times (**from this time forth, and even forevermore**).

i. "When we go out in youth to begin life, and come in at the end to die, we shall experience the same keeping. Our exits and our entrances are under one protection." (Spurgeon)

ii. "*Your going out and your coming in* is not only a way of saying 'everything'...in closer detail it draws attention to one's ventures and enterprises (cf. Ps. 126:6), and to the home which remains one's base; again, to pilgrimage and return." (Kidner)

iii. "He has not led me so tenderly thus far to forsake me at the very gate of heaven." (Adoniram Judson, cited in Spurgeon)

Psalm 122 – Coming to the House of the LORD and the City of God

Psalm 122 carries the title **A Song of Ascents. Of David**. *It is one of the four Songs of Ascents that is specifically attributed to King David. He wrote it both for what Jerusalem was in his day, and for what it would become under his son and their successors. David perhaps never made pilgrimage from a great distance to one of the major feasts, but he wrote Psalm 122 in the voice of one who did, and who had arrived at the Holy City.*

"David wrote it for the people to sing at the time of their goings up to the holy feasts at Jerusalem. It comes third in the series, and appears to be suitable to be sung when the people had entered the gates, and their feet stood within the city." (Charles Spurgeon)

A. Coming to Jerusalem.

1. (1) The joy of coming to God's house.

I was glad when they said to me,
"Let us go into the house of the LORD."

a. **I was glad when they said to me**: David had in mind both the community (**when they said**) and the individual (**I was glad**). He pictured the individual coming together with the group to **go into the house of the LORD**. That invitation and the acceptance of it made him **glad**.

i. Boice reflected on David's possible motive in writing Psalm 122: "It is reasonable to suppose that he wrote it both to express joy in his new capital city and to encourage love for and loyalty toward it as the focal point of the nation's political life and worship."

b. **Let us go into the house of the LORD**: During David's days there was never a temple, but he knew one would be built, having extensively planned and prepared for it (1 Chronicles 22:2-16). It's possible that David wrote here of the pilgrimage to the tabernacle, which did exist in his day and was regarded as the **house of the LORD**. It's more likely that David wrote this psalm in anticipation of the pilgrims who would come to the **house of the LORD** built by Solomon.

i. It is wonderful to think of David's extensive preparation for the people of Israel to come to the temple, especially for the required feasts three times a year.

ii. "That House was supreme in importance because it was the House of Jehovah. Jehovah, the God of Grace, is the One around Whom the people gather." (Morgan)

c. **Let us go into the house of the LORD**: Coming to God's house made David happy, though he knew that no building could contain God in all His glory and greatness. At **the house of the LORD** he could focus his thoughts, prayers, worship, and receiving of God's word in the community of God's people in a special way, and David was **glad** for that.

i. Too many don't know the gladness David sang of, either because they don't **go into the house of the LORD**, or because they do go and it isn't a **glad** thing for them.

ii. We should **go into the house of the LORD**. It is good and important for us to gather with God's people for prayers, worship, and receiving of God's word. The gathering should be formal and ordered *enough* so that it is regarded as a gathering of God's **house** – not everyone doing their own thing, but God's people coming together for His glory and their benefit in His house.

iii. Our going to God's **house** should be a **glad** thing. This isn't the same as saying it should be *entertaining*, especially in an age when entertainment is a dangerous idol. Not everything that happens at the **house of the LORD** must be *fun*, but it should all be *good*, both welcoming to the not-yet-believer and good for those who are believers in Jesus.

iv. If going to the **house of the LORD** is not a **glad** thing, the problem may be in the heart of the one who comes or it may be in what happens at the house of the LORD – but the problem should be prayerfully diagnosed and lovingly addressed.

2. (2) The happy arrival.

Our feet have been standing
Within your gates, O Jerusalem!

a. **Our feet have been standing within your gates**: Most regard this as David's description of the joyful statement of the pilgrim who has finally arrived. The most important aspect is the evident joy and gladness at coming to the destination.

> i. "This is the song of the singer, no longer distanced from the City, and Temple, but having arrived therein. It is the song of first impressions." (Morgan)

b. **Within your gates, O Jerusalem**: They came to **Jerusalem** because that was where David set up the tabernacle and where the ark of the covenant and the altar of sacrifice were. Later, Solomon built the temple in **Jerusalem** that David planned and prepared for.

B. Describing Jerusalem.

1. (3-4) A prosperous, unified city.

Jerusalem is built
As a city that is compact together,
Where the tribes go up,
The tribes of the LORD,
To the Testimony of Israel,
To give thanks to the name of the LORD.

a. **Jerusalem is built**: David had conquered the city of Jerusalem, taking it from the Jebusites who held it as a Canaanite stronghold. He **built** the city in his own day, and David rejoiced in declaring, **Jerusalem is built**.

> i. "It matters not how wicked or degraded a place may have been in former times, when it is sanctified to the use and service of God it becomes honourable. Jerusalem was formerly Jebus – a place where the Jebusites committed their abominations, and where were all the miseries of those who hasten after another God. But now, since it is devoted to God's service, it is a city – 'compact together,' 'the joy of the whole earth.'" (Plumer, cited in Spurgeon)

b. **A city that is compact together**: David's city of Jerusalem was not large, but it was not a disordered collection of tents and shacks. It was **built**, and built together in an orderly way (**compact together**). It was a real city.

> i. "During David's reign and for some time thereafter, Jerusalem was a small city located on the crest of Mount Zion and Mount Moriah, bounded on two sides by steep descents to the Kidron and Tyropaeon valleys, and thus no more than half a mile in breadth. It had a dramatic setting for one approaching it from a distance, and its tight structure would have impressed anyone observing it." (Boice)

ii. "Furthermore, it is not erected as a set of booths, or a conglomeration of hovels, but as a city, substantial, architectural, designed, arranged, and defended." (Spurgeon)

iii. "The expression '*bound firmly together*' [**compact together**] uses… the same verb as is found in the instructions for making the tent of worship: 'couple the tent together that it may be one whole' (Exod. 26:11). Such was the blueprint; such will be the ultimate reality (Rev. 21:10ff.)." (Kidner)

iv. "A church should be one in creed and one in heart, one in testimony and one in service, one in aspiration and one in sympathy. They greatly injure our Jerusalem who would build dividing walls within her; she needs compacting, not dividing." (Spurgeon)

c. **Where the tribes go up**: One of the reasons David conquered Jerusalem and established it as the capital of both the political and religious life of Israel was because it did not previously belong to a specific tribe, being under Canaanite occupation. Since it belonged to no tribe, it belonged to all the tribes, and the **tribes of the Lord** could come together as one at Jerusalem and the house of the Lord.

i. "Note that Israel was one people, but yet it was in a sense divided by the mere surface distinction of tribes; and this may be a lesson to us that all Christendom is essentially one, though from various causes we are divided into tribes. Let us as much as possible sink the tribal individuality in the national unity, so that the church may be many waves, but one sea; many branches, but one tree; many members, but one body." (Spurgeon)

ii. Christians today should reflect this same unity even with their diversity. "There is no such oneness in all the world as among true Christians; and this the very heathens observed and commended. As the curtains of the tabernacle were joined by loops, so were they by love. And as the stones of the temple were so close cemented together that they seemed to be all but one stone, so was it among the primitive saints." (Trapp)

iii. "Wherever my brethren meet, in whatever section of the Church on earth, so long as they belong to the one Church, the Body of Christ, nothing shall stay me from wishing them prosperity and peace. They may not recognize me here, but five minutes in Heaven will do away with all these earthly estrangements." (Meyer)

d. **To the Testimony of Israel**: This describes the ark of the covenant, which was often called by this title (Exodus 25:22, Exodus 27:21, Numbers 1:53).

Representing the throne of God and His presence in Israel, **the Testimony of Israel** was the center of the tabernacle and later the temple.

> i. Matthew Poole explained why the ark of the covenant was sometimes called **the Testimony of Israel**: "…the tables of the covenant [were] laid up in it, which are called God's testimony, and the tables of the testimony."

> ii. Many commentators (such as Adam Clarke) regard this psalm as written by and for exiles returning from the Babylonian captivity. The reference to the ark of the **Testimony** argues against that idea, because it was *not* part of the temple when the exiles returned.

e. **To give thanks to the name of the LORD**: The primary purpose of the feasts of Israel was for the people of God to come together and give Him **thanks**. Their appreciation for what He had done gave them faith for what He would do in the future.

> i. "Note that the object of these pilgrim feasts was *to give thanks*, not primarily to seek unity or prosperity. These were gifts over and above the occasion, not its *raison d'être*; whereas pagan worship was all too blatantly a means to securing what one wanted: cf. Hosea 2:5." (Kidner)

> ii. "The unity of the city reflected the unity of the tribes on these special occasions. The Israelite tribes came together for the purpose of praising 'the name of the Lord'. It was an act of loyalty, as the Lord had commanded them to present themselves before him." (VanGemeren)

2. (5) A city of justice and righteous rule.

For thrones are set there for judgment,
The thrones of the house of David.

a. **For thrones are set there for judgment**: As the seat of government for Israel, Jerusalem was where their main courts **for judgment** were established. Jerusalem was to be a city of *justice*, where good was honored and where evil was corrected.

> i. These **thrones** were for dispensing judgment, and may have been visible at the gates of the city (Ruth 4:1-12, Matthew 19:28).

b. **The thrones of the house of David**: David's **house** was established to reign over Israel. Saul's house never reigned, supplying really only one king. David's lineage reigned in Jerusalem and will forever reign in the Messiah, the Son of David.

C. Praying for Jerusalem.

1. (6-8) The exhortation to pray and the prayer itself.

Pray for the peace of Jerusalem:
"May they prosper who love you.
Peace be within your walls,
Prosperity within your palaces."
For the sake of my brethren and companions,
I will now say, "Peace *be* within you."

a. **Pray for the peace of Jerusalem**: David exhorted pilgrims coming to the Holy City to **pray for the peace** of the city. Jerusalem's name itself marks it as the city of peace (Hebrews 7:2), but in reality it has known much war and conflict, which continue to this day. It is good to **pray** for the often-elusive **peace of Jerusalem**.

> i. "In a church one of the main ingredients of success is internal peace: strife, suspicion, party-spirit, division, – these are deadly things. Those who break the peace of the church deserve to suffer, and those who sustain it win a great blessing." (Spurgeon)

b. **May they prosper who love you**: David continued by giving a prayer for Jerusalem. The prayer included a blessing for those who **love** the city, and a direct request for **peace** and **prosperity** for the city.

> i. Kidner on **peace** and **prosperity**: "They are the proper fruits of justice, the subject of verse 5."

> ii. "The word 'prosper' conveys an idea which is not in the original. The Hebrew word means to be secure, tranquil, at rest, spoken especially of one who enjoys quiet prosperity: Job 3:26; 12:6. The essential idea is that of quietness or rest; and the meaning here is, that those who love Zion will have peace." (Barnes, cited in Spurgeon)

> iii. "This is the *form of prayer* that they are to use: 'May *prosperity* ever reside within thy walls, on all the people that dwell there; and tranquillity within thy palaces or high places, among the *rulers* and *governors* of the people.'" (Clarke)

c. **For the sake of my brethren and companions**: David prayed for blessings for those who loved and prayed for Jerusalem, but the blessing was not only for the individual but for the community of those who cared for the peace of Jerusalem, those who said, **"Peace be within you."**

> i. A "play of words lies in the interchange of 'peace' and 'prosperity,' which are closely similar in sound in the Hebrew." (Maclaren)

> ii. "The repetition of the desire displays the writer's high valuation of the blessing mentioned; he would not again and again have invoked peace had he not perceived its extreme desirableness." (Spurgeon)

2. (9) The reason to pray and to seek good for Jerusalem.

Because of the house of the LORD our God
I will seek your good.

a. **Because of the house of the LORD our God**: David understood that the gladness and goodness of the pilgrim toward God's city was not primarily political in nature. It wasn't because of loyalty to a political party, leader, or philosophy. It was because **the house of the LORD** was established there.

i. "The Psalmist declareth the two motives, which induced him to utter his best wishes, and use his best endeavours, for the prosperity of Jerusalem; namely, love of his brethren, whose happiness was involved in that of their city; and love of God, who had there fixed the residence of his glory." (Horne)

ii. "Through it all it is evident that the glory of city and Temple consists in the fact that they are the city and house of Jehovah. It is not a song of buildings or of material magnificence. It is rather the song of assembly, of testimony, of judgment, of peace, of prosperity. These all issue from the supreme fact of Jehovah's presence." (Morgan)

iii. This has a special application for the Christian under the New Covenant. For us, the church is the **house of the LORD**, with Jesus the Head and Son of the house (Hebrews 3:5-6, Hebrews 10:21, 1 Peter 2:5, 1 Peter 4:17). What makes the church special is that it is *God's* habitation, *His* house. His presence makes it special.

iv. Ancient Jerusalem had political, economic, and social importance. Yet the most important reason to love and care for Jerusalem was because of **the house of the LORD**. Christians should have the same great care for and focus upon the work of God's house.

b. **I will seek your good**: Just as it was good for pilgrims in Israel to **seek** the good of Jerusalem *for the sake of God's house*, so Christians today can and should **seek** the **good** of society for the sake of God's house.

i. **I will seek**: "It is not a careless, loose seeking after it, almost as indifferently as a woman seeks after a pin which she has dropped; no, no; effort is implied." (Irons, cited in Spurgeon)

ii. "First we love it (verse 6) and then we labour for it, as in this passage: we see its good, and then seek its good." (Spurgeon)

Psalm 123 – Looking to the LORD for Mercy in Affliction

This psalm is simply titled **A Song of Ascents.** *It is another in the series of psalms sung by pilgrims on their way to Jerusalem at feast time. These songs give us a pattern of preparation to meet with God and His people.*

"This Psalm (as ye see) is but short, and therefore a very fit example to show the force of prayer not to consist in many words, but in fervency of spirit. For great and weighty matters may be comprised in a few words, if they proceed from the spirit and the unspeakable groanings of the heart, especially when our necessity is such as will not suffer any long prayer. Every prayer is long enough if it be fervent and proceed from a heart that understandeth the necessity of the saints." (Martin Luther, cited in Charles Spurgeon)

A. The afflicted looks to the LORD.

1. (1) Where to look.

**Unto You I lift up my eyes,
O You who dwell in the heavens.**

> a. **Unto You I lift up my eyes**: The psalmist declares his intention and action – to lift up his eyes to the LORD. This means that his eyes are not on his circumstances or himself, but on the LORD.

> > i. "It is good to have some one to look up to. The Psalmist looked so high that he could look no higher. Not to the hills, but to the God of the hills he looked." (Spurgeon)

> b. **O You who dwell in the heavens**: By remembering where God is, the psalmist grows in trust and confidence. Earth may have no mercy or help, but heaven has plenty of mercy and help.

> > i. We see a progression in these Psalms of Ascent, beginning with Psalm 120.

- In Psalm 120 we lament our surroundings.

- In Psalm 121 we lift our eyes to the hills of Zion.

- In Psalm 122 we delight in the house of the LORD.

- In Psalm 123 we look above the hills to the LORD in heaven.

ii. "The goal of the pilgrim is not Jerusalem, as important as that city was, or even the temple in Jerusalem, as important as it was, but God himself, whose true throne is not anywhere on earth but in heaven." (Boice)

2. (2) How to look.

Behold, as the eyes of servants *look* to the hand of their masters,
As the eyes of a maid to the hand of her mistress,
So our eyes *look* to the LORD our God,
Until He has mercy on us.

a. **As the eyes of servants look to the hand of their masters**: The example pictures a waiter or a butler standing behind his master seated at dinner. The servant looks to the hand of his master for the slightest indication of need or want, to instantly meet the need. With that same intensity, devotion, and steadfastness, the psalmist looks to God.

i. "They should stand where they can see Him; they should have their gaze fixed upon Him; they should look with patient trust, as well as with eager willingness to start into activity when He indicates His commands." (Maclaren)

ii. "This is not an endorsement of slavery, of course. It is a way of saying that the disciple's dependence on God and submission to God should be no less total than the most obedient servant of an earthly master." (Boice)

iii. Morgan says the picture of the servants looking to the hands of the master suggests at least three things:

- *Dependence*: The hands of the master provide all that is needed.

- *Submission*: The hands of the master direct the servant's work.

- *Discipline*: The hands of the master correct the servant.

iv. "Here, then, is the true way of looking for help from Jehovah. It is that of dependence, obedience, and response to correction." (Morgan)

b. **So our eyes look to the LORD our God**: The psalmist *waited* to mention God by name, so as to build a sense of anticipation. The looking is fully described before the One looked to is named.

i. "The psalmist creates a suspense by drawing out the use of the divine name." (VanGemeren)

ii. "Do we look to God like that – reverently, obediently, attentively, continuously, expectantly, singly, submissively, imploringly? Probably not, but we should." (Boice)

iii. "Creation, providence, grace; these are all motions of Jehovah's hand, and from each of them a portion of our duty is to be learned; therefore should we carefully study them, to discover the divine will." (Spurgeon)

iv. "We have too long acted on our own initiative; let us wait on our exalted Lord for the indication of his will." (Meyer)

c. **Until He has mercy on us**: This is how long the psalmist will focus his attention toward the LORD. He does not demand an immediate answer, but will persevere patiently until the LORD extends His mercy.

B. The afflicted pleads for mercy.

1. (3) The request for mercy.

Have mercy on us, O LORD, have mercy on us!
For we are exceedingly filled with contempt.

a. **Have mercy on us**: The psalmist wasn't content to only wait for mercy; he begged for it. He demonstrated that waiting on the LORD is not a passive thing. He repeated the request for **mercy**, showing the intensity of his plea. The Master he looked to would look upon him and help.

b. **For we are exceedingly filled with contempt**: The psalmist needed God's intervention and mercy because he felt filled with the contempt put on him by others.

i. **Exceedingly filled**: "The Hebrew word here used means "to be saturated"; to have the appetite fully satisfied – as applied to one who is hungry or thirsty. Then it comes to mean to be entirely full, and the idea here is, that as much contempt had been thrown upon them as could be; they could experience no more." (Barnes, cited in Spurgeon)

ii. Sometimes others show contempt to us, and it just rolls off like drops of water. Other times we take contempt from others and we let it fill us – sometimes until we are **exceedingly filled**. These times lay us low and make us feel that only the mercy of God can save us.

iii. **Contempt**: "It is illuminating that *contempt* is singled out for mention. Other things can bruise, but this is cold steel. It goes deeper into the spirit than any other form of rejection." (Kidner)

2. (4) The reason mercy is needed.

Our soul is exceedingly filled
With the scorn of those who are at ease,
With the contempt of the proud.

a. **With the scorn of those who are at ease**: This **scorn** is never easy to bear, but it is especially painful when it comes from those who seem to be **at ease**, who seem to have few problems or difficulties in life.

i. "This had become the chief thought of their minds, the peculiar sorrow of their hearts. Excluding all other feelings, a sense of scorn monopolized the soul and made it unutterably wretched." (Spurgeon)

ii. "The reason people ridicule what they oppose, aside from it being so easy, is that it is demoralizing and frequently effective. It is effective because it strikes at the hidden insecurities or weaknesses that almost everybody has." (Boice)

iii. "The injurious effect of freedom from affliction is singularly evident here. Place a man perfectly at ease and he derides the suffering godly, and becomes himself proud in heart and conduct." (Spurgeon)

b. **With the contempt of the proud**: This made the contempt heaped on the psalmist even worse – knowing it came from the **proud** and arrogant. Yet the psalmist was satisfied to wait for God's mercy.

i. "The proud think so much of themselves that they must needs think all the less of those who are better than themselves. Pride is both contemptible and contemptuous." (Spurgeon)

ii. Nevertheless, this psalm is filled with the unspoken confidence that the mercy of God will triumph over the contempt of the proud.

iii. "This sweet psalm, with all its pained sense of the mockers' gibes and their long duration, has no accent of impatience." (Maclaren)

iv. Contempt "…can be an honour (Acts 5:41), and it is something Christ Himself accepted and made redemptive." (Kidner)

v. "To set the life toward worship in an ungodly age is ever to be the object of scorn and contempt. What matters it? The eyes of Jehovah's pilgrims are lifted to the throne set high above all the tumult and strife of tongues." (Morgan)

Psalm 124 – Thanking God for the Help Only He Can Bring

This psalm is titled **A Song of Ascents. Of David**. *Psalm 122:4 mentions that the pilgrims gathered in Jerusalem to give thanks. Here we see David leading Israel in giving thanks to God for past help and expressing confidence in His continuing help.*

Despite the attribution to David, several commentators connect this psalm with exiles returning from Babylon. James Montgomery Boice answered this well: "The expressions of the psalm ('when men attacked us,' 'swept us away,' 'escaped like a bird') sound more like a military attack and deliverance from it than captivity." It is best to keep the connection with David, considering it an earnest plea for Israel to thank God for deliverance past and present.

"In the year 1582, this Psalm was sung on a remarkable occasion in Edinburgh. An imprisoned minister, John Durie, had been set free, and was met and welcomed on entering the town by two hundred of his friends. The number increased till he found himself in the midst of a company of two thousand, who began to sing, as they moved up the long High Street, 'Now Israel may say,' etc. They sang in four parts with deep solemnity, all joining in the well-known tune and Psalm. They were much moved themselves, and so were all who heard; and one of the chief persecutors is said to have been more alarmed at this sight and song than at anything he had seen in Scotland." (Horatius Bonar, cited in Charles Spurgeon)

A. Gratitude for God's help.

1. (1-2) The help of God when under the threat of men.

"If it had not been the LORD who was on our side,"
Let Israel now say—
"If it had not been the LORD who was on our side,
When men rose up against us,"

> a. **If it had not been the LORD who was on our side**: Twice in the first two verses of this psalm, David called Israel to recognize that their help was

141

in God alone. It wasn't just that Yahweh was present, but that He actively worked on behalf of His people (**on our side**).

i. "The phrase 'had been on our side' (*hayah lanu*) is the past tense of Immanuel ('God is with us'). Thus the community confesses that God has been with them in their past history." (VanGemeren)

ii. "Here is an If which cannot be an *if*. It is never a matter of uncertainty whether the Lord will be on our side or not. For the Lord Jesus in His incarnation and death has taken His place beside us forevermore. He is always on our side, so long as we keep His paths and walk in His ways." (Meyer)

iii. "This repetition is not in vain. For whilst we are in danger, our fear is without measure; but when it is once past, we imagine it to have been less than it was indeed. And this is the delusion of Satan, to diminish and obscure the grace of God." (Luther, cited in Spurgeon)

b. **Let Israel now say**: David thought it necessary that *all* God's covenant people recognize this. It wasn't enough for he or a few others to do this; it was the duty of all **Israel** to know and to **say** that God was their absolutely essential help.

c. **When men rose up against us**: There were many times in David's reign and before when this was true, but perhaps the most likely time referred to here was when the Philistines threatened to overwhelm Israel at the start of David's reign (2 Samuel 5:17-25). When **men** opposed the people of God, God stepped in to help.

i. "As a psalm of David, this gives us a rare insight into the early peril of his kingdom, particularly from the Philistines, who had thought to see the last of Israel when they shattered the kingdom of Saul. 2 Samuel 5:17ff. shows how serious the threat was, and how little confidence David placed in his own power to survive it." (Kidner)

ii. "It is easy to see how a psalm praising God's protection from the early days of Israel's national history might be incorporated into the songs pilgrims sang on their way to Jerusalem, which David had made his capital." (Boice)

2. (3-5) The disaster that could have happened had not God helped.

"Then they would have swallowed us alive,
When their wrath was kindled against us;
Then the waters would have overwhelmed us,
The stream would have gone over our soul;
Then the swollen waters
Would have gone over our soul."

a. Then they would have swallowed us alive: Continuing the thought from the emphatic repetition in the first two verses (if God had not helped Israel), David tells of what have happened: they would have been destroyed by their enemies. Yahweh wasn't one of many possible solutions to their problem; He and He alone was their savior.

    i. "One thought runs through it all, that the sole actor in their deliverance has been Jehovah. No human arm has been bared for them; no created might could have rescued them from the rush of the swelling deluge." (Maclaren)

    ii. "We have often involved ourselves in entanglements, through our own disobedience; but we have never been able to extricate ourselves from them. Escape has always come by His action." (Morgan)

    iii. **Their wrath was kindled against us**: "Anger is never more fiery than when the people of God are its objects. Sparks become flames, and the furnace is heated seven times hotter when God's elect are to be thrust into the blaze." (Spurgeon)

b. Then the waters would have overwhelmed us: David poetically described their potential ruin. The danger was like being **swallowed** alive by a giant beast, or like being drowned when waters **overwhelmed**.

    i. "The metaphor of water as a destructive force is common in the Old Testament (cf. Psalm 18:16; 42:7; 69:1-2, 15; Isaiah 8:7-8; Lamentations 3:54) because of the destructive torrential rains known to that part of the world." (VanGemeren)

c. Then the swollen waters: The idea here is of a rushing river, not the rising flood. In the poetic picture, they were in danger of being swept away by the torrent.

d. Gone over our soul: David again used repetition to emphasize the idea that the danger was not only political or economic; it had to do with the very soul, with *life* at the deepest levels. From these great dangers, God was their deliverer.

    i. David poetically described many of the troubles that face our **soul**:

- Sometimes our troubles swallow and devour us.
- Sometimes our troubles overwhelm us like a flood.
- Sometimes our troubles sweep us away like a torrent.

B. Praise to the LORD who helps.

1. (6-7) Praise for the help received.

Blessed *be* **the** LORD,
Who has not given us *as* **prey to their teeth.**
Our soul has escaped as a bird from the snare of the fowlers;
The snare is broken, and we have escaped.

a. **Blessed be the** LORD: As in other places in the Book of Psalms, the thought is not bestowing a blessing upon Yahweh, but on thanking, praising, and announcing Him as **blessed**. It is a powerful expression of thanks and praise.

i. "When we look back on life, as the psalmist does here, we become aware of the myriad instances of Divine protection. We were not so vividly conscious at the time; we might even have had fits of depression and counted ourselves bereft. But if we narrowly consider the perils from which we have been rescued, when we were about to be swallowed up quick, we become convinced that He was there." (Meyer)

ii. "The redeemed are astonished, upon looking back, at the greatness of the danger to which they had been exposed." (Horne)

b. **Who has not given us as prey to their teeth**: David again described their danger poetically – first as being delivered from a beast with grinding **teeth**, then as deliverance from a trap (**snare**) set for birds. With God's help, the people of God were safe from destruction and loss of liberty.

i. **Prey to their teeth**: "This is not quite the same figure as that of verse 3. In these jaws we feel the slower agonies of defeat, like the tearing and grinding of the prey." (Kidner)

ii. **As a bird from the snare**: "The comparison of the soul to a bird is beautiful [Psalm 11:1]. It hints at tremors and feebleness, at alternations of feeling like the flutter of some weak-winged songster, at the utter helplessness of the panting creature in the toils." (Maclaren)

iii. "Fowlers have many methods of taking small birds, and Satan has many methods of entrapping souls. Some are decoyed by evil companions, others are enticed by the love of dainties; hunger drives many into the trap, and fright impels numbers to fly into the net." (Spurgeon)

iv. "As the bird could not get out of the snare, so the soul cannot escape from temptation; but God can bring it out, and he works the rescue. Hear this, ye that are slaves to drunkenness: God can deliver you. You that have fallen into licentiousness hear it – God can deliver you. Whatever the sin that has birdlimed [trapped] you, that gracious hand which once was nailed to the cross can set you free." (Spurgeon)

v. "Save us, O God, from the rage and the subtlety of our spiritual adversary; save us from his teeth, when he would devour; from his snares, when he would deceive." (Horne)

vi. Here are two more poetic pictures of that which may trouble our **soul**:

- Sometimes our troubles grind us to powder.
- Sometimes our troubles capture us like a trap or snare.

2. (8) Confidence in the continuing help of God.

Our help *is* in the name of the LORD,
Who made heaven and earth.

a. **Our help is in the name of the LORD**: We sense a bit of defiance in this declaration. The nations find their supposed help in their supposed deities; God's people confidently find their **help** in **the name of the LORD**.

i. "Experience should breed confidence...write up experiences therefore, oft rub them over, and then conclude as here." (Trapp)

ii. "The great lesson of this Psalm, from the beginning to the end...is that for every deliverance, whether of a temporal or spiritual nature, we should, in imitation of the saints above, ascribe 'Salvation to God and the Lamb.'" (Horne)

iii. "If Jehovah had not helped, how great would have been the calamity! But He has helped, and the sigh which trembles with the consciousness of past peril, merges into the glad song: Blessed be Jehovah." (Morgan)

b. **Who made heaven and earth**: It was not a vain confidence. The same God who created **heaven and earth** was mighty to help His people.

i. "When we worship the Creator let us increase our trust in our Comforter. Did he create all that we see, and can he not preserve us from evils which we cannot see?" (Spurgeon)

Psalm 125 – As the Mountains Surround Jerusalem

This song is titled **A Song of Ascents**. *Like the others in the series of 15 Songs of Ascents, it was especially appropriate for those pilgrims on their way to Jerusalem for one of the three annual major feasts of Israel.*

"We can imagine the pilgrims chanting this song when [walking] the city walls." (Charles Spurgeon)

A. The people of God and Mount Zion.

1. (1) The permanent standing of the people of God.

Those who trust in the LORD
***Are* like Mount Zion,**
***Which* cannot be moved, *but* abides forever.**

> a. **Those who trust in the LORD**: What follows is a promise made to those who put their **trust in the LORD**. We can't properly put our trust in Him until we remove our trust in other things. He alone is our refuge and strength.
>
> > i. "The phrase, *Those who trust in the Lord,* shows one of the several facets of our relationship named in the Old Testament, along with the mention of those who 'fear', 'love' and 'know' him; a personal bond too intimate to be a passing liaison." (Kidner)
> >
> > ii. "There is a false trust in Zion, a trust that does not go beyond the mere city or presumes on the commitment of God to preserve the city." (Boice)
> >
> > iii. "All that deal with God must deal upon trust, and he will give comfort to those only that give credit to him, and make it appear they do so by quitting other confidences, and venturing to the utmost for God. The closer our expectations are confined to God, the higher our expectations may be raised." (Henry, cited in Spurgeon)

iv. "It is a good thing to understand much, and to trust in the Lord with growing knowledge, but, dear soul, if you do not know much, yet if you are trusting in the Lord, you shall be as Mount Zion, which cannot be removed." (Spurgeon)

b. **Are like Mount Zion, which cannot be moved**: The pilgrim who came from afar was impressed with the stature and standing of **Mount Zion**, the prominent hill upon which Jerusalem was established. The one who believes and trusts in the LORD is promised the same security, and he or she **abides forever**. Our place in His love, His new life, and His gracious purpose lasts forever and **cannot be moved**.

- Some people are like the sand, ever shifting and unstable (Matthew 7:26).
- Some people are like the sea, restless and unsettled (Isaiah 57:20, James 1:6).
- Some people are like the wind, uncertain and inconsistent (Ephesians 4:14).
- "Believers are like a mountain – strong, stable, and secure. To every soul that trusts him the Lord says, 'Thou art Peter.'" (Page, cited in Spurgeon)

  i. "Jehovah is their rock foundation, their encompassing protection, their enthroned King. In Him is all their strength and confidence." (Morgan)

  ii. "It is bedrock, high and secure. Moreover, it is surrounded by other mountains, which the writer compares to God, who likewise surrounds his people." (Boice)

  iii. "Is it not strange that wicked and idolatrous powers have not joined together, dug down this mount, and carried it into the sea, that they might nullify a promise in which the people of God exult! Till ye can carry Mount Zion into the Mediterranean Sea, the church of Christ shall grow and prevail." (Clarke, cited in Spurgeon)

2. (2) The great security of the people of God.

As the mountains surround Jerusalem,
So the LORD surrounds His people
From this time forth and forever.

a. **As the mountains surround Jerusalem**: Jerusalem is not set upon one hill, but established among a series of hills. God's **people** can trust that Yahweh will **surround** and protect them **as the mountains surround**

Jerusalem. The pilgrim coming to Jerusalem saw these mountains and with this song made spiritual application from the geography.

b. **So the LORD surrounds His people**: God promised not only to be present with His people, but also to be *all around* them. He would **surround** them, so that nothing can get to them unless it first pass through Him.

i. **As the mountains surround Jerusalem**: "Mount Zion is not the highest peak in the mountain range around Jerusalem. To its east lies the Mount of Olives, to its north Mount Scopus, to the west and south are other hills, all of which are higher than Mount Zion. Surrounded by mountains, Mount Zion was secure, by its natural defensibility." (VanGemeren)

ii. "It is surrounded with other *mountains*, at no great distance, as if placed in the midst of an amphitheatre." (Clarke)

iii. "The mountains around the holy city, though they do not make a circular wall, are, nevertheless, set like sentinels to guard her gates. God doth not enclose his people within ramparts and bulwarks, making their city to be a prison; but yet he so orders the arrangements of his providence that his saints are as safe as if they dwelt behind the strongest fortifications." (Spurgeon)

iv. "It is a beautiful conception. Around the chosen city the mountains stood like sentinels, leaving no part without its barrier. So is God around us, and this enables us to understand how His permissions may become His appointments.... The assaults of our foes are at least permitted by God, and His permissions are His appointments." (Meyer)

v. **His people**: "We are here taught that the Lord's people are those who trust him, for they are thus described in the first verses." (Spurgeon)

b. **From this time forth and forever**: This promise *abides* for the people of God – those who trust Him (verse 1). God's surrounding protection will be with believers **forever**, even as Jesus promised His presence to His people to the end of the age (Matthew 28:20).

i. "Note, it is not said that Jehovah's power or wisdom defends believers, but he himself is round about them: they have his personality for their protection, his Godhead for their guard." (Spurgeon)

ii. We must never separate verse 1 from verse 2; the promise of verse 2 has the condition of trust in verse 1. "In the days when these people failed in faith, the surrounding mountains failed to secure safety to Zion. It was overcome and trodden down." (Morgan)

B. Righteousness among the people of God.

1. (3) Righteousness in the land.

For the scepter of wickedness shall not rest
On the land allotted to the righteous,
Lest the righteous reach out their hands to iniquity.

a. **For the scepter of wickedness shall not rest on the land allotted to the righteous**: This was the protection God promised to His people who trusted in Him. In Israel's history, that **scepter of wickedness** only rested on the land when God's people were stubbornly unrighteous and untrusting in Him.

i. **Scepter of wickedness**: "This may or may not point to foreign domination: the heathen have no monopoly of sin." (Kidner)

ii. "Rod [**scepter**], here, may be taken for *persecution*, or for *rule*; and then it may be thus interpreted: 'The wicked shall not be permitted to *persecute always*, nor to have a *permanent rule*.'" (Clarke)

iii. "Regardless of how evil the times, they knew that the Lord had promised never to permit the wicked to prevail over the righteous." (VanGemeren)

iv. The pilgrims on their journey to Jerusalem would see much of **the land allotted to the righteous** as they traveled. They could rightly reflect on this promise and determine that they would be those who trusted in God. They were the **righteous** ones who had received God's allotment of the land.

b. **Lest the righteous reach out their hands to iniquity**: God knows that the rule of the wicked could provoke even the godly to sin through rebellion or frustration. This is one of the reasons why God promised not to allow the wicked to rule **on the land allotted to the righteous**.

i. "It needs Divine wisdom to determine how long a trial must last in order that it may test faith, thereby strengthening it, and may not confound faith, thereby precipitating feeble souls into sin. He knows when to say, 'It is enough.'" (Maclaren)

ii. "If evil were to prevail, it might be an occasion for some of the godly to be tempted, to lose heart, and to fall away. For the sake of God's people, wickedness must come to an absolute end!" (VanGemeren)

iii. "God (saith Chrysostom) does like a lute player, who will not let the strings of his lute be too slack, lest it mar the music, nor suffer them to be too hard stretched or screwed up, lest they break." (Trapp)

2. (4-5) Righteousness in the heart.

Do good, O LORD, to *those who are* good,
And to *those who are* upright in their hearts.
As for such as turn aside to their crooked ways,
The LORD shall lead them away
With the workers of iniquity.
Peace *be* upon Israel!

a. **Do good, O LORD, to those who are good**: One of the primary features of the Old Covenant God made with the Israelites at Mount Sinai was the principle of blessing their obedience and cursing their disobedience. Here, the singer simply prayed that God would fulfill that aspect of the covenant and **do good** for those **who are good**.

i. The amazing greatness of the revelation of the gospel of Jesus Christ is that God did good for those who are not good. We remember that *in due time Christ died for the ungodly* (Romans 5:6) and *God demonstrates His own love toward us, in that while we were still sinners, Christ died for us* (Romans 5:8).

ii. **To those who are upright in their hearts**: "The 'good and upright in heart' are they who stand steady in every change of circumstances; who complain not of God's dispensations, but, believing everything to be best which he ordains, adhere to him with a will entirely conformed to his, in adversity no less than in prosperity." (Horne)

b. **As for such as turn aside to their crooked ways**: Under the Old Covenant there was blessing for the good, but many curses for the wicked. The singer pictured these **workers of iniquity** being led out of the land in exile.

i. "…who are not *faithful*; who *give way to sin*; who *backslide*, and walk in a *crooked way*, widely different from the *straight way* of the *upright*, *yesharim*, the *straight* in heart; they shall be *led forth* to punishment *with the common workers of iniquity*." (Clarke)

ii. "The psalmist uses a vivid image to describe half-hearted adherents to the people of Jehovah: 'they bend their ways,' so as to make them crooked…. 'Those crooked, wandering ways'…can never lead to steadfastness or to any good." (Maclaren)

iii. **The LORD shall lead them away**: "It is important to notice the difference between the writer's *prediction* of God's sure judgment on the wicked and his *petition* for blessing on the righteous. He does not need to ask that the wicked will be judged, because their judgment is certain, sometimes sooner than either we or they expect!" (Boice)

c. **Peace be upon Israel**: Psalm 125 ends with a prayer pronouncing *shalom* upon Israel – essentially, that they would be the good that enjoy blessing and not be the wicked who suffer exile.

i. "We remember that Jerusalem means 'peace' (*shalom*). Thus, we are told, we shall not only be like Salem but shall have salem too." (Boice)

ii. "Finally the poet, stretching out his hands over all Israel, as if blessing them like a priest, embraces all his hopes, petitions, and wishes in the one prayer 'Peace be upon Israel!'" (Maclaren)

Psalm 126 – Amazed at God's Work

This psalm is titled **A Song of Ascents**. *It is the seventh in the series of 15 songs for pilgrims coming to Jerusalem. This song likely was composed after the exile, in wondrous gratitude for God's restoration, and in prayer for a furtherance of that work.*

A. Joy beyond expression at the return from exile.

1. (1) The fulfillment of the joyful dream.

When the LORD brought back the captivity of Zion,
We were like those who dream.

    a. **When the LORD brought back the captivity of Zion**: The psalmist sang of a time when God set His people free from their captivity, and they were restored to Jerusalem (**Zion**). Most associate this with the return from exile under Ezra and Nehemiah, but it is also possible that it describes David's return from his brief exile from Jerusalem in Absalom's coup (2 Samuel 15-19).

        i. As one of the *Songs of Ascents*, we imagine these words in the mouths of pilgrims on the way to or having arrived at Jerusalem. Perhaps they considered their seasons away from Jerusalem as a symbolic **captivity**, and they celebrated the larger return from exile and their current, personal experience of such.

    b. **We were like those who dream**: With power and beauty, the poet described the sense of happy, grateful astonishment at the power and goodness of God in bringing back His people from **the captivity of Zion**. It seemed too good, too great to be true, *but it was true.*

        i. "We could not believe our own eyes and ears, but thought it to be but a dream or delusion of our own fancies; as is usual in matters of great joy, as Genesis 45:26, Luke 24:11, Acts 12:9." (Poole)

ii. "The people knew about the promises of restoration; but when the actual moment of restoration came, it was an overwhelming experience. They were like those 'who dreamed.' It all happened too quickly and seemed like a mirage." (VanGemeren)

iii. "It remained a vivid national memory (cf. the lively paraphrase in TEV [Today's English Version]: 'it was like a dream! How we laughed, how we sang for joy...how happy we were'), as inspiring as the outbreaks of revival in the Christian church." (Kidner)

iv. At times Christian revival has been described in these terms. J. Edwin Orr's book *All Your Need* records the description of J. Oswald Sanders of the 1936 revival at Ngaruawahia, New Zealand: "*For some time before Easter, a spirit of unusual expectancy had been kindled in our hearts by the Holy Spirit, but the reality far exceeded the expectation. Those of us who were responsible for the conduct of the camp had the great joy of sitting back and seeing God work in a sovereign way. We were as men that dreamed.*"

2. (2-3) Laughing, singing, proclaiming.

Then our mouth was filled with laughter,
And our tongue with singing.
Then they said among the nations,
"The LORD has done great things for them."
The LORD has done great things for us,
And **we are glad.**

a. **Then our mouth was filled with laughter**: They celebrated God's amazing work with **laughter** and **singing**. There was so much laughing that their **mouth was filled** with it.

i. "The mercy was so unexpected, so amazing, so singular that they could not do less than laugh; and they laughed much, so that their mouths were full of it, and that because their hearts were full too." (Spurgeon)

ii. "We must raise up ourselves with this consideration – that the gospel is nothing else but laughter and joy. This joy properly pertaineth to captives, that is, to those that feel the captivity of sin and death.... These are the disciples in whose hearts should be planted laughter and joy, and that by the authority of the Holy Ghost, which this verse setteth forth." (Luther, cited in Spurgeon)

b. **The LORD has done great things for them**: The sense of joyful amazement was not confined to the people of God. Onlooking **nations** had to proclaim that the work belonged to Yahweh, and that the work was truly **great**.

> i. "The liberty now granted was brought about in so extraordinary a way, that the very *heathens* saw that the hand of the great Jehovah must have been in it." (Clarke)

> ii. "These foreigners were no dreamers; though they were only lookers-on, and not partakers in the surprising mercy, they plainly saw what had been done, and rightly ascribed it to the great Giver of all good." (Spurgeon)

c. **The Lord has done great things for us**: The singer heard what the nations said, agreed with it, emphasized it with repetition, and personalized it. It became the declaration of what God had done **for us**.

> i. "Their [reluctant] acknowledgment is caught up triumphantly by the singer. He, as it were, thanks the Gentiles for teaching him that word." (Maclaren)

> ii. Boice suggested four occasions where many experience great joy and the sense that God has **done great things** in their Christian life:

> - The joy of salvation.
> - The joy of spiritual victory.
> - The joy of Christian fellowship.
> - The joy of a new work for God.

d. **And we are glad**: There is a joyful peace in the declaration. This is not a worked-up, hyped-up enthusiasm. This was the confident joy in what God had done, simply to declare **we are glad**.

> i. "This is a mere burst of ecstatic joy. O how happy are we!" (Clarke)

> ii. "There is a world of restrained feeling, all the more impressive for the simplicity of the expression, in that quiet 'We became glad.' When the heathen attested the reality of the deliverance, Israel became calmly conscious of it." (Maclaren)

B. The prayer and wise understanding.

1. (4) A prayer for continued deliverance.

Bring back our captivity, O Lord,
As the streams in the South.

a. **Bring back our captivity, O Lord**: The second half of this psalm does not deny the amazed joy of the first half, but it recognizes that there is still work yet to be done. The returning exiles (under Ezra or David) realized there was much work yet to do, and the restoration had only yet begun.

i. "So the song is a cry for more complete restoration." (Morgan)

ii. We may imagine the sense of one whose life is profoundly changed by Jesus Christ. They are grateful and amazed at what He has done, yet can in the next moment consider how much more needs to be done.

iii. "For the psalmist, as for us, memory of the past could have become mere nostalgia. Those were the days! we say; wonderful, but gone forever. In Psalm 126, the memory of those singing, laughter-filled days of the past becomes, not nostalgia, but the ground of a strong hope for even better days to come." (Boice)

b. **As the streams in the South**: The **streams in the South** flowed when the rain fell in faraway mountains. Those **streams** could appear suddenly and rush with a mighty flow, sometimes known as *flash floods*. The psalmist prayed for a mighty, sudden work of God to further the work of restoration among His people.

i. "To the south of favoured Judea stretched the dry and barren district, where in summer-time all the streams ceased to flow. That, to the singer, was the condition of the people. But in the autumn, the rains fill up the stony channels, a very river of life." (Morgan)

ii. "[There are] few transformations more dramatic than that of a dry gully into a torrent. Such can be the effect of a downpour, which can also turn the surrounding desert into a place of grass and flowers overnight." (Kidner)

iii. "They desired that their return might be as rapid and as *abundant* as the waters of those rivers." (Clarke)

iv. "However arid the land, He can send the revivifying streams." (Morgan)

2. (5-6) The cycle of sadness and joy.

Those who sow in tears
Shall reap in joy.
He who continually goes forth weeping,
Bearing seed for sowing,
Shall doubtless come again with rejoicing,
Bringing his sheaves *with him*.

a. **Those who sow in tears shall reap in joy**: The gladness of the first half of this psalm was real, but only part of the picture. With wisdom the psalmist reminded himself and all of us that great joy is often preceded by a season of **tears**, as if they are seeds we **sow** that will bring a crop of **joy** to be later reaped.

i. "In the first image (the sudden filling of the desert streams, v. 4), the results are sudden and unearned. In the second image (the harvest after the difficult work of plowing and sowing seed, vv. 5-6) the results come only after a long period of hard work and waiting." (Boice)

ii. "The two images of renewal (4b, 5-6) are not only striking: they are complementary. The first of them is all suddenness, a sheer gift from heaven; the second is slow and arduous, with man allotted a crucial part to play in it." (Kidner)

iii. This illustration puts a connection between the tears and the joy. We want to reap the joy without ever having sown the tears.

iv. F.B. Meyer noted that some farmers soak (steep) their seeds before sowing them, and then applied the idea: "It is well when Christian workers steep their lessons and addresses with their prayers and tears. It is not enough to sow; we may do that lavishly and constantly, but we must add passion, emotion, tender pity, strong cryings and tears."

v. "He drops a seed and a tear, a seed and a tear, and so goes on his way. In his basket he has seed which is precious to him, for he has little of it, and it is his hope for the next year. Each grain leaves his hand with anxious prayer that it may not be lost: he thinks little of himself, but much of his seed, and he eagerly asks, 'Will it prosper? shall I receive a reward for my labour?' Yes…doubtless you will gather sheaves from your sowing." (Spurgeon)

b. **He who continually goes forth weeping, bearing seed for sowing**: The idea is repeated and enlarged. Those who have endured much **weeping**, if they truly carry it as **seed for sowing** – holding and casting it with faith in God and in His promise – those may be assured of reaping a good harvest.

i. "The people were not to sit by idly, waiting for God to come through. They had to go out and sow, praying that the Lord would be true. The phrase 'seed to sow' (v. 6) is reminiscent of Haggai's encouragement to the people to sow whatever little they had left, because the Lord will bless them." (VanGemeren)

ii. "Both the going forth and the coming home are stressed by a doubling of the verb, and might be translated, 'He that surely goes forth weeping…will surely come home with shouts of joy.'" (Kidner)

c. **Shall doubtless come again with rejoicing**: Tears truly *sown* in faith will bring in time a true harvest of **rejoicing**, as if the reapers held heavy **sheaves** of grain. This is a powerful and great promise that our tears and sorrows need not be wasted, but can be sown for a joyful harvest received in a better season.

i. "Because the Lord has written *doubtless*, take heed that you do not doubt. No reason for doubt can remain after the Lord has spoken." (Spurgeon)

ii. In the joy of the present pilgrim gathering, we sense the singers enjoying that harvest, yet wisely understanding that there will be future tears to sow in faith.

iii. "O disciple of Jesus, behold an emblem of thy present labour, and thy future reward. Thou 'sowest,' perhaps, 'in tears;' thou doest thy duty amidst persecution and affliction, sickness, pain, and sorrow; thou laborest in the church, and no account is made of thy labours; no profit seems to arise from them.... Yet the day is coming when thou shalt 'reap in joy;' and plentiful shall by thy harvest." (Horne)

iv. "He guards the buried seed, and stands sponsor for the harvest. No sigh, no tear, no prayer, inspired by the Spirit of God can positively be lost or unproductive. Like your Lord, you shall yet see of the travail of your soul, and be satisfied." (Meyer)

v. Alexander Maclaren wondered how much encouragement and strength "...have been drawn for centuries from the sweet words of this psalm. Who can tell how many hearts they have braced, how much patient toil they have inspired? The psalmist was sowing seed, the fruit of which he little dreamed of, when he wrote them, and his sheaves will be an exceeding weight indeed."

vi. "For thus thy blessed Master 'went forth weeping, a man of sorrows, and acquainted with grief, bearing precious seed,' and sowing it around him, till at length his own body was buried, like a grain of wheat, in the furrow of the grave. But he arose, and is now in heaven; from whence he 'shall doubtless come again with rejoicing,' with the voice of the archangel and the trump of God, 'bringing his sheaves with him.'" (Horne)

Psalm 127 – God's Work in Building Houses, Cities, and Families

This psalm is titled **A Song of Ascents. Of Solomon**. *Most believe Solomon to be the author, yet it is possible that the psalm was composed by David* for *Solomon. Here, Solomon will be considered the author.*

"The strength of the Hebrew people in the past, and all that remains of it today, largely results from the keen sense which they ever cherished of the importance of the home and the family. The house, the city, labour, are all important to the conserving of the strength of the family." (G. Campbell Morgan)

A. Blessing upon daily life.

1. (1) God's work of building and guarding.

Unless the Lord builds the house,
They labor in vain who build it;
Unless the Lord guards the city,
The watchman stays awake in vain.

> a. **Unless the Lord builds the house**: Solomon understood that the work of man had its place, but it was of little ultimate use without the work and blessing of God. Without God's work and blessing, **they labor in vain who build it**.
>
> > i. "No house-building is successful which leaves God out of account. How have we seen men build only houses, with care and at great cost, only to see them crumble to pieces because God was forgotten!" (Morgan)
> >
> > ii. "A Latin motto says, *Nisi Dominus Frusta*. It comes from the first words of this psalm and means 'Without the Lord, Frustration.' It is the motto of the city of Edinburgh, Scotland, appearing on its crest, and is affixed to the city's official documents. It could be attached to the

lives of many who are trying to live their lives without the Almighty." (Boice)

iii. It is *possible* that the **house** built here is actually a family. "It may also signify the raising of a family, especially because this section precedes a unit in which the family is emphasized as a reward from the Lord (vv. 3-5). In the Old Testament it is usual to speak of a family as a 'house' even as we speak of a prominent family as a 'dynasty'." (VanGemeren)

iv. "It is a fact that *ben, a son*, and *bath, a daughter*, and *beith, a house*, come from the same root *banah, to build*; because sons and daughters build up a household, or constitute a *family*, as much and as really as stones and timber constitute a *building*." (Clarke)

b. **Unless the LORD guards the city**: The watchman has his role and should stay **awake**, but God's work and blessing are needed to truly guard the city.

c. **Builds the house...guards the city**: It's especially meaningful that *Solomon* wrote this psalm, because he knew what it was like to both build a house and guard a city. Wise Solomon understood that though God welcomed and even commanded human effort and participation, His work and blessing were more important.

i. "These would be splendid words to cut into granite over the entrance to all our homes, and to emblazon in gold in all the meeting places of those in civic authority. But better still let them be written in the heart of those who make homes, and guard and govern cities." (Morgan)

ii. "Note that the Psalmist does not bid the builder cease from labouring, nor suggest that watchmen should neglect their duty, nor that men should show their trust in God by doing nothing: nay, he supposes that they will do all that they can do, and then he forbids their fixing their trust in what they have done, and assures them that all creature effort will be in vain unless the Creator puts forth his power." (Spurgeon)

iii. "They, above all men, ought to implore the divine grace and benediction, who are employed either in building or defending the spiritual house and city of God." (Horne)

2. (2) The vanity of reliance on the strength of man.

It is **vain for you to rise up early,**
To sit up late,
To eat the bread of sorrows;
For **so He gives His beloved sleep.**

a. **It is vain for you to rise up early**: We gather that Solomon did not speak against hard work, because several of his proverbs praise the hard worker who rises early (Proverbs 6:6-11). From the first verse of this psalm, we understand that Solomon intended the *trust* many put in their hard work and the anxiety that showed reliance on self, not God (**to eat the bread of sorrows**).

i. **For you**: "He directs his speech to the persons forementioned, *the builders or watchmen*, of both which sorts there are many that use the following course." (Poole)

ii. "But the psalmist decries this as an inferior way of life if the hard work is only for the purpose of providing daily food and clothing for oneself and the family. The higher way of life begins with trusting the Lord in one's work." (VanGemeren)

iii. "Long hours do not mean prosperous work. The evening meal may be put off till a late hour; and when the toil-worn man sits down to it, he may eat bread made bitter by labour. But all is in vain without God's blessing." (Maclaren)

iv. **Bread of sorrows**: "…living a life of misery and labours, fretting at their own disappointments, eaten up with envy at the advancement of others, afflicted overmuch with losses and wrongs. There is no end of all their labours." (Manton, cited in Spurgeon)

b. **For so He gives His beloved sleep**: Men who are affected by reliance on their own work experience the anxiety that comes with it. God's blessing is to give His loved ones **sleep**. They can be at peace knowing that God's hand is at work and His eye watches even as they sleep.

i. **His beloved**: "…an allusion to Solomon's other name, Jedidiah, God's darling." (Trapp)

ii. "There may be a cryptic reference to himself by Solomon in the words 'those he loves' (v. 2). In Hebrew the words are actually 'his beloved,' the name God gave Solomon according to 2 Samuel 12:25: Jedidiah, meaning 'Beloved of Jehovah.'" (Boice)

iii. **Sleep**: "Begone, dull, worrying care! Let me rest sweet…close mine eyes and still my heart; Jesus, give me sleep, and in sleeping give me my heart's desire, that I may awake and be satisfied." (Meyer)

B. Blessing upon the family.

"The labours of mankind, first in building houses and cities, and then in guarding and securing their possessions, are undergone, not with a view to themselves alone, but to their families, which they would establish and perpetuate." (Horne)

1. (3) The reward of children.

Behold, children *are* a heritage from the LORD,
The fruit of the womb *is* a reward.

a. **Children are a heritage from the LORD**: Solomon considered the wisdom of trusting God in building a house (verse 1), but he also understood that a home is built by more than bricks and wood. He called upon all to see (**behold**) that children are a blessing.

i. "The Jew would ask, why is the house being built if it is not for the family? And why are the watchmen protecting the city if not for the families that live in it? Then as now, the family was the basic unit and most important element of society." (Boice)

ii. "Let the fruitful family, however poor, lay this to heart; 'Children are a heritage of the Lord; and the fruit of the womb is his reward.' And he who gave them will feed them; for it is a fact, and the *maxim* formed on it has never failed, 'Wherever God sends mouths, he sends meat.'" (Clarke)

iii. "He gives children, not as a penalty nor as a burden, but as a favour. They are a token for good if men know how to receive them, and educate them. They are 'doubtful blessings' only because we are doubtful persons." (Spurgeon)

b. **The fruit of the womb is a reward**: Sadly, though Solomon had 700 wives and 300 concubines (1 Kings 11:3), we know of only one of his specific descendants. Perhaps Solomon knew very little of this **reward**.

i. "This last was a fit lesson for Solomon, who, by so many wives and concubines, left but one only son that we read of, and him not of the wisest." (Trapp)

ii. "Like much of Solomon's wisdom, the lessons of this psalm, relevant as they were to his situation, were mostly lost on him. His building, both literal and figurative, became reckless (1 Kings 9:10ff.,19), his kingdom a ruin (1 Kings 11:11ff.) and his marriages a disastrous denial of God (1 Kings 11:1ff.)." (Kidner)

2. (4-5) Children like arrows.

Like arrows in the hand of a warrior,
So *are* the children of one's youth.
Happy *is* the man who has his quiver full of them;
They shall not be ashamed,
But shall speak with their enemies in the gate.

a. **Like arrows in the hand of a warrior**: In many ways children are like **arrows in the hand of a warrior.**

- They must be carefully shaped and formed.
- They must be guided with skill and strength.
- They must be given care or they will not fly straight.
- They must be aimed and given direction; they will not find direction on their own.
- They are, in some respects, only launched once.
- They are an extension of the warrior's strength and accomplishment.
- They have potential for much good or evil.

    i. **Like arrows**: "This similitude importeth that children must have more in them than nature; for arrows are no arrows by growth, but by art; so they must be such children, the knottiness of whose nature is refined and reformed, and made smooth by grace; and then they are cared for." (Trapp)

    ii. "…ready winged with duty and love, to fly to the mark; polished and keen, to grace and maintain the cause of their parents." (Horne)

    iii. "We shall see them shot forth into life to our comfort and delight, if we take care from the very beginning that they are directed to the right point." (Spurgeon)

    iv. "If it is a vain act to build a house without God or watch over a city without depending on God to preserve it, then it is even greater folly to try to raise a family without God." (Boice)

b. **Happy is the man who has his quiver full of them**: If children are a reward (verse 3), then there is great blessing and happiness in having many children.

    i. **Who has his quiver full of them**: "…who hath a numerous issue; which as it is a great blessing in itself, so Solomon's want of it made it more valuable in his eyes." (Poole)

    ii. "A quiver may be small and yet full; and then the blessing is obtained. In any case we may be sure that a man's life consisteth not in the abundance of children that he possesseth." (Spurgeon)

    iii. "I remember a great man coming into my house, at Waltham, and seeing all my children standing in the order of their age and stature, said, 'These are they that make rich men poor.' But he straight received this answer, 'Nay, my lord, these are they that make a poor man rich;

for there is not one of these whom we would part with for all your wealth.'" (Hall, cited in Spurgeon)

iv. "Many children make many prayers, and many prayers bring much blessing." (German proverb, cited in Spurgeon)

c. **But shall speak with their enemies in the gate**: The gate of an ancient city was a place of business and justice. This verse speaks of children of the godly having places of prominence and influence in their communities.

i. "As the arrows protect the warrior, so the godly man need not be afraid, when blessed with sons.... A house full of children, born before one becomes old...is a protection against loneliness and abandonment in society." (VanGemeren)

ii. "Nobody cares to meddle with a man who can gather a clan of brave sons about him." (Spurgeon)

iii. "The gate was the place where justice was administered, and where was the chief place of concourse. It is therefore improbable that actual warfare is meant; rather, in the disputes which might arise with neighbours, and in the intercourse of city life, which would breed enmities enough, the man with his sons about him could hold his own. And such blessing is God's gift." (Maclaren)

iv. "One can discover his ideal through his song. It is that of a prosperous city, its enemies kept outside its gates; and that of the secret of its prosperity as being the house well-built, in the spiritual and moral sense, and the families dwelling within such houses as being able to deal with its enemies in the gate." (Morgan)

Psalm 128 – The Blessed Family of Those Who Fear the LORD

*This psalm is titled **A Song of Ascents**. It is another of the 15 songs sung by travelers on their way to Jerusalem, usually for one of the three yearly feasts (Passover, Pentecost, and Tabernacles). Like Psalm 127, it has a focus on God's work in and through the family.*

"It is of real significance that these songs of home and of true civic consciousness are found among those which are sung on the way that leads to worship. It is ever good to carry into the place of our communion with God the interests of home and city. It is only by doing so that we can influence these for their lasting good." (G. Campbell Morgan)

A. The blessing described.

1. (1) Blessing to all who fear the LORD.

Blessed *is* every one who fears the LORD,
Who walks in His ways.

a. **Blessed is every one who fears the LORD**: The proper honor and respect the creature owes to the Creator is described as *the beginning of wisdom* in many places (Psalm 111:10, Job 28:28, Proverbs 1:7, and Ecclesiasts 12:13). It is to be expected that such wise living brings a blessing.

i. "Blessed above all the sons of men, and the author of blessing to them all, was the man Christ Jesus, because above them all, and for them all, he feared, he loved, and he obeyed." (Horne)

b. **Blessed is every one**: This blessing is available to all who will honor and respect God receive this. It isn't dependent on race, class, education, or even intelligence.

i. "Happiness belongeth not to the rich, the powerful, and the prosperous as such; but in every state and condition, blessed is the man that 'feareth Jehovah.'" (Horne)

164

c. **Who walks in His ways**: This explains what the psalmist meant by the fear of the LORD. It wasn't fundamentally a matter of having certain *feelings* toward God, but a matter of a life of obedience.

i. "The deepest and central truth concerning him is that he fears Jehovah. The reality of that fear is seen in that he walks in the ways of Jehovah. Such a man is indeed blessed, that is, happy, in the true sense of that word." (Morgan)

ii. "It is idle to talk of fearing the Lord if we act like those who have no care whether there be a God or no. God's ways will be our ways if we have a sincere reverence for him: if the heart is joined unto God, the feet will follow hard after him." (Spurgeon)

2. (2-3) Blessings described.

When you eat the labor of your hands,
You *shall be* happy, and *it shall be* well with you.
Your wife *shall be* like a fruitful vine
In the very heart of your house,
Your children like olive plants
All around your table.

a. **When you eat the labor of your hands, you shall be happy**: The psalmist had in mind the hard-working farmer who enjoys the food of his own work. Though an element of work is cursed since Adam's time (Genesis 3:17-19), at least a portion of this curse is taken away for the one who fears the LORD.

i. "Thy labour shall not be vain and fruitless, and the fruit of thy labours shall not be taken away from thee, and possessed by others, as God threatened to the disobedient, Deuteronomy 28, but enjoyed by thyself with comfort and satisfaction." (Poole)

ii. "That is, thou shalt reap and receive the sweet of thy sweat, whether it be of the brow or of the brain, according to the kind of thy calling." (Trapp)

iii. "Thou shalt not be exempted from *labour*. Thou shalt *work*: But God will *bless* and *prosper* that work, and thou and thy family shall eat of it. Ye shall all live on the produce of your own labour, and the hand of violence shall not be permitted to deprive you of it." (Clarke)

b. **Your wife shall be like a fruitful vine**: The one who fears the Lord may be blessed with a large, happy home. The home is happy in its very **heart**, and the children flourish. As they gather (**all around your table**) there is a sense of community and happiness.

i. The *vine* was a symbol not only of fruitfulness (here explicitly so) but of sexual charm (Song of Solomon 7:8ff.) and of festivity (Judges 9:13)." (Kidner)

ii. Though the idea of bearing children is found in the figure of the **fruitful vine**, it goes far beyond it. "Good wives are also fruitful in kindness, thrift, helpfulness, and affection: if they bear no children, they are by no means barren if they yield us the wine of consolation and the clusters of comfort." (Spurgeon)

iii. The psalmist took it for granted that God's people were married. This was and is often assumed among the Jewish people: "At this day every Jew is bound to marry about eighteen years of age, or before twenty, else he is accounted as one that liveth in sin." (Trapp, 1662)

iv. *Christianity* brought in the idea that singleness is also a calling of God, and that in some cases is to be preferred over being married. *Jesus was single.*

c. **Like a fruitful vine...like olive plants**: These were two important crops in ancient Israel. The grapes and wine from the **fruitful vine** and the oil from the **olive plants** were not necessities for survival, but they made life so much better. A happy marriage and flourishing children are not essential for survival, but greatly enrich life in their own way.

i. "The vine and the olive are two of the best fruits...both together implying that a great part of a man's temporal happiness consisteth in having a good wife and children." (Trapp)

ii. "What a charming cluster of images! The wife as a vine twining round the carved trellis work of the inner court of the [Middle Eastern] home – as though the woman gives the rich wine of life, which is love, as well as shadowing fertility and graceful beauty; whilst children as olive plants are sources of perennial joy. Would you have such a home? Its key-stone is the fear of grieving the Spirit of God." (Meyer)

iii. "Olive trees take a long time to mature and become profitable. Patiently cultivated, they become quite valuable and continue to produce a profitable crop for centuries, longer perhaps than any other fruit-producing tree or plant." (Boice)

iv. "Though the olive tree may not bear after it has been planted for forty years, it is a symbol of longevity and productivity. So are children within the household of faith! They are not like grass, which is here today but is gone tomorrow. Rather, they are olive trees that in due time bear their fruit." (VanGemeren)

v. "The interesting thing about these two images, vines and olive plants, is that they are biblical symbols of the abundant life. They are not food staples like wheat or corn. They symbolize rich blessing." (Boice)

3. (4) The promise of blessing repeated.

Behold, thus shall the man be blessed
Who fears the LORD.

a. **Thus shall the man be blessed**: As stated before in verse 1, there is assurance of blessing for all who honor and respect God the way that they should. We recognize that some people have genuinely feared the LORD, yet have not enjoyed all of the specific blessings described in verses 2-3.

- This is because the psalmist wrote this as his *desired* blessing for those who fear the LORD.

- This is because these are general descriptions of the blessed life in ancient Israel, and not universal promises to the people of God.

- This is because these are not the only blessings of life, and God may give other blessings in compensation to those who fear the LORD.

- This is because none of us perfectly fears the LORD.

  i. "If temporal blessings be granted him, he accepteth them as shadows of those which are eternal; if they are denied, he remembereth that they are only shadows, and are therefore denied, that he may fix his thoughts and affections more firmly on the substance." (Horne)

b. **Who fears the LORD**: This is a further condition upon these general promises. The honor and respect that the creature owes the Creator is essential.

B. The blessing pronounced.

1. (5) Blessing connected with Jerusalem.

The LORD bless you out of Zion,
And may you see the good of Jerusalem
All the days of your life.

a. **The LORD bless you out of Zion**: As another of the Songs of Ascents, it is natural for the singers of this psalm to think about the connection of blessing with Jerusalem. God has good for His people that will come **out of Zion**.

- When we consider that much of the teaching and ministry Jesus did was in Jerusalem, we see that we are blessed **out of Zion**.

- When we consider that Jesus died as a sacrifice and a substitute for our sins in Jerusalem, we see that we are blessed **out of Zion**.

- When we consider that Jesus rose from the dead and ascended to heaven from Jerusalem, we see that we are blessed **out of Zion**.

- When we consider that the gospel was first preached out of Jerusalem and the church was birthed there, we see we are blessed **out of Zion**.

b. **May you see the good of Jerusalem**: For the one who fears the LORD, it is a blessing *for* him to see **the good of Jerusalem**. It shows that there is a sense in which a happy home is not enough; we must also have care for our community and nation.

> i. "Blended with the sweet domesticity of the psalm is glowing love for Zion. However blessed the home, it is not to weaken the sense of belonging to the nation." (Maclaren)

> ii. "If piety can be too individualistic, and a family too self-contained, the final strophe takes care of both these dangers." (Kidner)

> iii. Instead, strong and happy homes are for **the good** of a city. "The strength of any city lies in its strong family life. The true strength of the family issues from its ordering in the fear of the Lord." (Morgan)

2. (6) Blessing connected with family.

Yes, may you see your children's children.
Peace *be* upon Israel!

a. **May you see your children's children**: The blessing to the one who fears the LORD goes beyond the holy city and impacts the holy family. The psalmist sees the blessing as enjoying grandchildren.

> i. Since the pilgrim journeys to Israel were often made as families, it made sense for there to be much attention given to family relationships in the Songs of Ascents.

b. **Peace be upon Israel**: The psalm ends with this happy and confident declaration. The psalmist understood that if the people of Israel did fear the LORD, this blessing of *shalom* would be evident in their community, in their family, and in the kingdom as a whole.

> i. "This ancient singer had a true conception of the obligations flowing from personal and domestic blessings. He teaches us that it is not enough to 'see children's children,' unless we have eyes to took for the prosperity of Jerusalem, and tongues which pray not only for those in our homes, but for 'peace upon Israel.'" (Maclaren)

Psalm 129 – Afflicted Yet Confident in God's Deliverance

This psalm is another of the series of fifteen titled **A Song of Ascents**. *As the pilgrims came to Jerusalem to remember God's many past deliverances (such as in the Feasts of Passover or Tabernacles), they prayed confidently for God's continued protection and the defeat of their many enemies.*

"Whereas most nations tend to look back on what they have achieved, Israel reflects here on what she has survived. It could be a disheartening exercise, for Zion still has its ill-wishers. But the singers take courage from the past, facing God with gratitude and their enemies with defiance." (Derek Kidner)

A. God's goodness to afflicted Israel.

1. (1-3) Israel afflicted but not destroyed.

"Many a time they have afflicted me from my youth,"
Let Israel now say—
"Many a time they have afflicted me from my youth;
Yet they have not prevailed against me.
The plowers plowed on my back;
They made their furrows long."

> a. **Many a time they have afflicted me from my youth**: The psalmist presented this as the testimony of Israel (**let Israel now say**). The covenant descendants of Abraham, Isaac, and Jacob have endured unique and evil affliction throughout their history.

> > i. "'Many a time,' Israel says, because she could not say how many times. She speaks of her assailants as 'they,' because it would be impossible to write or even to know all their names." (Spurgeon)

> > ii. "**From my youth**; from the time that I was a people, when I was in Egypt and came out of it, which is called the time of Israel's youth, Jeremiah 2:2, Ezekiel 23:3." (Poole)

169

iii. The statement is repeated twice for emphasis, and rightfully so. The Egyptians, the Canaanites, the Philistines, the Syrians, the Assyrians, the Babylonians, the Greeks, the Romans, the Roman Catholics, the kings of Europe, the Muslims, the Czars, and the Nazis all have done their best to wipe out the Jews. Yet they remain.

iv. One might say that the chief accomplishment of the Jewish people has been *survival*. "The Jews are the longest-enduring distinct ethnic people on the planet. They have been slandered, hated, persecuted, expelled, pursued, and murdered throughout their long existence, but they have survived intact." (Boice)

v. "These repetitions are after the manner of poetry: thus she makes a sonnet out of her sorrows, music out of her miseries." (Spurgeon)

b. **Yet they have not prevailed against me**: This is the happy testimony of Israel. Jew-hatred has raged against them for centuries, yet the enemies of the Jewish people have never ultimately succeeded or **prevailed against** them.

i. "What a wonder it is that Satan and man do not prevail against the saint! There is no way of accounting for it, except in God's election. Because God has chosen us for Himself, and redeemed us at great cost, He cannot afford to hand us over to the will of our enemies." (Meyer)

ii. "There is a forceful Christian battle cry, composed in Latin and placed next to the burning bush: *Nec tamen consumebatur!* It means 'Yet not consumed.' God's people may be oppressed, but they are never consumed." (Boice)

iii. "The right use of retrospect is to make it the ground of hope. They who have passed unscathed through such afflictions may well be sure that any tomorrow shall be as the yesterdays were, and that all future assaults will fail as all past ones have failed." (Maclaren)

iv. In a New Covenant context, we can be confident in Jesus' promise that the strategies of hell will never prevail against His church (Matthew 16:18). "The Church is invincible…. the Church shall stand firm, because founded on a rock." (Trapp)

c. **The plowers plowed on my back**: The psalmist described the many afflictions of Israel as if their enemies ran over their stretched-out bodies with a plow. This is a vivid picture of suffering and subjugation, being utterly laid low before one's foes.

i. "The afflicted nation was, as it were, lashed by her adversaries so cruelly that each blow left a long red mark, or perhaps a bleeding wound, upon her back and shoulders, comparable to a furrow which tears up the ground from one end of the field to the other." (Spurgeon)

ii. "The word *horsu*, which signifies to dig, or cut the ground, and so, to plow, is also used simply for cutting, carving, or engraving; see Exodus 35:33; Jeremiah 17:1." (Horne)

iii. "While there is evidently a sense of danger in the mind of the singer, there is an utter absence of despair." (Morgan)

2. (4) The God who delivers.

The LORD is righteous;
He has cut in pieces the cords of the wicked.

a. **The LORD is righteous**: God promised to preserve His covenant people of Israel, and His faithfulness in delivering them is a demonstration of His righteousness. The fact that the **LORD is righteous** means He has and will keep His promises to Israel.

i. "The survival of this people, so hated but so resilient, bore silent witness to their Preserver (as, one may feel, it has continued to do)." (Kidner)

b. **He has cut in pieces the cords of the wicked**: Israel's foes were strong and clever, but not greater than God, who could deliver. The ways the **wicked** restrained and enslaved God's people would be **cut in pieces**.

i. "The 'cords' denote the yoke as a whole, which was fastened to the neck of an animal (v. 4; cf. Jeremiah 30:8)." (VanGemeren)

B. Asking God to turn back those who hate Jerusalem.

1. (5-7) Shame for those who hate Zion.

Let all those who hate Zion
Be put to shame and turned back.
Let them be as the grass *on* the housetops,
Which withers before it grows up,
With which the reaper does not fill his hand,
Nor he who binds sheaves, his arms.

a. **Let all those who hate Zion be put to shame**: The psalmist prayed that not only would the Israelites be delivered from their enemies, but that God would also apply His righteousness to their enemies. They should be shamed and **turned back**.

i. Some take offence at the prayer the psalmist made against the enemies of Israel, yet there is really no basis for such offence. "It is striking in this case at least how mild these imprecations are. The psalmist is not asking that those who have harmed Israel be sent to hell, or even that they experience the same sufferings they have inflicted on others. He asks only that they and their designs might not prosper." (Boice)

ii. "At the heart of high and holy patriotism there must ever burn a divine anger with all that is opposed to the purpose and plan of God. To hate Zion is to hate God. To tolerate those who do so, is to be confederate with their wickedness." (Morgan)

iii. This is "…a proper wish, and contains within it no trace of personal ill-will. We desire their welfare as men, their downfall as traitors. Let their conspiracies be confounded, their policies be turned back. How can we wish prosperity to those who would destroy that which is dearest to our hearts?" (Spurgeon)

b. **Let them be as the grass**: Grass that grows in the rainy season (especially on the **housetops** of the ancient Middle East) quickly **withers** as the weather becomes warm and dry. He prayed that the present green season of Israel's enemies would be short-lived.

i. "The graphic image of the grass on flat housetops of clay, which springs quickly because it has no depth of earth, and withers as it springs, vividly describes the short-lived success and rapid extinction of plots against Zion and of the plotters." (Maclaren)

ii. "Thus, while the felicity of Zion's children is rooted and grounded in Christ, that of her enemies hath no foundation at all." (Horne)

iii. "Grass on the housetop is a nonentity in the world: the house is not impoverished when the last blade is dried up, and, even so, the opposers of Christ pass away, and none lament them. One of the fathers said of the apostate emperor Julian, 'That little cloud will soon be gone'; and so it was. Every sceptical system of philosophy has much the same history; and the like may be said of each heresy." (Spurgeon)

c. **With which the reaper does not fill his hand**: The grass of the previous verse was useless for the **reaper** or those who gather grain (**he who binds sheaves**). The psalmist wanted the uselessness of the wicked enemies of Israel to be exposed and evident to all.

i. "While the church subsisteth from generation to generation, the kingdoms and empires that have persecuted her, fade and wither away of themselves." (Horne)

ii. "Study a chapter from the 'Book of Martyrs,' and see if you do not feel inclined to read an imprecatory Psalm over Bishop Bonner and Bloody Mary." (Spurgeon)

2. (8) Denial of blessing for those who hate Zion.

Neither let those who pass by them say,
"The blessing of the Lord **be upon you;**
We bless you in the name of the Lord**!"**

> a. **Neither let those who pass by them say**: The psalmist prayed that these enemies of Israel would *not* enjoy **the blessing of the** Lord upon them. He prayed that the pleasant picture of happy harvest work found in Ruth 2:4 would never be fulfilled for these enemies of Israel.

> b. **We bless you in the name of the** Lord: The blessing of God is the greatest thing any human life can enjoy, giving goodness to every aspect of life. The psalmist prayed that *none* of this goodness would be given to those who hated Jerusalem and Israel.

>> i. "In harvest times men bless each other in the name of the Lord; but there is nothing in the course and conduct of the ungodly man to suggest the giving or receiving of a benediction." (Spurgeon)

Psalm 130 – Out of the Depths

This psalm is another in the series titled **A Song of Ascents**. *Psalm 130 begins with a personal testimony of God's rescue from the depths of guilt. From there, the author ascends step by step to a place where he can give confidence to others in their trust in God.*

Because Psalm 130 is marked by an awareness of sin and a powerful assurance of forgiveness, tradition numbers it among the seven penitential psalms (6, 32, 38, 51, 102, 130, 143).

"Luther, when he was buffeted by the devil at Coburg, and in great affliction, said to those about him, Come, let us sing that psalm, 'Out of the depths,' etc., in derision of the devil.... And surely this psalm is a treasury of great comfort to all in distress." (John Trapp)

"On the afternoon of that same day [which his heart was strangely warmed and he truly trusted in Jesus for salvation] John Wesley attended a vesper service at St. Paul's Cathedral, in the course of which Psalm 130 was sung as an anthem. Wesley was greatly moved by the anthem, and it became one of the means God used to open his heart to the gospel of salvation." (James Montgomery Boice)

A. Crying out to the God who helps and forgives.

1. (1-2) A cry from the depths.

Out of the depths I have cried to You, O LORD;
Lord, hear my voice!
Let Your ears be attentive
To the voice of my supplications.

> a. **Out of the depths I have cried to You**: Previously in the psalms there have been cries from the depths of the earth (Psalm 71:20) or the depths of the grave (Psalm 86:13). Once again, from a place of deep and overwhelming danger, the psalmist cries out to Yahweh, the covenant God of Israel.

i. People experience depths of poverty, sorrow, confusion, and pain. Yet the depth that the psalmist cried from here was the depth of the awareness and guilt of sin (verse 3). Many have been spiritually drowned in these depths.

ii. "Self-help is no answer to the depths of distress, however useful it may be in the shallows of self-pity." (Kidner)

iii. "In this Psalm we hear of the pearl of redemption, verses 7 and 8: perhaps the sweet singer would never have found that precious thing had he not been cast into the depths. 'Pearls lie deep.'" (Spurgeon)

b. **Lord, hear my voice**: Translators use the same word *Lord* to translate both the name *Yahweh* in the first line of this psalm, and *Adonai* in the second line. Each word is a title or name for the God of the Bible, the Creator of heaven and earth. Here, the psalmist called out to *Adonai*, His master and ruler, asking Him to **hear** his **voice**, knowing that for God to hear His people is to help His people.

i. "As Jehovah marks [God's] unchangeable faithfulness to his promises of delivering his people, so Adonai marks his Lordship over all hindrances in the way of his delivering them." (Fausset, cited in Spurgeon)

ii. "Twice he here nameth the Lord, as desirous to take hold of him with both his hands." (Trapp)

c. **Let Your ears be attentive**: The plea to God is emphasized using repetition as a poetic tool.

i. "It is better for our prayer to be heard than answered. If the Lord were to make an absolute promise to answer all our requests, it might be rather a curse than a blessing." (Spurgeon)

2. (3-4) The great forgiveness of God.

If You, LORD, should mark iniquities,
O Lord, who could stand?
But *there is* forgiveness with You,
That You may be feared.

a. **If You, LORD, should mark iniquities**: In asking for God to help, the psalmist also understood that he had no confident reason to ask or to be heard by God *apart* from His great forgiveness. Without this graciousness, no one could **stand** before Yahweh Adonai (**You, LORD...O Lord**).

i. **Should mark iniquities**: "The word rendered above 'mark' is literally *keep* or *watch*, as in Psalm 130:6, and here seems to mean *to take account of*, or retain in remembrance, in order to punish." (Maclaren)

ii. "'Tis true, the Lord marks all iniquity to know it, but he doth not mark any iniquity in his children to condemn them for it: so the meaning of the Psalm is, that if the Lord should mark sin with a strict and severe eye, as a judge, to charge it upon the person sinning, no man could bear it." (Caryl, cited in Spurgeon)

iii. "If thou shouldst set down every deviation in thought, word, and deed from thy holy law; and if thou shouldst call us into judgment for all our infidelities, both of heart and life; O Lord, who could stand? Who could stand such a trial, and who could stand acquitted in the judgment?" (Clarke)

iv. **Who could stand?** "*To stand* is a judicial phrase, and notes a man's being absolved or justified, upon an equal trial, as Psalm 1:5, Romans 14:4, where it is opposed to falling." (Poole)

b. **But there is forgiveness with You**: Years of previous relationship with God had taught the psalmist that there is, in fact, **forgiveness** with God. When we are hit hard with our awareness of sin, it can be hard to believe, but it is true: **there is forgiveness with** God.

i. **There is forgiveness with You**: "You may not find forgiveness with other people. Your husband or your wife may not forgive you, if you have wronged him or her. Your children may not forgive you. Your coworkers may not forgive you. You may not even be able to forgive yourself. There is one who will, and that one is God. Write down where you can see and reflect on it often: Our God is a forgiving God." (Boice)

ii. **There is forgiveness with You**: "And when God once speaks forgiveness, it can never be unspoken. Fear and doubt and misgiving may question, but cannot revoke it." (Meyer)

iii. "The word rendered 'forgiveness'…. literally means cutting off, and so suggests the merciful surgery by which the cancerous tumour is taken out of the soul." (Maclaren)

iv. "When Luther was in great trouble of soul, he was comforted by one who said to him, 'Dost thou not believe thy Creed?' 'Yes,' replied Luther, 'I believe the Creed.' 'Well, then,' rejoined the other, 'one article in it is, "I believe in the forgiveness of sins."' Luther's heart was lightened at once by the remembrance of the words in this psalm, 'there is forgiveness.' It may be that you have sinned many times and grievously; but 'there is forgiveness.' Though a child of God, you have gone far astray from him; but 'there is forgiveness.' You have backslidden sadly and horribly; but 'there is forgiveness.' The devil comes and howls at you, and tells you that your doom is sealed, and your damnation is sure; but 'there is forgiveness.' Oh, blessed sentence!" (Spurgeon)

c. **That You may be feared**: One of the great purposes of God's great forgiveness is to build a sense of gratitude and reverence in those He forgives. His pardon should lead to purity and His forgiveness to an appropriate fear of displeasing the One who has been so gracious.

i. "Those who have been forgiven are softened and humbled and overwhelmed by God's mercy, and they determine never [again] to sin against such a great and fearful goodness. They do sin, but in their deepest hearts they do not want to, and when they do they hurry back to God for deliverance." (Boice)

ii. "It was a Welshman in the midst of the wonderful revival of 1905 who rendered verse Psalm 130:4, 'There is forgiveness with Thee – enough to frighten us!' which if not accurate translation is fine exposition." (Morgan)

iii. "God's lovingkindness is so great and so wonderful, that the apprehension of it fills the soul with such a sense of His love that it is frightened. Frightened, that is, not at God, but at sin." (Morgan)

iv. "He is feared, not only because of his great judgment and harshness, but also because of his great love in forgiving. The godly respond with godly fear and love." (VanGemeren)

v. "The hammer of the law may break the icy heart of man with terrors and horrors, and yet it may remain ice still, unchanged; but when the fire of love kindly thaweth its ice, it is changed and dissolved into water – it is no longer ice, but of another nature." (Swinnock, cited in Spurgeon)

B. Wise speaking to self and Savior.

1. (5-6) Speaking to the soul.

I wait for the LORD, my soul waits,
And in His word I do hope.
My soul *waits* for the Lord
More than those who watch for the morning—
***Yes, more than* those who watch for the morning.**

a. **I wait for the LORD, my soul waits**: Having made his cry from the depths to God (verses 1-2), the singer then determined to **wait** upon God and the rescue He would bring.

b. **In His word I do hope**: The waiting was not passive or inactive. The psalmist used the time to actively set his **hope** upon God's promises, revealed in His **word**.

c. **My soul waits for the Lord**: Here, using the word *Adonai*, the psalmist again expressed his trust in *Yahweh Adonai* (**the L**ORD**...the Lord**). This phrasing used both *Yahweh*, the name for the covenant God of Abraham, Isaac, and Jacob; and *Adonai*, the normal name for a master or lord.

d. **More than those who watch for the morning**: The poet used a vivid image to express his patient anticipation in waiting on God. We see a watchman in the darkness of the early morning, scanning the horizon for the first sign of the dawn. The watchman doesn't doubt that morning *will* come, but only wonders *when*, and watches for it diligently. So it was for the singer who watched for God and the help God promised to bring.

> i. Some think **those who watch** were military guards, others think they were priests waiting for dawn so the morning sacrifices could be started for the day. It doesn't really matter if the watchmen were military or priestly; they waited for the morning with certain expectation that it would come.

> ii. "With equal earnestness have the faithful since looked out for the dawning of that last morning, which is to abolish sin, and put an end to sorrow." (Horne)

2. (7-8) Speaking to the people of God.

O Israel, hope in the LORD**;**
For with the LORD **there is mercy,**
And with Him *is* abundant redemption.
And He shall redeem Israel
From all his iniquities.

a. **O Israel, hope in the L**ORD: With this verse the phrasing turns from the personal to the public. What the psalmist learned in waiting upon God and trusting Him from the depths is now put to use as he calls upon Israel to put their **hope** in Yahweh Adonai.

> i. **Hope in the L**ORD: The psalmist put his faith and hope in the Lord Himself, not in the mercy or redemption God would bring. He looked to the Giver before the gift.

> ii. "Cease looking for the water, and look for the well. You will more readily see the Savior than see salvation, for he is lifted up, even he who is God, and beside him there is none else. You will more easily fix your eye on Jesus than upon justification, sanctification, or any other separate blessing." (Spurgeon)

b. **For with the LORD there is mercy**: What he learned in his personal life, he can put to application for the whole nation. When God's people humbly look to Him, there is **mercy** and **abundant redemption** for both the individual and the community.

i. **Abundant redemption**: "Are our sins great? with God there is mercy, matchless mercy. Are our sins many? with God is plenteous redemption, *multa redemptio;* he will multiply pardons as we multiply sins, Isaiah 55:7." (Trapp)

c. **He shall redeem Israel from all his iniquities**: This is the confident conclusion to the psalm, demonstrating trust that God *will* indeed bring the redemption and rescue to both the individual and the nation overwhelmed in the depths of their sin. What God has demonstrated in the private life, He will also perform for the community that cries out to Him.

i. "Nothing could be further from the shut-in gloom and uncertainty of 'the depths' than this. The singer is now liberated from himself to turn to his people and to hold out hopes that are far from tentative." (Kidner)

Psalm 131 – David's Humble, Learned Contentment in the LORD

This psalm is titled **A Song of Ascents. Of David**. *Commentators suggest two possible occasions for its composition. The first may be when Saul hunted David, and David was repeatedly accused of ambition for the throne of Israel. The second may be David's in response to his wife, Michal, when she accused him of being vulgar and undignified after he danced in the procession of bringing the ark of the covenant into Jerusalem (2 Samuel 6:16-23).*

Whatever the occasion was, this short psalm is a beautiful denial of pride, arrogance, and selfish ambition. "It is one of the shortest Psalms to read, but one of the longest to learn. It speaks of a young child, but it contains the experience of a man in Christ." (Charles Spurgeon)

A. David declares his humble heart.

1. (1a) David renounces pride and arrogance.

LORD, my heart is not haughty,
Nor my eyes lofty.

> a. **LORD, my heart is not haughty**: David learned to reject *pride*. David came before the Lord in conscious humility. He understood the principle explained in Proverbs and quoted twice in the New Testament: *God resists the proud, but gives grace to the humble* (Proverbs 3:34, James 4:6, 1 Peter 5:5).

> > i. "The psalm begins with an emphatic reference to Yahweh…'O Yahweh, my heart.' In the presence of the covenant God, the psalmist has experienced how wonderful complete submission to God is." (VanGemeren)

> b. **Nor my eyes lofty**: David learned to reject *arrogance*. Under the influence of pride, we become arrogant and look down on other people.

Though David had accomplished great things and had a great destiny in front of him, he didn't go around thinking of himself as better than others.

> i. "Arrogance is an expression of pride. It is the proud who are arrogant, but arrogance goes beyond pride in that it is pride looking down on other people." (Boice)

2. (1b) David renounces selfish ambition.

Neither do I concern myself with great matters,
Nor with things too profound for me.

a. **Neither do I concern myself with great matters**: David learned to reject *selfish ambition*, and he chose not to pursue **things too profound** for him. He did not set his focus on promotion or position above what God had appointed in the present season. Jesus taught us to accept a lower place (Luke 14:8-11) and wait patiently for God to lift us up in His wisdom and timing.

> i. There are godly aspirations (Philippians 3:12-14) and then there are selfish ambitions (2 Corinthians 12:20, Galatians 5:20, Philippians 1:16 and 2:3). One way to distinguish between them is to look for a focus on God (related to spiritual aspirations) or a focus on self (selfish ambition).

> ii. "Frequently, too, we exercise ourselves in great matters by having a high ambition to do something very wonderful in the church. This is why so very little is done. The great destroyer of good works is the ambition to do great works." (Spurgeon)

> iii. "It is...difficult to recognize unruly ambition as a sin because it has a kind of superficial relationship to the virtue of aspiration – an impatience with mediocrity, and a dissatisfaction with all things created until we are at home with the Creator, the hopeful striving for the best God has for us." (Peterson, cited in Boice)

> iv. "The young man who is quite content to begin with preaching in a little room in a village to a dozen is the man who will win souls. The other brother, who does not [consider] preaching till he can preach to five thousand, never will do anything, he never can." (Spurgeon)

> v. "Fill your sphere, brother, and be content with it. If God shall move you to another, be glad to be moved; if he move you to a smaller, be as willing to go to a less prominent place as to one that is more so. Have no will about it." (Spurgeon)

b. **Great matters...things too profound**: These can also apply to some intellectual or mental pursuits that may become expressions of pride. In pride, we can *demand* to know aspects of God's will or mind. This was Job's sin, of which he repented (Job 40:1-5, 42:1-6).

i. David understood the principle of Deuteronomy 29:29: *The secret things belong to the* LORD *our God, but those things which are revealed belong to us and to our children forever, that we may do all the words of this law.*

B. David declares his contented heart.

1. (2) Contentment like a weaned child.

Surely I have calmed and quieted my soul,
Like a weaned child with his mother;
Like a weaned child *is* my soul within me.

a. **Surely I have calmed and quieted my soul**: Instead of proud pursuits, David determined to find satisfaction and serenity of **soul**, content with God and His works. Those who feel constantly driven to do and achieve more in their relationship with God should learn some of what David here learned.

i. David phrased this with an emphasis on what *he* did. Of course it was ultimately the work of God within him, but it was vitally connected to his own will and choices. God didn't do this *for* him; God used the operation of David's choice. We must choose to calm and quiet our soul.

ii. "Oh the wonder of quiet contentment with God! He has enjoyed the walk with God in which he 'stilled' ('composed') himself and 'quieted' (i.e., 'silenced' or 'found rest,' Psalm 62:1,5) his soul (v. 2)." (VanGemeren)

b. **Like a weaned child with his mother**: A child not-yet weaned embraces his mother with the thought of food and immediate satisfaction. A **weaned child** embraces his mother out of a desire for love, closeness, and companionship. Such was David's humble desire to draw near to God.

i. God is beyond what we normally think of as gender; He is neither male nor female. Yet overwhelmingly, God is represented to us as a *Father*. This is one of the few passages where God is represented in some way as a mother. Others include Isaiah 49:15 and Isaiah 66:13.

ii. "Weaning was one of the first real troubles that we met with after we came into this world, and it was at the time a very terrible one to our little hearts. We got over it somehow or other." (Spurgeon)

c. **Like a weaned child is my soul**: The phrase is repeated for emphasis. The process of weaning may seem strange and terrible to the child, but it is necessary for the child's development. The **weaned child** comes to realize that the denial of one of the mother's gifts does not mean denial of the mother's presence. He comes to love the mother herself instead of the gift received from her.

i. We regard the process of weaning as natural, but the child likely regards it as a battle. What David wrote of here was contentment with God that did not come *naturally*, but through victory over what comes naturally and the habits associated with previous experience.

ii. "The weaned child with its mother is the child who has learned to be independent of that which seemed indispensible, and indeed was so at one time." (Morgan)

iii. "He is no longer angry with his mother, but buries his head in that very bosom after which he pined so grievously: he is weaned *on* his mother rather than *from* her." (Spurgeon)

iv. "Weaned from what? Self-sufficiency, self-will, self-seeking. From creatures and the things of the world – not, indeed, as to their use, but as to any dependence upon them for his happiness and portion." (Jay, cited in Spurgeon)

v. When God allows things or circumstances in our life that wean us from things we have relied on, we should never despise it. "Blessed are those afflictions which subdue our affections, which wean us from self-sufficiency, which educate us into Christian manliness, which teach us to love God not merely when he comforts us, but even when he tries us." (Spurgeon)

2. (3) Exhorting Israel to find the same contentment.

O Israel, hope in the LORD
From this time forth and forever.

a. **O Israel, hope in the LORD**: God's people could only learn and live the lesson David sang of in this short psalm if they set their **hope in the LORD**, and in nothing else. Nothing or no one else gives the same assurance.

i. "See how lovingly a man who is weaned from self thinks of others! David thinks of his people, and loses himself in his care for Israel." (Spurgeon)

ii. "The secret of victory over feverish ambition is divulged in the psalmist's appeal to Israel to hope in the Lord." (Morgan)

iii. There is the testimony of David's experience that he wanted the people of God in general to enjoy. "Act all as I have done; trust in him who is the God of justice and compassion; and, after you have suffered awhile, he will make bare his arm and deliver you." (Clarke)

iv. "The last verse rouses us from contemplating David to following his example and that of his greater Son: not through introspection but through being weaned from insubstantial ambitions to the only solid fare that can be ours. 'My food is to do the will of him who sent me, and to accomplish his work' (John 4:34)." (Kidner)

v. "Let his faithful people hope and trust, not in themselves, their wisdom, or their power, but in Jehovah alone, who will not fail to exalt them." (Horne)

b. **From this time forth and forever**: The decision to place one's **hope in the LORD** must have a beginning point, and that point should be *now* (**from this time**). From there, it should go **forth and forever**, never ending.

i. **Forever**: "Weaning takes the child out of a temporary condition into a state in which he will continue for the rest of his life: to rise above the world is to enter upon a heavenly existence which can never end." (Spurgeon)

ii. It will endure forever, but it does have a beginning. "If there is any unconverted person here who cannot understand all this, I pray the Lord to make him a child first, and then make him a weaned child." (Spurgeon)

Psalm 132 – Remembering the Promise to David and Beyond

This psalm is another in the series of fifteen titled **A Song of Ascents**. *It has no author associated with it in the title. Some believe David was the author, and some believe it was written after the exile. James Montgomery Boice made the case for Solomon as the author: "Since verses 8-10 are quoted in 2 Chronicles 6:41-42 as part of Solomon's prayer at the dedication of the temple, the psalm probably dates from Solomon's reign even though the title does not identify it as Solomon's psalm."*

The coming of the ark of the covenant to Jerusalem is referred to in verses 6-9 of this psalm. Psalm 24 and Psalm 68 also refer to this event, which is described more fully in 1 Chronicles 15-16.

Psalm 132 is allued to twice in the New Testament: Stephen alludes to Psalm 132:5 in Acts 7:46, and Peter alludes to Psalm 132:11 in Acts 2:30.

A. A heart for the house of the LORD.

1. (1-5) David's heart for the house of God.

LORD, remember David
And all his afflictions;
How he swore to the LORD,
And vowed to the Mighty One of Jacob:
**"Surely I will not go into the chamber of my house,
Or go up to the comfort of my bed;
I will not give sleep to my eyes
Or slumber to my eyelids,
Until I find a place for the LORD,
A dwelling place for the Mighty One of Jacob."**

    a. **LORD, remember David and all his afflictions**: The singer began by remembering David, the great king of Israel – and all the **afflictions** he endured.

i. Apart from the Messiah (who is given the title *Son of David*), David the son of Jesse is acknowledged as Israel's greatest king. Yet he had to endure a remarkable number of **afflictions**. All the following were true of David:

- He was despised and criticized by his family.
- He was placed in many life-and-death struggles.
- He was accused of treason and treachery.
- He was attacked by the connected, powerful, and ruthless.
- He lived many years as a fugitive, a wanted man.
- He had family, home, friends, and career taken from him.
- He experienced a significant season of backsliding.
- He accepted as the king only reluctantly.
- He faced many enemies in battle through many wars.
- He openly criticized and despised by his wife.
- He suffered because of his own sin and scandal.
- He endured great conflict and problems among his own children.
- He suffered a coup staged by his son, followed by a civil war.
- He was openly despised and criticized by some of his subjects.

ii. The psalmist asked God to look upon and **remember** both David himself and **all his afflictions**. He prayed, "Lord, consider the man and consider his troubles. Let none of them be forgotten or wasted."

iii. The **afflictions** of David always suggest the afflictions of his Greater Son: "That God would 'remember' the far greater 'afflictions' sustained for our sake by the Messiah in the days of his humiliation, when through much tribulation, he accomplished our redemption, and entered into his glory, is the petition preferred, in these words, by us Christians." (Horne)

iv. The individual Christian can take comfort that God does **remember** all the **afflictions** endured unto His glory. "Thus God still bends over the scenes of the life-work of His children. The chapel where a McCheyne pleaded with his congregation; the South Sea Island, where a Williams poured out his blood; the dark forests in which a Brainerd wrestled for his Indians; the great Continent, where a Moffat, a Livingstone, a Hannington wrought, prayed, and suffered. He remembers David and all his afflictions." (Meyer)

b. **How he swore to the LORD**: The poet asked Yahweh to remember a specific oath David made unto Him. The oath itself is not recorded in 2 Samuel 7, but the heart behind it was recorded there.

i. "Wearied with a stormy life, he might well have left it to others to care for the work.... He will put his own comfort second, God's service first." (Maclaren)

c. **Until I find a place for the LORD, a dwelling place for the Mighty One of Jacob**: David was absolutely dedicated to building God a temple, a **dwelling place**. David's dedication to this was so complete that he vowed to refuse himself many comforts of life until the job was finished.

i. After David built himself a fine palace, he felt guilty that a mere tent represented God's dwelling place. David asked Nathan the prophet for permission to build the temple, and Nathan orginally said yes. Soon afterward, God told Nathan that David was not to build Him a temple, but his son would (2 Samuel 7).

ii. David did not *build* that **place for the LORD**, but he did **find** it. "We find by 1 Chronicles 16:43, that he did not bless, and consequently did not inhabit his own house, until he had brought the ark to Zion, where the temple was afterwards erected." (Horne)

iii. God excused David from his obligation to build a temple. Yet God was so pleased with David's heart that He promised to build *David* a house, a lasting dynasty over Israel (2 Samuel 7).

iv. "And we find that he would have acted in all things according to his oath and vow, had God permitted him. But even after the Lord told him that Solomon, not he, should build the house he still continued to show his good will by collecting treasure and materials for the building, all the rest of his life." (Clarke)

v. David's passion speaks to us in at least two ways:

- We should have a passionate drive to enjoy God's presence in our own lives, that our hearts would truly be His home.
- We should have a passionate drive for the blessing and benefit of the house of God, the community of His people.

vi. "I wish that this same zeal would take firm hold of all Christians. How many there are who dwell in their ceiled houses while the house of God lies waste! They can provide abundantly for themselves; but for God's cause, for God's gospel, for a place wherein the poor may meet for the preaching of the Word, they do not seem to care." (Spurgeon)

vii. **The Mighty One of Jacob**: "The designation 'Mighty One of Jacob' derives from Genesis 49:24 and signifies the marvelous manner in which the Lord had protected, guided, and blessed Jacob. The epithet connotes the great strength of the Lord as the Divine Warrior." (VanGemeren)

2. (6-9) Our heart for the house of God.

Behold, we heard of it in Ephrathah;
We found it in the fields of the woods.
Let us go into His tabernacle;
Let us worship at His footstool.
Arise, O Lord, to Your resting place,
You and the ark of Your strength.
Let Your priests be clothed with righteousness,
And let Your saints shout for joy.

a. **Behold, we heard of it**: Most all commentators understand **it** here to mean the ark of the covenant and the tabernacle associated with it. This would be the remembrance of the season before David brought the ark (and, presumably the tabernacle) into Jerusalem. The ark was lost, and under David's direction it was found.

i. "The location of the ark seems to have been forgotten during the reign of Saul when it was at Keriath-jearim (1 Chronicles 13:3), and it was only found there later (in David's day) after a time of serious searching." (Boice)

b. **Let us go into His tabernacle**: As one of the Songs of Ascents, this song was sung by pilgrim travelers going to the temple in Jerusalem, mainly at feast times. They remembered and understood David's great heart for God's house and used it to inspire them as they said, "**Let us go into His tabernacle; let us worship at His footstool.**"

c. **Arise, O Lord, to Your resting place**: The pilgrims on their journey remembered the words of Moses in the wilderness, who called out when the ark traveled, *Rise up, O Lord! Let Your enemies be scattered, and let those who hate You flee before You* (Numbers 10:35).

i. Though the **ark of** God's **strength** had found its resting place, this was still an appropriate saying for a pilgrim people.

d. **Let Your priests be clothed with righteousness**: When they sang of the goodness and glory of God's temple, they also remembered the position of His **priests**. It was fitting for them to be known for **righteousness** in life, and this would make God's **saints shout for joy**.

i. "The pure vestments of the priests were symbols of stainless character, befitting the ministers of a holy God. The psalmist prays that the symbol may truly represent the inner reality." (Maclaren)

ii. When God's servants are not **clothed with righteousness**, it can cause God's people to lose some of their **joy**. "[There is] no surer sign of God's gracious presence with a people, than a powerful ministry, clothed with inward purity and holiness, represented by the holy garments." (Trapp)

B. The promise of God's blessing.

1. (10) A prayer for blessing on the Messiah.

For Your servant David's sake,
Do not turn away the face of Your Anointed.

a. **For Your servant David's sake**: God promised that He would not forsake the sons of David (2 Samuel 7:14-16). When the psalmist prayed this, he prayed for the fulfillment of a promise God had already made.

i. "For his sake all those who are anointed in him are accepted. God blessed Solomon and succeeding kings, for David's sake; and he will bless us for Jesus' sake." (Spurgeon)

b. **Do not turn away the face of Your Anointed**: The singer asked that the favor of God would never be taken from His **Anointed**. There is a sense in which every king of David's line was God's anointed, but this looks to the ultimate **Anointed** one – the Messiah Himself, Jesus Christ. This is ultimately a prayer for blessing on God's Messiah, the **Anointed** Son of David.

i. "The prayer upholds David by the special designations 'your servant' (*ebed*; cf. 27:9) and 'your anointed one' (*masiah*; cf. 2:2; 84:9; 89:20). These designations apply to David and to all his descendants who were anointed as kings over Israel or Judah." (VanGemeren)

2. (11-12) God's promise to David.

The Lᴏʀᴅ has sworn *in* truth to David;
He will not turn from it:
"I will set upon your throne the fruit of your body.
If your sons will keep My covenant
And My testimony which I shall teach them,
Their sons also shall sit upon your throne forevermore."

a. **The Lᴏʀᴅ has sworn in truth to David**: Earlier (verse 2) the singer remembered how David made a solemn oath to God. In return, God made a solemn oath to David, as recorded in 2 Samuel 7:5-16. God would never **turn from** such an oath.

> i. There was definitely a connection between the two oaths. "Jehovah's promise to establish a dynasty in Zion was made to the man who undertook to provide a Tabernacle for God in the midst of the City." (Morgan)

> ii. "Though the narrative in Samuel pertaining to the promises to David (2 Sam 7:12-16) makes no mention of an oath, here it is a poetic expression for the certainty of God's promise to David (cf. 89:3,35)." (VanGemeren)

b. **I will set upon your throne the fruit of your body**: The psalmist remembered the promises God made to David in 2 Samuel 7:12-16. These were the promises God confirmed with an oath.

> i. **Forevermore**: "This was conditional with respect to the posterity of David. They have been driven from the throne, because they did not keep the Lord's covenant, but the true David is on the throne." (Clarke)

3. (13-15) God's promise to Zion.

For the Lord has chosen Zion;
He has desired *it* for His dwelling place:
"This *is* My resting place forever;
Here I will dwell, for I have desired it.
I will abundantly bless her provision;
I will satisfy her poor with bread.

a. **For the Lord has chosen Zion**: The connection is made between the choice of David and his descendants and God's choice of Jerusalem (**Zion**) as His sacred **dwelling place**, the place He **desired**.

> i. The Bible is based on historical facts – real people, real events, and real places. God could have chosen any place on earth to be the stage on which His drama of redemption was displayed, and He deliberately chose Zion. His dwelling is in no way *restricted* to Jerusalem and the land of Israel, but it is significant that this was the place He **desired**.

> ii. **The Lord has chosen Zion**: "The human response was all too often cynical, treating God's choice as something to be exploited: a shelter against his judgment (Jer. 7, especially verses 8-15) or an asset to be commercialized (Matt. 21:12f.)." (Kidner)

b. **This is My resting place forever**: Once the ark of the covenant came into Jerusalem, there was to be no more traveling for the tabernacle. The tabernacle, the temple, the altar, and the ark would never rest in another place than Jerusalem.

i. "This is the joy of our souls, for surely we shall rest in God, and certainly our desire is to dwell in him. This also is the end of our fears for the church of God; for if the Lord dwell in her, she shall not be moved; if the Lord desire her, the devil cannot destroy her." (Spurgeon)

ii. There is a sense in which this section of the psalm takes the previous requests and answers them beyond all expectation. "The people had asked God to come to his resting place as the ark was brought to Jerusalem; God says that he will sit enthroned there 'for ever and ever.' They asked righteousness for the priests; God promises to clothe the priests with salvation, which is a greater concept. The people asked that the saints might sing for joy; God promises that they will sing for joy forever." (Boice)

iii. "The Divine promises teach the great truth that God over-answers our desires, and puts to shame the poverty of our petitions by the wealth of His gifts. He is 'able to do exceeding abundantly above all that we ask or think.'" (Maclaren)

c. **I will abundantly bless her provision**: God promised to have a special material blessing on Jerusalem and Israel, especially as part of the blessings for obedience connected to the Mosaic Covenant (Deuteronomy 7:13; 28:8-12).

i. "I will plentifully provide for Jerusalem, and all that live in her or resort to her for worship; nor shall they seek my face in vain." (Poole)

ii. **I will satisfy her poor with bread**: "Dainties I will not promise them; a sufficiency, but not a superfluity; poor they may be, but not destitute." (Trapp)

ii. Bishop George Horne, writing in the 1700s, had an interesting observation on this promise: "What a dreadful reverse of all this do we behold in the present state of the once glorious, but now desolated, Jerusalem!"

4. (16-18) God's promise to His servants.

I will also clothe her priests with salvation,
And her saints shall shout aloud for joy.
There I will make the horn of David grow;
I will prepare a lamp for My Anointed.
His enemies I will clothe with shame,
But upon Himself His crown shall flourish."

a. **I will also clothe her priests with salvation**: Earlier in verse 9 the singer prayed that the priests would be clothed with righteousness. Now he declared a promise from God that He would also clothe the **priests with salvation**.

i. When those who serve as God's representatives are clothed **with salvation**, the people of God **shall shout aloud for joy**.

b. **There I will make the horn of David grow; I will prepare a lamp for My Anointed**: Jerusalem would be the place where the strength promised to David and his descendants would **grow**. God prepared a light (**a lamp**) for His Messiah, the ultimate **Anointed** One.

i. "The three terms, *horn, lamp* and *crown*, scarcely need comment, with their evident implications of strength, clarity and royal dignity. But note that the word used for *crown* (the same as for the high priest's mitre) draws attention to the fact that it symbolized the king's hallowing. Not power alone, but holiness is this king's – our King's – glory." (Kidner)

ii. **The horn of David grow**: "…a metaphor taken from those goodly creatures, as stags, and such like; whose chiefest beauty and strength consisteth in their horns, especially when they bud and branch abroad." (Playfere, cited in Spurgeon)

iii. "**A lamp;** a successor or succession to continue for ever in his family, as this phrase is expounded, 1 Kings 11:36, 15:4; and particularly one eminent and glorious light, to wit, the Messias, who shall come out of his loins, and revive and vastly enlarge his kingdom." (Poole)

iv. "That this verse doth mystically refer to Christ, the Jews confess…. So saith Rabbi Saadiah, 'The lamp is the king, which illuminates the nations:' and Kimchi, 'The horn of David, is the Messias.'" (Horne)

c. **His enemies I will clothe with shame**: Any and all who oppose God's Messiah will end in **shame**, but the Anointed One's **crown shall flourish**. His reign will prosper and last forever.

i. "Their shame they will be unable to hide, it shall cover them: God will array them in it for ever, and it shall be their convict dress to all eternity." (Spurgeon)

Psalm 133 – The Blessed Unity of God's People

Of the fifteen psalms in the series, Psalm 133 is the last of the four attributed to King David in the title: **A Song of Ascents. Of David.** *We don't know exactly when David composed this song, but one likely occasion was when David was finally received as king over all the tribes of Israel, ending a terrible season of national division and discord.*

"It could date from the crowning of David at Hebron when the leaders of the nation were, for a time at least, of one heart and mind (see 2 Samuel 5:1; 1 Chronicles 12:38-40)." (James Montgomery Boice)

A. The blessing declared.

1. (1) Unity among God's people is **good** and **pleasant**.

Behold, how good and how pleasant *it is*
For brethren to dwell together in unity!

> a. **Behold**: Psalm 133 begins with an exhortation to **behold** – that is, to take notice. What follows is important and deserves our attention.

>> i. "It is a wonder seldom seen, therefore behold it! It may be seen, for it is the characteristic of real saints – therefore fail not to inspect it! It is well worthy of admiration; pause and gaze upon it! It will charm you into imitation, therefore note it well!" (Spurgeon)

> b. **How good and how pleasant it is for brethren to dwell together in unity**: David draws our attention to something **good** and **pleasant** – unity among the people of God.

>> • It is **good** because it reflects God's heart and purpose of unity among His people (also described in John 17:20-23, Ephesians 1:9-10).

>> • It is **pleasant** because it makes life together as God's people so much more enjoyable than seasons when constant bickering and conflict dominate.

c. **How good and how pleasant**: Not everything that is good is pleasant, and not everything that is pleasant is good. Unity among God's people is such a remarkable blessing because it is both **good** and **pleasant** – and both to a high degree, indicated by the repetition of **how**.

i. "Precious and profitable, sweet and delectable…dainty and goodly, as Revelation 18:14. Communion of saints is the next happiness upon earth to communion with God." (Trapp)

d. **For brethren to dwell together**: David had in mind the relationship that God's people have with one another, not with the world around them. Believers should work to have good and peaceable relationships with all others (Romans 12:18), but here the focus is on relationships among God's people.

e. **For brethren to dwell together in unity**: This **unity** is tested, because these brethren **dwell together**. In many ways it is easier to have some kind of unity with those distant. To **dwell together** means the bonds of unity and peace will be at times tested.

i. This song was especially relevant for pilgrims travelling together to Jerusalem. "During the pilgrimages, the Jews enjoyed an ecumenical experience on their way toward and in Jerusalem. The pilgrims came from many different walks of life, regions, and tribes, as they gathered for one purpose: the worship of the Lord in Jerusalem." (VanGemeren)

B. The blessing described.

1. (2) Like oil on the head.

It is **like the precious oil upon the head,**
Running down on the beard,
The beard of Aaron,
Running down on the edge of his garments.

a. **It is like the precious oil upon the head**: In the ancient Middle East, it was common to anoint one's head with oil, sometimes as a greeting entering a home (Luke 7:46). This was done to refresh the one receiving the oil, and to give a good smell from the fragrance that came from the perfumed oils. Among God's people, unity refreshes and makes a pleasant atmosphere for all.

i. "The anointing oil intended for the head (Exod. 29:7) was not confined to it, nor could its fragrance be contained. Exodus 29:21 provided explicitly that after the pouring of the oil on the head, some was to be sprinkled on the robes: 'and he and his garments shall be holy'." (Kidner)

b. **Running down on the beard, the beard of Aaron**: The picture in words shows that unity is a *rich and abundant* blessing – as this oil overflowed the head and came down the beard. It also shows that unity is a *rare and precious* blessing, because the suggestion is that this was holy anointing oil, which was not to be imitated (Exodus 30:22-33).

> i. Christian unity is "...far beyond that common friendship so highly extolled by Cicero, and other heathens; and is therefore here fitly compared to that nonesuch [perfect] odoriferous ointment." (Trapp)

> ii. This is a unity of holiness. "That anointing oil, poured upon Aaron, was the oil of consecration, and symbolized his separation from all evil; it was the oil of holiness." (Morgan)

> iii. "The odour of this must have been very agreeable, and serves here as a metaphor to point out the exquisite excellence of brotherly love." (Clarke)

> iv. "What a sacred thing must brotherly love be when it can be likened to an oil which must never be poured on any man but on the Lord's high-priest alone!" (Spurgeon)

c. **The beard of Aaron**: The oil upon the priest's head was good as an instrument of refreshing and greeting, as it would be for anyone else. Yet for Aaron (as high priest), it also was part of his consecration to priestly service (Exodus 29:7), which led to so many other good things.

- Service unto God and His people.
- Atonement of sins.
- Offerings of peace, fellowship, and thanksgiving.
- Compassionate ministry to the people of God.

> i. The illustration is wonderful. When there is unity among God's people, it is not only good and pleasant in itself, but it also leads to so many other good things. When the people of God struggle with each other, there are so many other good things they are not doing and enjoying.

> ii. God intended the priests to represent His righteousness and salvation to a watching world. Spiritually speaking, this anointing made that possible. Unity among God's people has a similar effect.

d. **Running down on the edge of his garments**: What an abundant blessing unity is! It is like oil poured out so richly that it flows from the head to the beard, and then down to the very edge of the priest's **garments**.

i. There is some debate whether the **edge of his garments** refers to the collar (as Maclaren and others say) or to the bottom hem of his priestly robes. Either way, it was an impressive flow of oil.

ii. Boice commented on the New International Version translation of verse 2 (...*running down on the beard, running down on Aaron's beard, down on the collar of his robe*): "In verse 2 the threefold repetition 'running down,' 'running down,' and 'down' – the Hebrew uses the same verb each time – emphasizes that the blessing of Aaron's anointing was from above himself, that is, from God." (Boice)

iii. "In short, true unity, like all good gifts, is from above; bestowed rather than contrived, a blessing far more than an achievement." (Kidner)

2. (3) Like the dew of the mountains.

It is **like the dew of Hermon,**
Descending upon the mountains of Zion;
For there the Lord **commanded the blessing—**
Life forevermore.

a. **It is like the dew of Hermon**: King David used a second word picture to show how wonderful unity is among the people of God. It is also like the rich **dew** that covers Mount **Hermon**, making it green and moist. It is a distinct contrast to the dry wilderness found in other parts of Israel. Unity among God's people makes life thriving and healthy.

i. "On this mountain the dew is very copious. Mr. Maundrell says that 'with this dew, even in dry weather, their tents were as wet as if it had rained the whole night.'" (Clarke)

ii. "The dew was ever the agent of renewal, of refreshment, of fertilizing force: that out of which life was maintained in strength." (Morgan)

iii. "It refreshes the thirsty ground and quickens vegetation; so fraternal concord, falling gently on men's spirits, and linking distant ones together by a mysterious chain of transmitted good, will help to revive failing strength and refresh parched places." (Maclaren)

iv. "To the Jew it seemed as though the Hermon range overtowered the land and was able to drop its dews across the intervening distance upon the mountains of Zion. Thus, from the glory of His exaltation Jesus drops the dew of the Holy Spirit as blessing upon the lowlands of our life – that blessing which is life forevermore." (Meyer)

b. **Descending upon the mountains of Zion**: This blessing comes upon Jerusalem, which David established as the center for Israel's worship. In Jerusalem their unity would be displayed and enjoyed.

> i. "This dew is not to be taken literally [in Jerusalem], for the falling of the dew availed very little to the refreshment or improvement of the hills of Zion and Moriah, especially as now they were filled with buildings; but allegorically, for the favour or blessing of God, which is frequently called and compared to the dew, as Proverbs 19:12, Isaiah 18:4, Hosea 14:5, Micah 5:7." (Poole)

c. **The LORD commanded the blessing–life forevermore**: The blessing of unity is something God *commands*, something the previously cited New Testament passages teach (John 17:20-23, Ephesians 1:9-10, Romans 12:18). Since we will have **life forevermore** with the people of God, we should work hard to enjoy unity with them now.

> i. "O for more of this rare virtue! Not the love which comes and goes, but that which dwells; not that spirit which separates and secludes, but that which dwells together; not that mind which is all for debate and difference, but that which dwells together in unity." (Spurgeon)

> ii. "O, come the day when division shall cease, and enmity be done away; when the tribes of the spiritual Israel shall be united in a bond of eternal charity, under the true David, in the Jerusalem which is above; and saints and angels shall sing this lovely Psalm together!" (Horne)

Psalm 134 – *The* L*ORD* *Bless You from Zion*

This is the last of the series of fifteen psalms with the title **A Song of Ascents**. *It is a call to the priests and Levites of the temple to continue their service of praise, with the answer of a blessing back to the people.*

Charles Spurgeon suggested that the scene was of pilgrims departing Jerusalem in the darkness of early morning, calling out to the priests and Levites who stood watch at the temple. The pilgrims then receive the blessing spoken back to them.

A. The blessing pronounced unto the LORD.

1. (1) A call for servants to bless the LORD.

Behold, bless the LORD,
All *you* servants of the LORD,
Who by night stand in the house of the LORD!

 a. **Behold, bless the LORD**: As in several other places in the Book of Psalms, this does not mean to **bless** in the sense that a greater bestows a blessing on a lesser. God is infinitely greater than man, and man could never give a blessing to God. The idea is that it blesses and honors God when His creatures praise Him and thank Him appropriately.

  i. **Behold**: "I believe *hinneh* should be taken here in the sense of *take heed!* Be upon your guard." (Clarke)

  ii. **Bless the LORD**: "That is, speak good of his name: tell the wonders he has wrought, and show that his name is exalted." (Clarke)

  iii. "Be not content with praise, such as all his works render to him; but, as his saints, see that ye 'bless' him. He blesses you; therefore, be zealous to bless him." (Spurgeon)

  iv. "Do not stand there like statues, silent and idle, but employ your hearts and tongues in singing forth the praises of the Lord." (Poole)

 b. **All you servants of the LORD**: The **servants** of God have special reason to bless Him. If the **servants of the LORD** do not praise Him, who will?

- They partner with God in His work, which is a special privilege.
- They enjoy the nearness that comes with working together with God.
- They receive special strength and anointing as they serve Him.
- They have new and exciting challenges of faith.

i. Since this is addressed to **servants of the LORD**, this psalm shows us that *praise* should be added to all our work. We can imagine a temple guard asking, "Isn't it enough that I do my work and stand watch through the night?" The answer is: "No, that isn't enough. To all your work, add praise – **bless the LORD, all you servants of the LORD**.

ii. "Not one of you should serve him as of compulsion, but all should bless him while you serve him; yea, bless him for permitting you to serve him, fitting you to serve him, and accepting your service." (Spurgeon)

iii. "Those who have made their way to Jerusalem to worship and have completed their devotions are now returning home, singing this song. They will not be able to worship in the temple again until their next journey. As they leave the city, they are encouraged to know that the priests will be remaining behind to represent them at the temple and so they will be worshiping God there continually." (Boice)

iv. G. Campbell Morgan also understood these priests and Levites, these **servants of the LORD**, to be representative of the whole community of God's people. He applied the same principle to Christian worship in a modern age. A small gathered group, in some way, represents the large and mighty body of Christ.

c. **Who by night stand in the house of the LORD**: The singer probably had in mind the priests or Levites who had special duties at the temple, including **night** watches at **the house of the LORD**.

i. "We read, 1 Chronicles 9:33, that the Levitical singers were 'employed in their work day and night;' to the end, doubtless, that the earthly sanctuary might bear some resemblance of that above, where, St. John tells us, the redeemed 'are before the throne of God, and serve him day and night in the temple.' Revelation 7:15." (Horne)

ii. **Stand in the house of the LORD**: "The priestly and Levitical ministry is often designated by the verb 'stand' (cf. Psalm 135:2; Deuteronomy 10:8)." (VanGemeren)

iii. "...not only by day, but also and especially by night, when their watch was more necessary. See Exodus 27:21, Leviticus 8:35, 1 Samuel

3:3. As you watch by night when others sleep, so do you utter the praises of God when others are silent." (Poole)

iv. "Even when they were placed in a dungeon, bleeding from their beatings, Paul and Silas sang praise to God at night (Acts 16:25)." (Boice)

v. **By night**: "It is comparatively easy to bless the Lord in the daytime, when sunshine lies like His smile on nature, and all the world is full of music, and our lives flow on quietly and peacefully. It does not take much grace to bless the Lord then. But when night has draped the earth and hushed the homes of men to solitude, and we stand amid the shadows that lurk around us in the sanctuary, facing the inexplicable mysteries of Providence, of history, of life and death; then the song falters on our lips, and chokes our utterance." (Meyer)

2. (2) Blessing God with uplifted hands.

Lift up your hands *in* the sanctuary,
And bless the LORD.

a. **Lift up your hands**: The lifting of **hands** was not only the common posture for prayer among the ancient Hebrews; it was also appropriate for praise. It displayed the anticipation of gratefully receiving from God, and the sense of surrender to Him.

i. "The lifting up of the hands was a gesture in prayer, it was an intimation of their expectation of receiving blessings from the Lord, and it was also an acknowledgment of their having received the same." (Pierce, cited in Spurgeon)

b. **Lift up your hands in the sanctuary**: It may be that **sanctuary** is used more generally here, referring to the temple area as a whole. Yet, only the priests or Levites had access to the **sanctuary** (temple building) itself.

i. "So it may speak of worshipping 'in holiness'…and be the passage underlying 1 Timothy 2:8, 'lifting up holy hands'." (Kidner)

ii. "One readeth it, out of the Hebrew, Lift up your hands, sanctuary, that is, ye sanctuary men." (Trapp)

c. **And bless the LORD**: The idea is repeated for emphasis. God's people should give Him their thanks, honor, praise, and glory.

i. "They are exhorted to fill the night with prayer as well as watchfulness, and to let their hearts go up in blessing to Jehovah. The voice of praise should echo through the silent night and float over the sleeping city." (Maclaren)

B. The blessing received from the LORD.

1. (3) The Creator's blessing.

The LORD who made heaven and earth
Bless you from Zion!

a. **The LORD who made heaven and earth**: The psalmist looked to God as Creator of all things, and appealed to the God of all might, design, and wisdom with the prayer that follows.

> i. Most commentators see this as a reference to the priestly blessing described in Numbers 6:23-27.

> ii. "The blessing extends to all of life, wherever the people of God may go or live, because Yahweh, the covenant God ("Lord"), is "the Maker of heaven and earth," i.e., the Great King of the universe (see 121:2)." (VanGemeren)

> iii. "Is it possible for Him to have made heaven and earth, and not to be able to bless the soul whom He has not created only, but redeemed! He cannot fail to bless those that bless." (Meyer)

b. **Bless you from Zion**: The idea is that blessing from the God of all creation flows **from Zion** unto each of His people wherever he or she may be. This is a beautiful and fitting close to the Songs of Ascents. The people came to Zion in pilgrimage to bless the LORD, singing the songs of Psalms 120-134. The Songs of Ascents end with the idea that God's blessing went with each of them **from Zion**. The blessing doesn't remain in Jerusalem, but flows from there.

> i. **Bless you** uses the *singular*, not the plural. This is because the idea is drawn from Numbers 6:23-27, and also because God's blessing comes to us not only as a community, but also as individuals. He loves and blesses us *each one*.

> ii. "Zion cannot bless us; the holiest ministers can only wish us a blessing; but Jehovah can and will bless each one of his waiting people." (Spurgeon)

> iii. This spiritual conception of God was different than pagan ideas. The psalmist understood that God's power and influence weren't limited to Jerusalem. The God who had the Creator's claim to all **heaven and earth** was no local deity; He could bless in Zion and **from Zion**.

> iv. "So the thought is that if we bless God in our worship, as we must, then God will also bless us abundantly in our daily lives. This is the only ultimate goal of any Christian: to bless God and to be blessed by him." (Boice)

Psalm 135 – Praise for the Creator and the Redeemer

Psalm 135 is of note for its use of other passages from the Hebrew Scriptures. Almost every verse quotes the words or the idea of another Old Testament passage, including four different psalms, two passages from Deuteronomy, two from Jeremiah, and two from Exodus. Derek Kidner wrote of Psalm 135, "Every verse of this psalm either echoes, quotes or is quoted by some other part of Scripture."

"The reader will be struck by the many allusions as well as direct citations to other passages of Scripture. The end result of the psalmist's artistry is that the inspired creation stands on its own, even though it is dependent on other Scriptures for its poetic, liturgical, and idiomatic expressions." (Willem VanGemeren)

A. The good God, Creator and Redeemer.

1. (1-2) A call to praise Yahweh.

Praise the LORD!
Praise the name of the LORD;
Praise *Him*, O you servants of the LORD!
You who stand in the house of the LORD,
In the courts of the house of our God,

> a. **Praise the LORD**: Psalm 135 begins and ends with this phrase. It is a call for stirring, passionate praise to God, but not one that runs only on the fuel of emotion. This psalm gives many reasonable, logical reasons why we should **praise the LORD**.

> > i. Meyer described the characteristics of praise: "In this, we adore God for all that He is in Himself. Forgetting our own petty interests and concerns, our *me* and *my* and *mine*, we take our stand with angels and archangels and all the host of heaven in crying, Thou art worthy, O holy, holy, holy Lord! Heaven and earth are full of Thy great glory. Glory be unto Thee, O God Most High!"

ii. "To worship is to quicken the conscience by the holiness of God, to feed the mind with the truth of God, to purge the imagination by the beauty of God, to open the heart to the love of God, to devote the will to the purpose of God." (Former Archbishop of Canterbury William Temple, cited in Boice)

b. **Praise the name of the LORD**: To praise **the name of the LORD** is to honor Him in all His character and attributes. The name was understood to represent the nature of the person.

c. **Praise Him, O you servants of the LORD**: As in the previous psalm (Psalm 134:1), this refers to the priests and Levites who would **stand in the house of the LORD** for priestly and temple duties.

d. **In the courts of the house of our God**: This may speak of the people of Israel in general, who as worshippers had no access to the **house of the LORD** (only priests could enter the holy place). The common man could stand **in the courts of the house of our God**. This was a call to *all* God's people to praise Him.

i. "…**in the courts**, where the people also had a place, 2 Chronicles 4:9, and are required to bear a part in this heavenly Hallelujah." (Trapp)

ii. "While the previous psalm greeted chiefly the Levites on night watch, this one has a great and varied throng in view, priestly and lay." (Kidner)

iii. "'Our God' signifies possession, communion in possession, assurance of possession, delight in possession. Oh the unutterable joy of calling God our own!" (Spurgeon)

2. (3-4) Reasons to praise the LORD.

Praise the LORD, for the LORD is good;
Sing praises to His name, for *it is* pleasant.
For the LORD has chosen Jacob for Himself,
Israel for His special treasure.

a. **For the LORD is good**: In listing reasons *why* Yahweh should be praised, the psalmist began with the simple declaration of God's goodness. This idea is presented many times in the Bible (as in Psalm 73:1 and 143:10; Mark 10:18).

i. "Do not only magnify the Lord because he is God; but study his character and his doings, and thus render intelligent, appreciative praise." (Spurgeon)

ii. "It is impossible to keep the reasons for praise out of the summons to praise." (Maclaren)

iii. We, as human beings, have ideas of **good** and evil because we are made in the image of God. Anyone who questions the goodness of God or His existence has to answer the question, "Where do we get our concept of good?"

iv. "What could be more basic than this, that God is good? Nothing at all, since this is God's essential nature." (Boice)

b. **Sing praises to His name**: One of the ways praise is shown is in song. God's people should be a singing people.

c. **For it is pleasant**: This is the second reason given to praise Yahweh – because it benefits the one who praises Him. This should never be the *primary* reason, because then worship has a focus on self-gratification. Yet worship does do us good, and there is nothing wrong with enjoying the fact that it is **pleasant**.

i. True praise is **pleasant**, "…an angelical exercise, and, to the spiritually minded man, very delicious. To others, indeed, who have no true notion of God but as of an enemy, it is but as music at funerals, or as the trumpet before a judge, no comfort to the mourning wife, or guilty prisoner." (Trapp)

d. **For the LORD has chosen Jacob for Himself**: The psalmist listed a third reason to praise God – His choosing of **Israel for His special treasure**. He did not choose Israel because they were great, but because He is great in love.

i. God told Israel this in Deuteronomy 7:7-8: *The LORD did not set His love on you nor choose you because you were more in number than any other people, for you were the least of all peoples; but because the LORD loves you, and because He would keep the oath which He swore to your fathers.*

ii. "God's choice exalts; for here the name is changed from Jacob, the supplanter, to Israel, the prince. The love of God gives a new name and imparts a new value; for the comparison to a royal treasure is a most honourable one." (Spurgeon)

iii. Israel was called to praise God because He chose them; this is also a reason for the New Covenant believer. "Shall not we Christians, then, praise the same gracious Lord, who hath chosen us out of the world, who hath given unto us his gospel, who dwelleth in us by his Spirit, and who, by that Spirit, maketh us more than conquerors over our spiritual adversaries?" (Horne)

iv. **For Himself**: "It does not say, 'unto heaven,' – 'unto certain privileges,' – 'unto certain favors.' All that is quite true, but it does not say so here: 'The Lord hath chosen Jacob unto himself.' Oh, what a blessed choice is this – to be chosen unto God!" (Spurgeon)

e. **His special treasure**: This fulfills the declaration of God in Deuteronomy 7:6: *For you are a holy people to the LORD your God; the LORD your God has chosen you to be a people for Himself, a special treasure above all the peoples on the face of the earth.*

> i. **His special treasure**: "The Hebrew word *segullah* signifieth God's special jewels, God's proper ones, or God's secret ones, that he keeps in store for himself, and for his own special service and use. Princes lock up with their own hands in secret their most precious and costly jewels; and so doth God his." (Brooks, cited in Spurgeon)

3. (5-7) Praising God who creates all things.

For I know that the LORD is great,
And our Lord *is* above all gods.
Whatever the LORD pleases He does,
In heaven and in earth,
In the seas and in all deep places.
He causes the vapors to ascend from the ends of the earth;
He makes lightning for the rain;
He brings the wind out of His treasuries.

a. **I know that the LORD is great, and our Lord is above all gods**: In declaring the greatness of God, the singer used two great titles or names for God. Yahweh, the covenant God of Israel (the **LORD**) **is great**, and Adonai, the Master of all (**Lord**) **is above all gods**. God is exalted above all the pretended deities of the pagans.

> i. **I know that the LORD is great**: "On what a firm foundation does the psalmist plant his *foot – 'I know!'* One loves to hear men of God speaking in this calm, undoubting, and assured confidence, whether it be of the Lord's goodness or of the Lord's greatness." (Bouchier, cited in Spurgeon)

> ii. **All gods**: "…or worshipped as gods by the heathen people. And therefore seeing they commonly praise and extol their idols, it becometh you not to be silent as to the praises of your God." (Poole)

b. **Whatever the LORD pleases He does**: The psalmist exalted Yahweh as having ultimate power, with the ability to do whatever He desires. His power extends everywhere, **in heaven and in earth**, and **in the seas** and **from the ends of the earth**.

i. **In the seas and in all deep places**: "…in the visible seas, and in those invisible depths, both of earth, and of the waters which are contained in the bowels of the earth." (Poole)

c. **He makes lightning for the rain**: This exalts Yahweh over the Canaanite idol Baal, who was thought of as the god of weather. Baal was sometimes depicted as holding a bolt of lightning, and was believed to be the one who sent **the rain**. The singer rebuked this, and sang of Yahweh as the Lord over **lightning**, **rain**, and **the wind**.

i. "The heathen divided the great domain; but Jupiter does not rule in heaven, nor Neptune on the sea, nor Pluto in the lower regions; Jehovah rules over all." (Spurgeon)

ii. "The Psalmist teacheth us to restore the celestial artillery to its rightful owner, Jehovah, the God of Israel, and the Creator of the universe." (Horne)

4. (8-12) Praising God who redeems His people.

He destroyed the firstborn of Egypt,
Both of man and beast.
He sent signs and wonders into the midst of you, O Egypt,
Upon Pharaoh and all his servants.
He defeated many nations
And slew mighty kings—
Sihon king of the Amorites,
Og king of Bashan,
And all the kingdoms of Canaan—
And gave their land *as* **a heritage,**
A heritage to Israel His people.

a. **He destroyed the firstborn of Egypt**: Yahweh also exalted Himself over the supposed gods of the Egyptians. This psalm refers back to the many plagues God inflicted on Egypt (**He sent signs and wonders into the midst of you**), with the greatest of them being the judgment of death on **the firstborn of Egypt**.

i. "Egypt was the theatre of the grand contest between the God of Israel and the gods of the heathen." (Horne)

ii. **Upon Pharaoh and all his servants**: "God's servants are far better off than Pharaoh's servants: those who stand in the courts of Jehovah are delivered, but the courtiers of Pharaoh are smitten all of them, for they were all partakers in his evil deeds." (Spurgeon)

b. **He defeated many nations**: Once Israel was free from Egypt, Yahweh also showed His greatness over all supposed gods by defeating **nations** and **mighty kings** that attacked His people.

i. "Psalmists are never weary of drawing confidence and courage for today from the deeds of the Exodus and the Conquest." (Maclaren)

ii. "The victories over *Sihon* and *Og* are recounted in Numbers 21:21ff., 21:33ff.; cf. Deuteronomy 3:11." (Kidner)

iii. "These two kings were the first to oppose, and they were among the most notable of the adversaries: their being smitten is therefore a special object of song for loyal Israelites." (Spurgeon)

c. **And gave their land as a heritage**: God demonstrated His greatness over all the gods of the Canaanites by defeating **the kingdoms of Canaan** and giving their land to Israel, as a **heritage** to them – something passed on from generation to generation.

i. "Canaan was their heritage because they were the Lord's heritage, and he gave it to them actually because he had long before given it to them by promise." (Spurgeon)

B. Exalting God in all His greatness.

1. (13-14) The greatness of God's fame.

Your name, O LORD, *endures* forever,
Your fame, O LORD, throughout all generations.
For the LORD will judge His people,
And He will have compassion on His servants.

a. **Your name, O LORD, endures forever**: In light of Yahweh's incomparable greatness (just declared in the previous verses), the singer praised His unchanging **name** and His never-ending **fame**.

i. "God does not change. He is immutable, to use the proper theological word for his unchangeability. God is not only good; but he will also always be good. He is always the same in his eternal attributes. We will never find him to be less good than he has been to us in the past." (Boice)

ii. **Your fame**: "The name was to increase in significance, as the Lord increased his activities in the history of redemption and revealed more of himself in history and revelation." (VanGemeren)

b. **For the LORD will judge His people**: The good and great God **will** bring justice, righteousness, and **compassion** to His people. His goodness and greatness are *for* them, not against them.

i. "He will do them justice against their enemies." (Clarke)

2. (15-18) The greatness of God in contrast to the empty folly of idols.

The idols of the nations *are* silver and gold,
The work of men's hands.
They have mouths, but they do not speak;
Eyes they have, but they do not see;
They have ears, but they do not hear;
Nor is there *any* breath in their mouths.
Those who make them are like them;
***So is* everyone who trusts in them.**

a. **The idols of the nations are silver and gold**: This is a striking contrast to the greatness of the all-powerful God who reigns in heaven. The goodness and greatness of Yahweh make the puny idols, **the work of men's hands**, seem even emptier and more foolish.

i. "The psalmist returns to the motif of vanity of idolatry by an extensive quotation from Psalm 115:4-8." (VanGemeren)

b. **They have mouths, but they do not speak**: As in several other passages in the Hebrew Scriptures, the Bible mocks those who make or worship idols. The one who makes the statue has a mouth, eyes, and ears superior to the idol itself.

i. **Eyes they have, but they do not see**: "The eyes of idols have frequently been very costly; diamonds have been used for that purpose; but of what avail is the expense, since they see nothing?" (Spurgeon)

ii. "If they cannot even see us, how can they know our wants, appreciate our sacrifices, or spy out for us the means of help? What a wretched thing, that a man who can see should bow down before an image which is blind!" (Spurgeon)

iii. "The Rev. John Thomas, a missionary in India, was one day travelling alone through the country, when he saw a great number of people waiting near an idol temple. He went up to them, and as soon as the doors were opened, he walked into the temple. Seeing an idol raised above the people, he walked boldly up to it, held up his hand, and asked for silence. He then put his fingers on its eyes, and said, "It has eyes, but it cannot see! It has ears, but it cannot hear! It has a nose, but it cannot smell! It has hands, but it cannot handle! It has a mouth, but it cannot speak! Neither is there any breath in it!" Instead of doing injury to him for affronting their god and themselves, the natives were all surprised; and an old Brahmin was so convinced of his folly by what Mr. Thomas said, that he also cried out, "It has feet, but cannot run away!" The people raised a shout, and being ashamed of their stupidity, they left the temple, and went to their homes." (Cited in Spurgeon's *Treasury of David*)

c. **Those who make them are like them**: Though man is greater than the idol he makes, the creation and honoring of idols make a man or a woman *lower*. Idolatry never exalts man, but rather brings him low.

i. "It is forever true that man becomes like his god, approximates in character and conduct to that which he yields his homage." (Morgan)

ii. "If we worship things that people produce, we will become as impotent and empty as those things, but if we worship God, by the grace of God we will become like God." (Boice)

iii. "Like the material things idolaters serve, idolaters are spiritually dead, they are the mere images of men, their best being is gone, they are not what they seem. Their mouths do not really pray, their eyes see not the truth, their ears hear not the voice of the Lord, and the life of God is not in them." (Spurgeon)

iv. "To put anything of our own creation, whether wealth, or fame, or power, in the place of God, is to begin a process of degradation, the end of which is destructive of everything of high possibility in life." (Morgan)

3. (19-21) The people of God called to bless and praise Yahweh.

Bless the Lord, O house of Israel!
Bless the Lord, O house of Aaron!
Bless the Lord, O house of Levi!
You who fear the Lord, bless the Lord!
Blessed be the Lord out of Zion,
Who dwells in Jerusalem!
Praise the Lord!

a. **Bless the Lord, O house of Israel**: In a series of three statements, this psalm closes with a call to the descendants of **Israel**, **Aaron**, and **Levi** to honor God and give Him the recognition He deserves.

b. **You who fear the Lord, bless the Lord**: This may be a call to Gentiles who honored God to also join with Israel, the priests, and the Levites in praising and honoring Yahweh.

i. "It may be that this verse is intended to bring in God-fearing men who were not included under Israel, Aaron, and Levi. They were Gentile proselytes, and this verse opens the door and bids them enter." (Spurgeon)

c. **Blessed be the** L<small>ORD</small> **out of Zion**: Jerusalem was (and is) a special place to God, but His praise, His goodness, His greatness extend **out of Zion**. He is not a local deity; His power and greatness are not limited to Zion.

> i. **Who dwells in Jerusalem**: "This clause may be added either to distinguish the true God from the gods which were worshipped in other places and countries; or as a reason why they should bless God, because he had blessed and honoured that place with his gracious and glorious presence." (Poole)

d. **Praise the** L<small>ORD</small>: It is fitting for such a soaring psalm to end as it began – to declare God's praise, and to call upon others to do so also.

Psalm 136 – God's Never-Ending Mercy

Psalm 136 is a special psalm, with each one of its 26 verses repeating the sentence, His mercy endures forever. *Psalm 118 repeated that affirmation five times. Throughout the Hebrew Scriptures, the phrase has somewhat of a liturgical sense to it, as if the assembled people of Israel said or sung this in response to the direction of the Levites leading singing and worship. Ezra 3:11 indicates that this encouragement was part of a responsive singing among God's people:* And they sang responsively, praising and giving thanks to the LORD: "For He is good, For His mercy endures forever toward Israel."

The sentence is used several other times in the Old Testament, each time in the context of some kind of public praise or declaration. His mercy endures forever *is found:*

- In David's psalm of praise recorded in 1 Chronicles 16:7 (16:34).
- In the assignments of the priests in David's day (1 Chronicles 16:41).
- In Israel's praise at the dedication of Solomon's temple (2 Chronicles 5:13, 7:3, 7:6).
- In the record of the LORD's victory over the Ammonites as they praised (2 Chronicles 20:21).
- In the future praise by Israel after the destruction suffered in the Babylonian conquest (Jeremiah 33:10-11).
- In the dedication of Ezra's temple (Ezra 3:11).

We picture a great multitude of the people of God gathered in the temple courts. A priest or Levite would call out a reason to give God thanks, and His people would respond with, "For His mercy endures forever."

"In Jewish tradition Psalm 136 has been called the Great Hallel (or Great Psalm of Praise). It does not use the words hallelu jah, *but it is called the Great Hallel for the*

way it rehearses God's goodness in regard to his people and encourages them to praise him for his merciful and steadfast love." (James Montgomery Boice)

A. The enduring mercy of God from the beginning of time.

1. (1-4) The enduring mercy of God in His essential nature, who He is.

Oh, give thanks to the LORD, for *He is* good!
For His mercy *endures* forever.
Oh, give thanks to the God of gods!
For His mercy *endures* forever.
Oh, give thanks to the Lord of lords!
For His mercy *endures* forever:
To Him who alone does great wonders,
For His mercy *endures* forever;

> a. **Oh, give thanks to the LORD, for He is good**: As in the previous psalm, Psalm 136 gives thanks and praise to God for His *goodness*. The fact that God **is good** is fundamental to all that He is and does. We know that *God is love* (1 John 4:8 and 4:16), and that love is an expression of His goodness. This is a wonderful reason to give Yahweh **thanks**.

> > i. "*Give thanks* is not the whole meaning of this word…and therefore calls us to thoughtful, grateful worship, spelling out what we know or have found of God's glory and his deeds." (Kidner)

> > ii. "He is good beyond all others; indeed, he alone is good in the highest sense; he is the source of good, the good of all good, the sustainer of good, the perfecter of good, and the rewarder of good. For this he deserves the constant gratitude of his people." (Spurgeon)

> > iii. Because we are made in God's image (Genesis 1:26-27), we know something of what is good. However, we are fallen (Romans 5:19), and our knowledge of good is corrupted. Yet our entire concept of *good* is rooted in God and His goodness.

> > iv. Those who question God's goodness do so according to some standard of what is good and what is evil. The very existence of that standard connects them to something beyond themselves – back to the Creator who made them in His image.

> b. **For His mercy endures forever**: This is the first of 26 times this phrase is repeated in this psalm. It was probably the answer of the congregation of Israel to each first line spoken by the priests or Levites.

> > i. 1 Chronicles 16:37-41 suggests that **His mercy endures forever** was sung daily as part of the morning and evening sacrifices.

ii. "Most hymns with a solid, simple chorus become favourites with congregations, and this is sure to have been one of the best beloved." (Spurgeon)

iii. The greatest demonstration of the always-enduring **mercy** of God was seen in the person and work of Jesus Christ, the Savior of the world.

c. **His mercy endures forever**: The declaration proclaims that God's *hesed* (**mercy**) never ends and will always be given to His people.

i. **Mercy** is the translation of the great Hebrew word *hesed*, which may be understood as Yahweh's grace, His loyal love, His covenant love unto His people. Some scholars have overemphasized its covenant aspect, taking too much *feeling* from the word. *Hesed* combines loyalty to a covenant with true love and mercy.

ii. For centuries it was translated with words like *mercy, kindness*, and *love*. In 1927, a scholar named Nelson Glueck (among others) argued that the real idea behind *hesed* was "covenant loyalty" and not so much love or mercy. However, many disagreed and there is no good reason for changing the long-held understanding of *hesed* and taking it as a word that mainly emphasizes covenant loyalty (see R. Laird Harris on *hesed* in the *Theological Wordbook of the Old Testament*).

d. **Give thanks to the God of gods...to the Lord of lords**: Reasons are repeatedly found to thank and praise God. Here each reason is connected to *who God is*. He is greater than any of the supposed **gods** or **lords** of the nations. This idea may be drawn from Deuteronomy 10:17.

i. **LORD.... God.... Lord**: "The opening stanzas refer to the One to Whom reference is made throughout, by the three great names by which He as known: *Jehovah*, the title of grace (verse 1); *Elohim*, the name of might (verse 2); and *Adonai*, the title of sovereignty (verse 3)." (Morgan)

ii. **The Lord of lords**: "All lords in the plural are summed up in this Lord in the singular: he is more lordly than all emperors and kings condensed into one." (Spurgeon)

e. **To Him who alone does great wonders**: God's people were invited to praise Him as the God of true power and miraculous **wonders**. Most of the rest of this psalm describes many of these **great wonders**, that were and are an expression of His great **mercy**, His *hesed* to His people.

i. "The attributes here mentioned are those of 'goodness' and 'power;' the one renders him willing, the other able to save; and what can we desire more, but that he should continue to be so?" (Horne)

ii. "His works are all great in wonder even when they are not great in size; in fact, in the minute objects of the microscope we behold as great wonders as even the telescope can reveal." (Spurgeon)

iii. It is true that God **alone does great wonders**, and the following lines tell us that creation is the beginning (not the end) of those wonders.

2. (5-9) The enduring mercy of God in His work as Creator.

To Him who by wisdom made the heavens,
For His mercy *endures* forever;
To Him who laid out the earth above the waters,
For His mercy *endures* forever;
To Him who made great lights,
For His mercy *endures* forever—
The sun to rule by day,
For His mercy *endures* forever;
The moon and stars to rule by night,
For His mercy *endures* forever.

a. **To Him who by wisdom made the heavens**: Here the singer refers back to Genesis 1 and points to God's creative work as a demonstration of His never-ending **mercy** to His people.

i. "The psalm looks at the story of Creation from an original point of view, when it rolls out in chorus, after each stage of that work, that its motive lay in the eternal lovingkindness of Jehovah. Creation is an act of Divine love." (Maclaren)

ii. "As far back as the creation his eye had travelled, and all through the stormy, troubled days he could detect the silver thread of mercy. Oh that we had his eyes to see always the love of God!" (Meyer)

iii. "There are no iron tracks, with bars and bolts, to hold the planets in their orbits. Freely in space they move, ever changing, but never changed; poised and balancing; swaying and swayed; disturbing and disturbed, onward they fly, fulfilling with unerring certainty their mighty cycles. The entire system forms one grand complicated piece of celestial machinery; circle within circle, wheel within wheel, cycle within cycle." (*The Orbs of Heaven*, cited by Spurgeon)

b. **Laid out the earth above the waters**: In this section, the work of God as Creator is described with elements from the first four days of creation (Genesis 1:1-19). Because each of these is an expression of His never-ending mercy toward His people, we can say that God created the heavens and the earth with His people in mind.

i. "The heavens above and the earth beneath declare the wisdom of their great Maker, and proclaim aloud, to an intelligent ear, the divinity of the hand that formed them. The heavens display the love of God to man; the earth teaches the duty of man to God." (Horne)

ii. "Paul echoed the same truths in Lystra when he taught the Gentiles there that God 'has shown kindness by giving you rain from heaven and crops in their seasons; he provides you with plenty of food and fills your hearts with joy' (Acts 14:17)." (Boice)

iii. The theme of creation in this psalm "…invites the Christian not to wrangle over cosmological theories but to delight in his environment, known to him as no mere mechanism but a work of 'steadfast love'. No unbeliever has grounds for any such quality of joy." (Kidner)

B. The enduring mercy of God to His people.

1. (10-15) The enduring mercy of God in the deliverance from Egypt.

To Him who struck Egypt in their firstborn,
For His mercy *endures* **forever;**
And brought out Israel from among them,
For His mercy *endures* **forever;**
With a strong hand, and with an outstretched arm,
For His mercy *endures* **forever;**
To Him who divided the Red Sea in two,
For His mercy *endures* **forever;**
And made Israel pass through the midst of it,
For His mercy *endures* **forever;**
But overthrew Pharaoh and his army in the Red Sea,
For His mercy *endures* **forever;**

a. **To Him who struck Egypt in their firstborn**: The previous psalm mentioned the deliverance from Egypt and the striking of the firstborn (Psalm 135:8-9). Here again God is praised as the One who rescued Israel from their slavery and degradation in Egypt – another expression of His never-ending **mercy**.

i. The singer recounted God's great wonders flowing seamlessly from the work of creation described in Genesis 1 to the work of deliverance described in Exodus. We rightly regard (or should regard) the Exodus account as historical, describing *what really happened*. Therefore, the context and flow of this psalm demonstrates that what God described in Genesis 1 *really happened*. The psalmist does not treat them differently, as if one were a legend and the other actual history.

b. **To Him who divided the Red Sea in two**: God did not only bring the Israelites out of Egypt, but He also delivered them from Pharaoh's attempt to re-capture them. In **mercy** to Israel, God **overthrew Pharaoh and his army in the Red Sea**.

i. God's use of history in this psalm is important. As in countless other places in the Scriptures, God used His work in the past to give hope, faith, and confidence to His people both for the moment and for the future.

ii. "The word for dividing the Red Sea is peculiar. It means to hew in pieces or in two, and is used for cutting in halves the child in Solomon's judgment [1 Kings 3:25]; while the word 'parts' [two] is a noun from the same root, and is found in Genesis 15:17, to describe the two portions into which Abraham clave the carcasses. Thus, as with a sword, Jehovah hewed the sea in two, and His people passed between the parts, as between the halves of the covenant sacrifice." (Maclaren)

iii. **Overthrew Pharaoh and his army**: "…as in Hebrew, *shaked off.* The word is applicable to a tree shaking off its foliage, Isaiah. 33:9. The same word is used in Exodus 14:27: 'And the Lord overthrew (*shook off*) the Egyptians in the midst of the sea.'" (Barnes, cited in Spurgeon)

2. (16-22) The enduring mercy of God from the wilderness to the Promised Land.

To Him who led His people through the wilderness,
For His mercy *endures* forever;
To Him who struck down great kings,
For His mercy *endures* forever;
And slew famous kings,
For His mercy *endures* forever—
Sihon king of the Amorites,
For His mercy *endures* forever;
And Og king of Bashan,
For His mercy *endures* forever—
And gave their land as a heritage,
For His mercy *endures* forever;
A heritage to Israel His servant,
For His mercy *endures* forever.

a. **To Him who led His people through the wilderness**: This short statement is a reminder of many mighty and loving acts of God. Yahweh provided guidance, food, water, structure, leadership, healing, victory, and many other things to Israel **through the wilderness**.

i. "It was an astonishing miracle of God to support so many hundreds of thousands of people in a wilderness totally deprived of all necessities for the life of man, and that for the space of *forty* years." (Clarke)

ii. "…through that vast howling wilderness, where there was neither way nor provision; through which none but the Almighty God could have safely conducted them." (Poole)

iii. This was a great demonstration of God's never-failing **mercy**. "Their conduct in the wilderness tested his mercy most severely, but it bore the strain; many a time he forgave them; and though he smote them for their transgressions, yet he waited to be gracious and speedily turned to them in compassion." (Spurgeon)

b. **To Him who struck down great kings**: The previous psalm described the defeat of **Sihon king of the Amorites** and **Og king of Bashan**, as well as the giving of Canaan to Israel **as a heritage** (Psalm 135:10-12). These were all demonstrations of the never-ending **mercy** of God.

i. **Great kings**: "Great, as those times accounted them, when almost every small city had their king; Canaan had thirty and more of them. Great also in regard of their stature and strength; for they were of the giant's race, Deuteronomy 3:11-13, Amos 2:9." (Trapp)

ii. "The Lord who smote Pharaoh at the beginning of the wilderness march, smote Sihon and Og at the close of it." (Spurgeon)

iii. **And slew famous kings**: "What good was their fame to them? As they opposed God they became infamous rather than famous. Their deaths made the Lord's fame to increase among the nations while their fame ended in disgraceful defeat." (Spurgeon)

3. (23-25) The enduring mercy of God in ongoing deliverance and help.

Who remembered us in our lowly state,
For His mercy *endures* forever;
And rescued us from our enemies,
For His mercy *endures* forever;
Who gives food to all flesh,
For His mercy *endures* forever.

a. **Who remembered us in our lowly state**: The song makes a sharp yet skillful transition from God's great wonders of the past to His faithful help in the present. It is good for us to look to the past for evidence that **His mercy endures forever**, but even better for us to see the evidence in our own day.

i. "After all, 'his steadfast love endures for ever', and the refrain is designed to show the relevance of every act of God to every singer of the psalm." (Kidner)

ii. **Rescued us from our enemies**: "Sin is our enemy, and we are redeemed from it by the atoning blood; Satan is our enemy and we are redeemed from him by the Redeemer's power; the world is our enemy, and we are redeemed from it by the Holy Spirit." (Spurgeon)

b. **Who gives food to all flesh**: The psalmist asked God's people to praise and thank Him not only for His work as *deliverer*, but also as *provider*. This is more evidence of God's never-ending **mercy**, which is extended to **all flesh**, not only to Israel.

i. **Food to all flesh**: "…by whose *universal providence* every intellectual and animal being is supported and preserved. The appointing every *living thing food*, and that sort of food which is suited to its nature, (and the nature and habits of animals are endlessly diversified,) is an overwhelming proof of the wondrous providence, wisdom, and goodness of God." (Clarke)

ii. "He promised to Noah and to all 'flesh' to sustain it with his grace (cf. Genesis 9:8-17). Here the psalmist makes use of the word 'flesh'… and thus makes an allusion to God's promise (cf. Genesis 9:11, 15-17)." (VanGemeren)

4. (26) Gratitude to the God of enduring mercy.

Oh, give thanks to the God of heaven!
For His mercy *endures* forever.

a. **Oh, give thanks to the God of heaven**: In directing us to do this, the psalmist not only had in mind our appropriate gratitude, but also reminds us that the God of Israel, the God of Abraham, Isaac, and Jacob, is **the God of heaven**. He is the God who really exists and really reigns.

i. **God of heaven**: "Therefore the final call to praise, which rounds off the psalm by echoing its beginning, does not name Him by the Name which implied Israel's special relation, but by that by which other peoples could and did address Him, "the God of heaven," from whom all good comes down on all the earth." (Maclaren)

ii. "His mercy in providing heaven for his people is more than all the rest." (Trapp)

b. **For His mercy endures forever**: The singer has given us many reasons to respond to God with this statement, and we are persuaded. The never-ending **mercy** of God – His lovingkindness, His grace, His loyal love – will never stop finding a way to bless and help His people.

i. "And do you suppose that such mercy is going to fail you? It endureth forever! You fret and chafe like a restless little child; but you cannot fall out of the arms of God's mercy." (Meyer)

ii. Spurgeon suggested many things that Psalm 136 as a whole teaches:

- The past, present, or future will not end His mercy.
- The storms of life will not end His mercy.
- Distance from loved ones will not end His mercy.
- Death itself will not end His mercy.
- God's never-ending mercy should make us merciful to others.
- God's never-ending mercy should make us hopeful for others.
- God's never-ending mercy should make us hopeful for ourselves.

iii. "One night in February 358 A.D. the church father Athanasius held an all-night service at his church in Alexandria, Egypt. He had been leading the fight for the eternal sonship and deity of Jesus Christ, knowing that the survival of Christianity depended on it. He had many enemies – for political even more than theological reasons – and they moved the power of the Roman government against him. That night the church was surrounded by soldiers with drawn swords. People were frightened. With calm presence of mind Athanasius announced the singing of Psalm 136. The vast congregation responded, thundering forth twenty-six times, 'His love endures forever.' When the soldiers burst through the doors they were staggered by the singing. Athanasius kept his place until the congregation was dispersed. Then he too disappeared in the darkness and found refuge with his friends." (Boice)

iv. "Many citizens of Alexandria were killed that night, but the people of Athanasius's congregation never forgot that although man is evil, God is good. He is superlatively good, and 'his love endures forever.'" (Boice)

Psalm 137 – The Mournful Song of the Exiles

Because this psalm is a remembrance of Babylon, many commentators believe it was written after the return from exile. It may also have been written many years into the exile.

A. Singing to the self.

1. (1-3) Mourning by Babylon's rivers.

By the rivers of Babylon,
There we sat down, yea, we wept
When we remembered Zion.
We hung our harps
Upon the willows in the midst of it.
For there those who carried us away captive asked of us a song,
And those who plundered us *requested* mirth,
***Saying,* "Sing us *one* of the songs of Zion!"**

a. **By the rivers of Babylon**: This song of the exile puts us on the shore of one of Babylon's mighty rivers, likely the Euphrates. Judea and the whole of Israel had no mighty river comparable to the Euphrates, so it would certainly make an impression upon the forced refugee from Judea to Babylonia.

i. **Rivers of Babylon**: "These might have been the *Tigris* and *Euphrates*, or their *branches*, or *streams* that flowed into them. In their captivity and dispersion, it was customary for the Jews to hold their religious meetings on the banks of rivers. Mention is made of this in Acts 16:13, where we find the Jews of Philippi resorting to a *river side, where prayer was wont to be made.*" (Clarke)

ii. Based on verse 1, Horne suggested this cry of mourning from a repentant one: "O Lord, I am an Israelite, exiled by my sins from thy holy city, and left here to mourn in this Babylon, the land of my captivity. Here I dwell in sorrow, by these transient waters, musing on the restless and unstable nature of earthly pleasures."

b. **There we sat down, yea, we wept**: The immense **rivers of Babylon** said to the exiled one, *you're not home any more*. As they **remembered Zion**, they wept.

- They wept over the death of so many loved ones.
- They wept over the loss of almost everything they owned.
- They wept over the destroyed city of Jerusalem and her great temple.
- They wept over the agony of a forced march from Judea to Babylon.
- They wept over the cruelty of their captors.
- They wept over the loss of such a pleasant and blessed past.
- They wept over the forced captivity of their present.
- They wept over the bleak nature of their future.
- They wept over their sin that invited such judgment from God.

    i. "The English words are sad, even mournful, but the words have an even sadder sound in the Hebrew language. Verses 1-3, which lead up to and explain the pathetic question of verse 4, repeat nine times the pronoun ending *nu* (meaning 'we' or 'our'), which sounds mournful. It is like crying 'ohhh' or 'woe' repeatedly." (Boice)

c. **We hung our harps upon the willows**: The singer used poetic liberty to present a striking scene. Large willow trees grew on the shores of the great river, and because there were no songs left in these captives, they **hung** their **harps** on those willow trees.

    i. "Many singers were carried captives: Ezra 2:41. These would of course take their instruments with them." (Horne)

    ii. "The *arabim* or *willows* were very plentiful in Babylon. The great quantity of them that were on the banks of the *Euphrates* caused Isaiah, Isaiah 15:7, to call it *the brook* or *river of willows*." (Clarke)

    iii. "We notice that although the exiles were unable to sing the songs of Zion in Babylon, they nevertheless did not break their harps in pieces or throw them in the stream. Instead they hung them on the poplars, presumably saving them for what would surely be a better day." (Boice)

d. **Sing us one of the songs of Zion**: This was the cruel demand of **those who carried us away captive**. They asked for one of the famous **songs of Zion**. The ones who **plundered** the people of God now wanted them to entertain them. Yet there was no song left in them; their harps had been hung in the trees.

i. "So, like tipsy revellers, they called out 'Sing!' The request drove the iron deeper into sad hearts, for it came from those who had made the misery. They had led away the captives, and now they bid them make sport." (Maclaren)

ii. "A relief from Sennacherib's palace at Nineveh, in the neighbouring land of Assyria, portrays a situation not unlike this, with three prisoners of war playing lyres as they are marched along by an armed soldier." (Kidner)

iii. They did not sing, and as the following lines will show, they *could* not sing. "Yet, there was a song in the silence, not heard of the cruel oppressors, but heard of Jehovah Himself. It was the song of the heart, remembering Jerusalem, counting it the chief joy of life." (Morgan)

2. (4-6) A vow to remember Jerusalem, even in exile.

How shall we sing the LORD's song
In a foreign land?
If I forget you, O Jerusalem,
Let my right hand forget *its skill!*
If I do not remember you,
Let my tongue cling to the roof of my mouth—
If I do not exalt Jerusalem
Above my chief joy.

a. **How shall we sing the LORD's song in a foreign land?** Though their conquerors wanted them to sing for their own amusement, the song simply wasn't there. The songs of God's people were more than performances; they came from their relationship with God. It would take a long time to sing those songs **in a foreign land**.

i. "They sought to be amused by these people of a strange religion, and the request was in itself an insult of their faith. It was impossible, and they refused to sing the song of Jehovah. To have done so would have been to play traitor to their own lost city, and to all that their citizenship stood for." (Morgan)

ii. F.B. Meyer took the idea of not being able to sing and used it as an admonishment for Christians: "You have ceased singing lately. The joy of your religious life has vanished. You pass through the old routine, but without the exhilaration of former days. Can you not tell the reason? It is not because your circumstances are depressed, though they may be; for Paul and Silas sang praises to God in their prison. Is not disobedience at the root of your songlessness? You have allowed some little rift to come within the lute of your life, which has been slowly widening, and now threatens to silence all. And you never will be able to resume that song until you have put away the evil of your doing, and have returned from the land of the enemy."

b. **If I forget you, O Jerusalem**: The singer vowed that he would never forget God's holy city, and even gave a curse upon himself if he did. If he did **forget**, then his **right hand** could lose its skill to play the harp. If he failed to **remember**, then his **tongue** would lose its ability to sing.

i. "The godly could not forget Jerusalem and everything it stands for: covenant, temple, presence and kingship of God, atonement, forgiveness, and reconciliation. They vowed never to forget God's promises and to persevere, waiting for the moment of redemption." (VanGemeren)

ii. **Forget its skill**: "In the Hebrew it is only *forget*, without expressing what, to intimate the extent and generality of this wish; Let it forget or be disenabled not only for playing, but for every action in which it was formerly used." (Poole)

iii. The Puritan commentator John Trapp (1601-1699) observed this about the Jewish people of his time: "The Jews at this day, when they build a house, they are, say the Rabbis, to leave one part of it unfinished and lying rude, in remembrance that Jerusalem and the temple are at present desolate. At least, they use to leave about a yard square of the house unplastered, on which they write, in great letters, this of the psalmist, 'If I forget Jerusalem,' etc., or else these words, *Zecher leehorban,* that is, The memory of the desolation (Leo Modena of the Rites of the Jews)."

B. Singing about the nations.

1. (7) Remember Edom.

Remember, O Lord, against the sons of Edom
The day of Jerusalem,
Who said, "Raze *it*, raze *it*,
To its very foundation!"

a. **Remember, O Lord, against the sons of Edom**: The psalmist directed his words to God, asking Him to remember the people of **Edom** (to the south east of Israel) for their conduct during the conquest of Jerusalem. In this case, the call to **remember** was a call to oppose and to judge.

i. "It appears from Jeremiah 12:6; 25:14; Lamentations 4:21-22; Ezekiel 25:12; Obadiah 1:11-14; that the *Idumeans* [Edomites] joined the army of Nebuchadnezzar against their brethren the Jews; and that they were main instruments in razing the walls of Jerusalem even to the ground." (Clarke)

ii. The small book of Obadiah is a prophetic pronouncement against the Edomites for their part in the conquest of Judea. *Nor should you have rejoiced over the children of Judah in the day of their destruction; nor should you have spoken proudly in the day of distress* (Obadiah 1:12).

b. **Raze it, raze it, to its very foundation**: The Edomites were a sister-nation to Israel, having descended from Esau, the brother of Jacob (Israel). They should have supported and sympathized with Jerusalem when the Babylonians came against it. Instead, they enjoyed Jerusalem's agony and wanted the city to be completely destroyed.

i. "The word 'foundations'…implies more than the actual foundations of the walls of Jerusalem, as it also pertains to the God-established order in creation, in his rule, and in his election of a people to himself (cf. Psalm 24:2; 78:69; 89:11; 104:5). The Edomites were hoping for the destruction of the 'foundations' of Yahweh's rule on earth." (VanGemeren)

ii. "It is horrible for neighbours to be enemies, worse for them to show their enmity in times of great affliction, worst of all for neighbours to egg others on to malicious deeds." (Spurgeon)

2. (8-9) Judge Babylon.

O daughter of Babylon, who are to be destroyed,
Happy the one who repays you as you have served us!
Happy the one who takes and dashes
Your little ones against the rock!

a. **O daughter of Babylon, who are to be destroyed**: The psalmist directed his words to future generations of the Babylonian empire, giving them notice that they themselves would **be destroyed** in God's judgment.

i. It is interesting that the psalmist did not make this a prayer to God as he did regarding Edom in the previous verse. Perhaps he regarded the judgment of Babylon to be so certain that it didn't need his prayer, only his pronouncement, especially in light of other prophecies.

b. **Happy the one who repays you as you have served us**: This is a blessing on the one who brings judgment against the Babylonians, and a judgment corresponding to what the Babylonians **served** unto Jerusalem and Judea.

i. "There is ample evidence that 'to dash in pieces their little ones' was a common enough sequel to a heathen victory, and that Babylon had been in no mood for restraint at the fall of Jerusalem (2 Kings 25:7; Lamentations 5:11f.).” (Kidner)

c. **Happy the one who takes and dashes your little ones against the rock:** This awful blessing is understood in light of the previous line. No doubt the singer had seen this done to the **little ones** of Jerusalem, and the horrible image was seared upon his mind. He prayed that the Babylonians would get as they had given.

i. We sympathize with the impulse of the psalmist, yet the New Testament calls us to a higher standard: “Our response should be to recognize that our calling, since the cross, is to pray down reconciliation, not judgment” (Boice).

ii. “Perhaps, if some of their modern critics had been under the yoke from which this psalmist has been delivered, they would have understood a little better how a good man of that age could rejoice that Babylon was fallen and all its race extirpated.” (Maclaren)

iii. “Let those find fault with it who have never seen their temple burned, their city ruined, their wives ravished, and their children slain; they might not, perhaps, be quite so velvet-mouthed if they had suffered after this fashion.” (Spurgeon)

iv. The psalmist also may have known of Isaiah’s prophecy that announced that just this would happen: *Their children also will be dashed to pieces before their eyes* (Isaiah 13:16).

v. “Today the fortresses of ancient Edom are a desolate waste, and the site of ancient Babylon is a ruin. God cannot be mocked.” (Boice)

Psalm 138 – God's Promise to Honor His Word and to Complete His Work

This psalm is titled **A Psalm of David**. *Several commentators mention that it was fittingly placed next to Psalm 137, which described the inability of the psalmist to sing before the heathen. Psalm 138 is a declaration that even the kings of the nations will praise Yahweh.*

"This Psalm is wisely placed. Whoever edited and arranged these sacred poems, he had an eye to apposition and contrast; for if in Psalm 137 we see the need of silence before revilers, here we see the excellence of a brave confession. There is a time to be silent, lest we cast pearls before swine; and there is a time to speak openly, lest we be found guilty of cowardly non-confession." (Charles Spurgeon)

"There is a fine blend of boldness and humility from the outset: boldness to confess the Lord before the gods, humility to bow down before him." (Derek Kidner)

A. Declaration of praise for the past.

1. (1-2a) The declaration of praise.

I will praise You with my whole heart;
Before the gods I will sing praises to You.
I will worship toward Your holy temple,
And praise Your name

a. **I will praise You with my whole heart**: David began this song with a bold declaration – that he would hold nothing back in his **praise** to God. It would be done with all his being, with his **whole heart**.

i. **My whole heart**: "We need a broken heart to mourn our own sins, but a whole heart to praise the Lord's perfections." (Spurgeon)

ii. "'With the whole heart' leaves no room for mixed motives of divided devotion." (Morgan)

b. **Before the gods I will sing praises to You**: We can't imagine that David meant he would praise Yahweh in the actual presence of idols and images of other **gods**. There are three ideas about what David meant by his singing praise **before the gods** (*elohim*).

- Perhaps it was a declaration of allegiance to Yahweh and He alone, and **the gods** represent the idols of the heathen.

- Perhaps **gods** (*elohim*) in this context refer to angelic beings, as in a few other places in the Hebrew Scriptures.

- Perhaps **gods** refers to kings or judges, such as are spoken of later in verse 4.

  i. "A witness against the impotence of idols.... Praise belongs to the Lord alone and not to the gods of the nations, whose kings will have to submit to the Lord." (VanGemeren)

c. **I will worship toward Your holy temple**: Even when David was not at the temple, he recognized it as God's appointed place for worship and sacrifice. He would worship according to God's direction.

  i. "Wheresoever I am the face of my soul shall turn, like the needle of a dial, by sacred instinct, towards thee, in the ark of thy presence, in the Son of thy love." (Trapp)

2. (2b-3) Reasons for praise.

For Your lovingkindness and Your truth;
For You have magnified Your word above all Your name.
In the day when I cried out, You answered me,
***And* made me bold *with* strength in my soul.**

a. **For Your lovingkindness and Your truth**: David's praise was not empty adoration. It had reasons behind it, which were a basis for it. He thought of the great **lovingkindness** (*hesed*) of God toward him, and God's firmly established **truth**. Meditation on those gifts from God gave David a basis for his spirit of praise.

b. **For You have magnified Your word above all Your name**: Having mentioned God's **truth** in the previous line, now David considered the main way God's truth is communicated to us – through His **word**. God has such a high estimation of His **word** that He has **magnified** it **above** His very **name**, His character.

  i. This is a stunning and remarkable statement, showing the incredible regard God has for His own **word**. He holds His **word** in greater esteem than His very character or name.

ii. "It would be as if God is saying, 'I value my integrity above everything else. Above everything else I want to be believed.' The verse does not have to mean that God's other qualities are moved to second place." (Boice)

iii. Charles Spurgeon explained his confidence in complete, God-spoken, inspiration of the Bible: "We believe in plenary verbal inspiration, with all its difficulties, for there are not half as many difficulties in that doctrine as there are in any other kind of inspiration that men may imagine. If this Book be not the real solid foundation of our religion, what have we to build upon? If God has spoken a lie, where are we, brethren?"

c. **In the day when I cried out, You answered me**: David also had very practical reasons to praise and thank God. The LORD had **answered** and rescued him many times. When David's strength failed, God made him **bold with strength** in his **soul**.

i. We notice an important pattern in the reasons David gave for his praise. It is important to praise God for who He is, even more than for what He has done for us.

- First he gave God praise for who He is – a God of **lovingkindness** and **truth**.

- Then he gave God praise for His revelation – the **word**, magnified above His very name.

- Then he gave God praise for *what He had done* – God's response to David in a time of crisis.

ii. **Made me bold**: "The psalmist uses a remarkable expression, in saying that Jehovah had made him bold, or, as the word is literally, proud." (Maclaren)

iii. "If the burden was not removed, yet strength was given wherewith to bear it, and this is an equally effective method of help." (Spurgeon)

B. Declaration of confidence for the future.

1. (4-6) Praise from the kings of the earth.

All the kings of the earth shall praise You, O LORD,
When they hear the words of Your mouth.
Yes, they shall sing of the ways of the LORD,
For great *is* the glory of the LORD.
Though the LORD is on high,
Yet He regards the lowly;
But the proud He knows from afar.

a. **All the kings of the earth shall praise You**: David was king of Israel and gave praise to the LORD, but he also knew the day would come when **all the kings of the earth** would praise Him. They would praise Him in response to hearing **the words of** His **mouth** from those who proclaim.

    i. Morgan saw a connection between the answered prayer of verses 2-3 and the praise of kings described here: "The reason of praise is next declared to be that of lovingkindness and truth as already proved. The effect of praise is to be that of the revelation of God to others, who if they come to know Him, will also praise Him."

    ii. **When they hear the words of Your mouth**: "It probably means when those who know God declare his words to them. In other words, the psalm is acknowledging the need for the people of God to be missionaries." (Boice)

b. **They shall sing of the ways of the LORD**: The kings of the earth would not only praise Yahweh with words, but also in song. This was in response to their understanding that **great is the glory of the LORD**.

c. **Yet He regards the lowly**: David understood that God is great in glory and **on high**, yet He holds **the lowly**, the humble, in high regard. On the other hand, God keeps His distance from **the proud**.

    i. "Infinitely *great* as God is, he regards even the lowest and most inconsiderable part of his creation; but the *humble* and *afflicted* man attracts his notice particularly." (Clarke)

    ii. "**Unto the lowly**; unto such as are mean and obscure in the world; to me, a poor contemptible shepherd, whom he hath preferred before great princes, and to such as are little in their own eyes." (Poole)

    iii. David's statement that God **regards the lowly, but the proud He knows from afar** is another way of saying a truth from Proverbs 3:34 that is repeated twice in the New Testament: *God resists the proud, but gives grace to the humble* (James 4:6, 1 Peter 5:5).

    iv. "Low things he looketh close upon, that he may raise them higher; lofty things he knoweth afar off, that he may crush them down lower. The proud Pharisee pressed as near God as he could; the poor publican, not daring to do so, stood aloof off; yet was God far from the Pharisee, near to the publican." (Trapp)

    v. "Proud men boast loudly of their culture and '*the* freedom of thought,' and even dare to criticize their Maker: but he knows them from afar, and will keep them at arm's length in this life, and shut them up in hell in the next." (Spurgeon)

2. (7-8) David's firm confidence for the future.

Though I walk in the midst of trouble, You will revive me;
You will stretch out Your hand
Against the wrath of my enemies,
And Your right hand will save me.
The Lord will perfect *that which* **concerns me;**
Your mercy, O Lord, *endures* **forever;**
Do not forsake the works of Your hands.

a. **Though I walk in the midst of trouble, You will revive me**: As David considered the greatness of God and His kindness to the humble (verses 4-6), it gave him confidence that God would **revive** him in his present **trouble**. Understanding God's greatness and kindness builds our faith.

b. **Your right hand will save me**: When God's help came, it would come with all His skill and strength (**Your right hand**). God would defend David **against the wrath** of his **enemies**.

i. "Thou shall strike them with thy left hand, and save me with thy right." (Trapp)

ii. "Adversaries may be many, and malicious, and mighty; but our glorious Defender has only to stretch out his arm and their armies vanish." (Spurgeon)

c. **The Lord will perfect that which concerns me**: This was David's confident declaration. He knew that God had a plan concerning him, and this God of greatness and goodness would absolutely **perfect** that plan.

i. "This is the language of utmost confidence.... The hope is based, not upon the determination of the singer, but upon Jehovah." (Morgan)

ii. This is another way of stating the great promise of Philippians 1:6: *being confident of this very thing, that He who has begun a good work in you will complete it until the day of Jesus Christ.*

iii. David could think of the particular promise (2 Samuel 7) that God had made concerning him – that his descendants would rule forever, especially fulfilled in the Messiah. The principle is true for every believer regarding the promise and course of life God has appointed for him.

iv. Maclaren noted the connection between the phrases **the Lord will perfect** and **Your mercy, O Lord, endures forever**: "Because Jehovah's lovingkindness endures forever, every man on whom His shaping Spirit has begun to work, or His grace in any form to bestow its gifts, may be sure that no exhaustion or change of these is possible."

d. **Do not forsake the works of Your hands**: With confidence in the never-ending **mercy** (*hesed*) of Yahweh, David knew that God would never forsake him, who belonged to God by creation and redemption.

i. "Look upon the wounds of thy hands, and forsake not the works of thy hands, prayed Queen Elizabeth. And Luther's usual prayer was, Confirm, O God, in us that thou hast wrought, and perfect the work that thou hast begun in us, to thy glory; so be it." (Trapp)

ii. His creating hands formed our souls at the beginning; his nail-pierced hands redeemed them on Calvary; his glorified hands will hold our souls fast and not let them go for ever." (Burgon, cited in Spurgeon)

Psalm 139 – Praise and Prayer to the God Who Knows All and Is Everywhere

This magnificent psalm is titled **For the Chief Musician. A Psalm of David.** *It does not surprise us that such a significant psalm came from David's pen, who was "the sweet psalmist of Israel" (2 Samuel 23:1). The* **Chief Musician** *is thought by some to be the* LORD *God Himself, and others suppose him to be a leader of choirs or musicians in David's time, such as Heman the singer or Asaph (1 Chronicles 6:33, 16:4-7, and 25:6).*

"Let the modern wits, after this, look upon the honest shepherds of Palestine as a company of rude and unpolished clowns; let them, if they can, produce from profane authors thoughts that are more sublime, more delicate, or better turned; not to mention the sound divinity and solid piety which are apparent under these expressions." (Claude Fleury, cited in Charles Spurgeon)

A. The greatness of God touches my life.

1. (1-6) The all-knowing God knows me.

O LORD, You have searched me and known *me.*
You know my sitting down and my rising up;
You understand my thought afar off.
You comprehend my path and my lying down,
And are acquainted with all my ways.
For *there is* not a word on my tongue,
But behold, O LORD, You know it altogether.
You have hedged me behind and before,
And laid Your hand upon me.
Such knowledge *is* too wonderful for me;
It is high, I cannot *attain* it.

    a. **You have searched me and known me:** David prayed to Yahweh, understanding that He had personal knowledge of him. Pagans often thought that their gods were hostile or indifferent to men and women; David knew that the true God cared enough to have **searched** and **known** each man and woman.

- It's not just that God knows everything – *He knows me.*
- It's not just that God is everywhere – *He is everywhere with me.*
- It's not just that God created everything – *He created me.*

> i. "Any small thoughts that we may have of God are magnificently transcended by this psalm; yet for all its height and depth it remains intensely personal from first to last." (Kidner)

> ii. "All my postures, gestures, practices...whether I sit, stand, walk, lie; thou searchest and knowest all. Some search, but know not; thou dost both." (Trapp)

b. **You know my sitting down and my rising up**: David used this proverbial phrase to say that God knew *everything* about him, even the most everyday things. As Jesus would later say, God knows the number of hairs on our head (Matthew 10:30).

> i. "Even these inconsiderable and casual things are under thy continual notice. I cannot so much as *take a seat*, or *leave it*, without being marked by thee." (Clarke)

> ii. VanGemeren points out that when looking **You know** (verse 2) and *You covered* (verse 13) in the Hebrew grammar, the emphasis is on **You**. "This section continues the emphasis on divine involvement by an emphatic use of 'you'."

c. **You understand my thought afar off**: God not only knew the smallest aspects of David's everyday life; He also knew his *thoughts*. God knows our words before we speak them, and there is nothing of us hidden from the all-knowing God. As David wrote, You **are acquainted with all my ways**.

> i. "Divine knowledge is perfect, since not a single word is unknown, nay, not even an unspoken word, and each one is '*altogether*' or wholly known." (Spurgeon)

> ii. The fact that God knows every **word on my tongue** should affect my speech. Those who claim to be disciples of Jesus Christ, yet use profanity or impurity of speech, should remember that God hears and knows every word.

d. **You have hedged me behind and before**: The normal sense of a *hedge* in the Bible is of a protective barrier. God **hedged** David on every side, so that nothing could come to David unless it first passed through God's permission. What was true for David is true for all who trust in the LORD.

i. It can be very uncomfortable to know that you are always being watched. We may get nervous if we see video cameras monitoring us at all times. Yet our unease is based on the fact that we doubt the good intentions or good will of those who watch us. The child is comforted that a loving parent watches over him; when we are confident in the love and care of God our Father, His constant knowledge of us is a comfort rather than a curse.

e. **And laid Your hand upon me**: As with the hedge, this was an expression of God's love and care for David. This was not the hand of oppression, but the hand of grace.

i. "This statement of omniscience is characteristically vivid and concrete: not formulated as a doctrine but, as befits a psalm, confessed in adoration. This divine knowledge is not merely comprehensive, like that of some receptor that misses nothing, capturing everything alike. It is personal and active." (Kidner)

f. **Such knowledge is too wonderful for me**: David understood that God knew him *better than he knew himself*, a wonderful and humble place to be. We sometimes reject what God and His word say about us and our condition; we should recognize that He knows us better than we know ourselves.

i. **Too wonderful for me**: "I cannot grasp it. I can hardly endure to think of it. The theme overwhelms me. I am amazed and astounded at it. Such knowledge not only surpasses my comprehension, but even my imagination." (Spurgeon)

2. (7-12) The all-present God is with me.

Where can I go from Your Spirit?
Or where can I flee from Your presence?
If I ascend into heaven, You *are* there;
If I make my bed in hell, behold, You *are there*.
***If* I take the wings of the morning,**
***And* dwell in the uttermost parts of the sea,**
Even there Your hand shall lead me,
And Your right hand shall hold me.
If I say, "Surely the darkness shall fall on me,"
Even the night shall be light about me;
Indeed, the darkness shall not hide from You,
But the night shines as the day;
The darkness and the light *are* both alike *to You*.

a. **Where can I go from Your Spirit**: David considered the truth that God is present everywhere, and there is no corner or dimension of the universe hidden from Him. **Heaven** isn't too high and **hell** isn't too low; God is everywhere.

> i. "Here he argueth God's omniscience from his omnipresence." (Trapp)

> ii. "The psalmist is not trying to evade God, but he further amplifies that God's knowledge is beyond the ability of humans to grasp. The knowledge or discernment of God can never be limited to any particular place, because God's sovereignty extends to the whole created universe." (VanGemeren)

> iii. "The Psalmist speaks of God as a Person everywhere present in creation, yet distinct from creation. In these verses he says, '*Thy spirit... thy* presence...*thou* art there...*thy* hand...*thy* right hand...darkness hideth not from *thee.*' God is everywhere, but he is not everything." (Jones, cited in Spurgeon)

b. **Your Spirit?.... Your presence?** David probably did not have a deep understanding of Trinitarian theology, but by the inspiration of God he spoke of God's **Spirit** as an essential aspect of His being and **presence**.

> i. **From Your presence:** "*Mippaneycha*, 'from thy faces.' Why do we meet with this word so frequently in the *plural* number, when applied to God? And why have we his *Spirit*, and his *appearances* or *faces, both* here? A *Trinitarian* would at once say, 'The plurality of persons in the Godhead is intended;' and who can *prove* that he is mistaken?" (Clarke)

> ii. "The presence of God's glory is in heaven; the presence of his power on earth; the presence of his justice in hell; and the presence of his grace with his people." (Mason, cited in Spurgeon)

c. **If I make my bed in hell, behold, You are there**: David did not describe what we normally think of as *hell* – Gehenna (Matthew 10:28 and 18:9), the lake of fire (Revelation 20:14-15). The Hebrew word here is *sheol*, which normally has the sense of *the grave* or by implication *the afterlife*.

> i. Though David did not use the specific word for **hell**, the sense would be the same. Even in hell, God will be present because there is no place where God cannot be. Yet God's presence in hell will radiate none of His love and grace – only His righteous judgment.

> ii. "Heaven is the seat of his glory, creation the scene of his providence, and the grave itself will be the theatre of his power." (Horne)

iii. "Thou art in *heaven*, in thy glory; in *hell*, in thy vindictive justice; and in all *parts of earth, water, space, place*, or *vacuity*, by thy *omnipresence*." (Clarke)

d. **Wings of the morning**: This may well refer to the spread and speed of light as it fills the morning sky from the east to the west. Light itself can not outrun God's presence and knowledge.

i. "Light flies with inconceivable rapidity, and it flashes far afield beyond all human ken; it illuminates the great and wide sea, and sets its waves gleaming afar; but its speed would utterly fail if employed in flying from the Lord." (Spurgeon)

e. **Even there Your hand shall lead me**: David was so assured of the constant presence of God's **hand** of love and care that not even death and the grave could separate him from God's love – as Paul would later write in Romans 8:38-39. In fact, God's **right hand** – His hand of skill and strength – would **hold** David no matter what may come.

i. "The piety and charity which are patiently endured in the field, and on the bed of sickness; the misery and torment inflicted by persecution in the mines, the galleys, and the dungeons; all are under the inspection of Jehovah, and are noted down by him against the day of recompense." (Horne)

f. **Even the night shall be light about me**: God's presence with David was like a constant light in the darkness. As the pillar of cloud illuminated Israel in the wilderness (Exodus 13:21), so with God's presence **the night shines as the day**.

i. "Darkness may, indeed, conceal us and our deeds from the sight of men; but the divine presence, like that of the sun, turns night into day, and makes all things manifest before God." (Horne)

ii. "Darkness is light to Him, and has no hiding place from Him." (Morgan)

3. (13-16) The eternal God formed me.

For You formed my inward parts;
You covered me in my mother's womb.
I will praise You, for I am fearfully *and* wonderfully made;
Marvelous are Your works,
And *that* my soul knows very well.
My frame was not hidden from You,
When I was made in secret,
***And* skillfully wrought in the lowest parts of the earth.**
Your eyes saw my substance, being yet unformed.

And in Your book they all were written,
The days fashioned for me,
When *as yet there were* **none of them.**

a. **For You formed my inward parts**: The God of all knowledge and constant presence had the care and concern to personally form the child in his **mother's womb**. It speaks of the fact that God knew David from before his birth, as a child conceived and developing in the womb.

i. That fact that God knows and cares for children *in the womb* means that God's concern for life begins at conception. It means that God's people have a responsibility to also know and care for children in the womb.

ii. Some people argue for the moral right to have an abortion because the mother has the right to do as she pleases with her own body. Psalm 139 demonstrates that God sees *another person* in the mother's womb.

b. **I will praise You, for I am fearfully and wonderfully made**: David the son of Jesse was a remarkable man. He was a shepherd, a special forces soldier, a hero, a poet, and a king. In some respects, here he also added *scientist* to his accomplishments. With the mind of a trained biologist but the skill of a poet, David declared that he was **fearfully and wonderfully made**.

i. The workings of the human body are stunning in their design and execution. We know far more than David ever did about how we are **made**, and it should make us full of more awe and praise than David ever had.

ii. "Thy infinite power and wisdom, manifested in the rare and curious structure of man's body, doth fill me with wonder and astonishment, and with the dread of thy majesty." (Poole)

iii. "The Psalmist had scarcely peered within the veil which hides the nerves, sinews, and blood-vessels from common inspection; the science of anatomy was quite unknown to him; and yet he had seen enough to arouse his admiration of the work and his reverence for the Worker." (Spurgeon)

iv. "The greatest miracle in the world is man; in whose very body (how much more in his soul!) are miracles enough (between head and feet) to fill a volume." (Trapp)

v. "If we are marvelously wrought upon even before we are born, what shall we say of the Lord's dealings with us after we quit his secret workshop, and he directs our pathway through the pilgrimage of life? What shall we not say of that new birth which is even more mysterious than the first, and exhibits even more the love and wisdom of the Lord." (Spurgeon)

c. **And skillfully wrought in the lowest parts of the earth**: Here David used the phrase **lowest parts of the earth** to refer to any mysterious, unseen place. The process of a baby's formation in a mother's womb has always been as unseen and mysterious as that which happens **in the lowest parts of the earth**.

i. **Skillfully wrought**: "Hebrew *embroidered*; exquisitely composed of bones, and muscles, and sinews, and veins, and arteries, and other parts, all framed with such wonderful skill, that even heathens, upon the contemplation of all the parts of man's body, and how excellently they were framed, both for beauty and use, have broken forth into pangs of admiration and adoration of the Creator of man." (Poole)

ii. The work of God in fashioning the body of the individual has made some people wonder about the presence of birth defects, and what that may mean regarding God's work. We should regard such birth defects as injuries to God's original design, and even as a person may be injured out of the womb, so they can be injured while still in the womb and in the process of formation. Such injuries are the result of the fall and the corruption it introduced into the world, yet still the eye of faith can see the hand of God at work in what defects or injuries He would allow in His providence.

iii. **The lowest parts of the earth**: "The mysterious receptacle in which the unborn body takes shape and grows is delicately described as 'secret' and likened to the hidden region of the underworld, where are the dead. The point of comparison is the mystery enwrapping both." (Maclaren)

iv. "Much of the formation of our inner man still proceeds in secret; hence the more of solitude the better for us." (Spurgeon)

d. **Your eyes saw my substance, being yet unformed**: What David (and others) could not see, God could see perfectly. This is another demonstration of his perfect knowledge and care.

i. The Puritan commentator John Trapp had a strange statement on the phrase **was not hidden**: "Aquinas saith that at the resurrection the bodies of the saints shall be so clear and transparent that all the veins, humours, nerves, and bowels shall be seen, as in a glass. It is sure that they are so to God when first formed in the womb."

e. **In Your book they were all written, the days fashioned for me**: God's perfect knowledge did not only extend to the past, before David was born.

It also extended to the future, and God knew David's **days** as if they had been **written in a book.**

i. "The Lord's writing in the book (cf. Psalm 51:1; Psalm 69:28) refers to God's knowledge and blessing of his child 'all the days' of his life (cf. Ephesians 2:10). His life was written in the book of life, and each of his days was numbered." (VanGemeren)

B. Our response to the greatness of God.

1. (17-18) The precious nature of God's thoughts to me.

How precious also are Your thoughts to me, O God!
How great is the sum of them!
If **I should count them, they would be more in number than the sand;**
When I awake, I am still with You.

a. **How precious also are Your thoughts to me, O God**: David was filled with amazement and adoration by considering how God knew and cared for him. It is **precious** that God should think of us at all; it is beyond **precious** that He would think *well* of us and think *so often* of us.

i. **How precious**: "The root meaning of the word rendered 'precious' is weighty. The singer would weigh God's thoughts towards him, and finds that they weigh down his scales." (Maclaren)

ii. "He is not alarmed at the fact that God knows all about him; on the contrary, he is comforted, and even feels himself to be enriched, as with a casket of precious jewels. That God should think upon him is the believer's treasure and pleasure." (Spurgeon)

b. **If I should count them, they would be more in number than the sand**: David used a powerful image to illustrate the idea of how *often* God thinks of us. We imagine standing on a shore and wondering just how many grains of **sand** fill the beach – yet God's thoughts are **more in number.**

i. "Thoughts such as are natural to the Creator, the Preserver, the Redeemer, the Father, the Friend, are evermore flowing from the heart of the Lord. Thoughts of our pardon, renewal, upholding, supplying, educating, perfecting, and a thousand more kinds perpetually well up in the mind of the Most High." (Spurgeon)

ii. "You know that people are very proud if a king has merely looked at them; I have heard of a man who used to boast, all his life, that King George IV. – such a beauty as he was! – once spoke to him. He only said, 'Get out of the road;' but it was a king who said it, so the man felt greatly gratified thereby. But you and I, beloved, can rejoice that

God, before whom kings are as grasshoppers, actually thinks of us, and thinks of us often." (Spurgeon)

c. **When I awake, I am still with You**: Day or night, David thought of God because he knew the greatness of God's **thoughts to** him. At the waking of the day, the wonderful presence of God was **still with** him.

> i. "He awakes from sleep, and is conscious of glad wonder to find that, like a tender mother by her slumbering child, God has been watching over him, and that all the blessed communion of past days abides as before." (Maclaren)

> ii. The thoughts about the greatness of God's love "…are like a dream; but, unlike a dream, God's love is real. When awake the psalmist knows that he still enjoys God's presence." (VanGemeren)

> iii. "*When I awake* may therefore have its strongest sense, a glimpse of resurrection." (Kidner)

2. (19-22) Longing for righteousness and justice.

Oh, that You would slay the wicked, O God!
Depart from me, therefore, you bloodthirsty men.
For they speak against You wickedly;
Your enemies take *Your name* in vain.
Do I not hate them, O LORD, who hate You?
And do I not loathe those who rise up against You?
I hate them with perfect hatred;
I count them my enemies.

a. **Oh, that You would slay the wicked**: David abruptly shifted from a spirit of wonder and adoration to intense prayer against **the wicked** and against **bloodthirsty men**. It wasn't primarily because these men opposed David, but because they opposed God: **for they speak against You wickedly**. David's adoration filled him with zeal for God's honor.

> i. "The abrupt change in the psalm from reverie to resolve is disturbing, but wholly biblical in its realism." (Kidner)

> ii. "Crimes committed before the face of the Judge are not likely to go unpunished.... God who sees all evil will slay all evil." (Spurgeon)

> iii. "A faithful servant hath the same interests, the same friends, the same enemies with his Master, whose cause and honor he is, upon all occasions, in duty bound to support and maintain." (Horne)

b. **Do I not hate them, O LORD, who hate You?** David was undeniably God's partisan. He wanted to be on God's side, and therefore even allowed himself to **hate** those who hated God. In fact, David boasted **I hate them with perfect hatred**, regarding them as **enemies**.

i. David went against a spirit also evident in our day – against the idea that we can love God without hating evil. It is entirely possible for a person to be *too* loving, and it corrupts his claimed love for God.

ii. "A good man hates, as God himself doth: he hates not the persons of men, but their sins; not what God made them, but what they have made themselves." (Horne)

iii. "We are neither to hate the men, on account of the vices they practice; nor to love the vices, for the sake of the men who practice them." (Horne)

3. (23-24) A humble prayer to a great God.

Search me, O God, and know my heart;
Try me, and know my anxieties;
And see if *there is any* wicked way in me,
And lead me in the way everlasting.

a. **Search me, O God, and know my heart**: David came to the God of perfect knowledge and constant presence knowing He was also a God of love, and could be trusted to **search** him and to **know** him at the deepest levels. This is also an admission that God knew David better than David knew himself, and that he needed God to **search** and **know** him.

i. David took his theological understanding of God's nature and attributes and applied it to his own personal discipleship. The nature and attributes of God were not mere theories; they were guides to David's spiritual growth.

ii. David knew that *he* could not know his heart at its depths, so he asked God to know it. "The ultimate word of Greek philosophy, 'Man, know thyself,' was really valuable because it brought man face to face with the impossible." (Morgan)

iii. "Very beautifully does the lowly prayer for searching and guidance follow the psalmist's burst of fire. It is easier to glow with indignation against evildoers than to keep oneself from doing evil. Many secret sins may hide under a cloak of zeal for the Lord." (Maclaren)

iv. "The rejection of evil arises from the psalmist's spirit of commitment to the Lord and not from pride. This is clear from his prayer, asking for God to discern his motives and his actions." (VanGemeren)

v. "I call upon you to be cautious in using this prayer. It is easy to mock God, by asking him to search you whilst you have made but little effort to search yourselves, and perhaps still less to act upon the result of the scrutiny." (Melvill, cited in Spurgeon)

b. **Try me, and know my anxieties**: David wanted God to examine him and look for *worry*. Such **anxieties** could be evidence of unbelief or misplaced trust.

c. **See if there is any wicked way in me**: David opened his soul completely before God, asking if there were any unknown or unperceived sins. This showed how much he *cared* for holiness in his life, and how *humble* he was in recognizing that there could be an unperceived **wicked way** in himself.

i. When prayed sincerely, this is something of a dangerous prayer – worthy, yet dangerous. "It is a serious thing to pray, because it invites painful exposures and surgery, if we truly mean it. Still it is what every wise believer should desire." (Boice)

ii. "The [King James Version] says 'wicked way'; but the [Revised Version] margin gives 'way of grief.' We may be in a way that causes God grief, even though it is not what men might term a way of wickedness." (Meyer)

d. **Lead me in the way everlasting**: David ended this majestic psalm by declaring his destination – **the way everlasting**. Trusting the God of complete knowledge and constant presence would bring David to **everlasting** life. The way of holiness prayed for in the previous lines was the **way everlasting**.

i. "We have been going in ways of grief. We desire to go in the way everlasting – the way of eternal life; the way which we shall never need to retrace; the way that touches the deepest life possible to the creature." (Meyer)

ii. "The final words could be translated 'the ancient way' as in Jeremiah 6:16 (cf. Revised Standard Version mg., New English Bible); but the majority of translators would appear to be right in rendering them *the way everlasting*, in contrast to the way of the wicked which will perish." (Kidner)

Psalm 140 – The Cry and Confidence of a Slandered Soul

This psalm is titled **To the Chief Musician. A Psalm of David.** *The theme is similar to many of David's other psalms, in which he cried out to God in a time of trouble. This trouble seems to be slander against him, perhaps when he was a fugitive escaping from Saul's court.*

The Chief Musician *is thought by some to be the* LORD *God Himself, and others suppose him to be a leader of choirs or musicians in David's time, such as Heman the singer or Asaph (1 Chronicles 6:33, 16:4-7, and 25:6). Charles Spurgeon remarked, "The writer wished this experimental hymn to be under the care of the chief master of song, that it might neither be left unsung, nor chanted in a slovenly manner."*

A. Evil men, their evil words, the evil plots.

1. (1-3) Praying for deliverance.

Deliver me, O LORD, from evil men;
Preserve me from violent men,
Who plan evil things in their hearts;
They continually gather together for war.
They sharpen their tongues like a serpent;
The poison of asps is under their lips. Selah

> a. **Deliver me, O LORD, from evil men**: Many times in David's life, he suffered under the presence and pressure of **evil** and **violent men**. This desperate song came from such a time, and shows its urgency by having no prelude of praise or contemplation. David went straight to his plea.
>
> > i. "The singer was being slandered by evil and violent men, who were prepared if occasion offered to add actual violence to their lying speech." (Morgan)

243

ii. "Slander and calumny must always precede and accompany persecution, because malice itself cannot excite people against a good man, as such; to do this, he must first be represented as a bad man." (Horne)

iii. "The persecuted man turns to God in prayer; he could not do a wiser thing. Who can meet the evil man and defeat him save Jehovah himself, whose infinite goodness is more than a match for all the evil in the universe?" (Spurgeon)

b. **Who plan evil things in their hearts**: Those **evil men** were known by the **evil things in their hearts**. Their evil actions were not accidents disconnected from their true nature, as shown in that they were always ready for conflict and **war**.

i. **Evil things in their hearts**: "It is an awful thing to have such a heart-disease as this. When the imagination gloats over doing harm to others, it is a sure sign that the entire nature is far gone in wickedness." (Spurgeon)

ii. **They continually gather together for war**: John Trapp noted that the Hebrew is "…they gather wars, as serpents gather poison to vomit out at others." (Trapp)

c. **They sharpen their tongues like a serpent**: The desire for **war** and **evil things** is often expressed in sharp and poisonous words. David felt both the sting and the poison of such men and their words.

i. "*Like a serpent*; either whetting their tongues, as serpents are said to whet theirs when they are about to bite; or rather, using words as sharp and piercing as the sting of a serpent." (Poole)

ii. "It was a common notion that serpents inserted their poison by their tongues, and the poets used the idea as a poetical expression, although it is certain that the serpent wounds by his fangs and not by his tongue. We are not to suppose that all authors who used such language were mistaken in their natural history any more than a writer can be charged with ignorance of astronomy because he speaks of the sun's travelling from east to west." (Spurgeon)

iii. **Asps**: "The word rendered '*adder*' [**asps**], *achsub*, occurs here only; and it is perhaps impossible to determine what species is intended. As the word, in its proper signification, seems to express coiling, or bending back – an act common to most serpents." (Kitto, cited in Spurgeon)

iv. Paul quoted verse 3 in Romans 3:13 as part of his description of man's deep sinfulness. In principle, Paul expanded the idea beyond

David's original sense and applied the concept to *all* humanity in its fallen condition.

d. **Selah**: This word indicates some kind of pause, either for a musical expression or for careful thought and meditation – or both. **Selah** is repeated three times in this psalm, and here indicates that the deep sinfulness of man is worthy of our careful consideration. We often think too little of God's greatness *and* too little of man's sinfulness.

i. "What emerges clearly from this passage is the evil that can arise, not from any pressure of circumstances but from a love of violence, cruelty and intrigue for their own sake." (Kidner)

ii. "We meet with *Selah* here for the first time since Psalm 89. From Psalm 90 to Psalm 140 no *Selah* occurs. Why omitted in these fifty we cannot tell any more than why so often recurring in others. However, there are only about forty psalms in all in which it is used." (Bonar, cited in Spurgeon)

2. (4-5) Praying for preservation.

Keep me, O LORD, from the hands of the wicked;
Preserve me from violent men,
Who have purposed to make my steps stumble.
The proud have hidden a snare for me, and cords;
They have spread a net by the wayside;
They have set traps for me. Selah

a. **Keep me, O LORD, from the hands of the wicked**: In the first portion of this psalm, David acknowledged the presence of **wicked** and **violent men**. With such a realistic view, he then requested of God, "**Preserve me from violent men.**"

i. "Thus David was hunted as a rebel, Christ was crucified as a blasphemer, and the primitive Christians were tortured as guilty of incest and murder." (Horne)

ii. "The 'wicked' may arrogantly desire, plan, and execute; but the Master of the universe cannot tolerate anarchy for long. To this end the plea changes into an imprecatory prayer." (VanGemeren)

b. **The proud have hidden a snare for me**: They hoped to make David trip over a series of hidden snares, **cords**, nets, and **traps**, many of which were expressed in their poisonous words (verse 3). David was not blind to the traps, but he had hope in God's help.

i. "They hunted David as they would a dangerous wild beast: one while striving to *pierce* him with the spear; another to *entangle* him in their snares, so as to take and sacrifice him before the people, on pretense of his being an *enemy to the state.*" (Clarke)

ii. "David's enemies wished to snare him in his path of service, the usual way of his life. Saul laid many snares for David, but the Lord preserved him." (Spurgeon)

iii. "How are 'the snares, the nets'…placed for us by that cunning and experienced artist, who takes care that nothing should appear in view, but the alluring baits of honour, pleasure, and profit, while of the toils we have no notice, till we find ourselves entangled and caught in them!" (Horne)

iv. "If a godly man can be cajoled, or bribed, or cowed, or made angry, the wicked will make the attempt. Ready are they to twist his words, misread his intentions, and misdirect his efforts; ready to fawn, and lie, and make themselves mean to the last degree so that they may accomplish their abominable purpose." (Spurgeon)

c. **Selah**: When David considered the *danger* coming from those who opposed him, it prompted a thoughtful pause.

B. Seeking God's help.

1. (6-8) Praying to the God of strength and salvation.

I said to the LORD: "You *are* my God;
Hear the voice of my supplications, O LORD.
O GOD the Lord, the strength of my salvation,
You have covered my head in the day of battle.
Do not grant, O LORD, the desires of the wicked;
Do not further his *wicked* scheme,
***Lest* they be exalted. Selah**

a. **You are my God**: David would worship no other god; his allegiance was to Yahweh alone. This devotion gave him confidence that God would **hear the voice of** his **supplications**. God doesn't just hear the words of the cry, but the **voice** of the cry. It is distinctive and meaningful to Him.

i. "'Thou art my God,' in opposition to the gods of the heathen. They may worship Baal and Asherah, but ' thou art my God.' I count other gods to be idols, the works of men's hands, and I despise them." (Spurgeon)

b. **O GOD the Lord, the strength of my salvation**: David cried out to Yahweh (**GOD**) his Master (**Lord**, *adonai*), recognizing *Him* as the Lord of his life, and no other god. The true God could actually help David, being **the strength of** his **salvation**.

i. "To himself, and to all others, his escape has been marvelous. How could it be accounted for, except that an unseen shield had been around him, covering his head in the day of battle." (Meyer)

c. **You have covered my head in the day of battle**: David knew many literal battles, but he also lived through many battles with lying and slanderous men. David testified that God had been his protection, his shield, his armor in those battles. According to Meyer (cited in Spurgeon), **day of battle** is better translated, "day of armor."

i. "That is to say, *God had been David's Armour-bearer*. The Lord had borne a shield before him; instead of the harness in which warriors put their confidence, God had covered David with a coat of mail [armor] through which no sword of the enemy could possibly cut its way." (Spurgeon)

d. **Do not grant, O LORD, the desires of the wicked**: In recognizing the supremacy of Yahweh, David realized that if God *were* to help the **wicked**, then they would **be exalted**. He prayed for God to work for His people and against **the desires of the wicked**.

e. **Selah**: When David considered the need for the wicked to be stopped in their evil plotting, it prompted a thoughtful pause.

2. (9-11) David's prayer regarding the wicked.

"*As for* the head of those who surround me,
Let the evil of their lips cover them;
Let burning coals fall upon them;
Let them be cast into the fire,
Into deep pits, that they rise not up again.
Let not a slanderer be established in the earth;
Let evil hunt the violent man to overthrow *him*."

a. **As for the head of those who surround me**: Since we don't know the exact occasion in David's life for this prayer, we don't know who he meant by **the head**. It could have been Saul, who was David's long and persistent enemy. It could have been Doeg, who was an evil, violent man who bore a false report against David (1 Samuel 21-22).

i. If this prayer is about Saul, it is another significant example of how David would not violently strike against Saul even when he had the opportunity (1 Samuel 24:1-7, 1 Samuel 26:7-11). David would not touch Saul; for all his sins and faults, Saul was God's anointed king. When David was attacked by Saul, he would pour out his heart in prayer to the LORD, entrusting Saul's punishment to God in heaven, rather than taking it in his own hands.

b. **Let the evil of their lips cover them**: David prayed for simple justice in regard to his enemies. He prayed they would be covered with the same **evil** they had spoken against others. Under the New Covenant, we are told not to return evil for evil (Romans 12:17), but we sympathize with David's cry for justice.

i. "Their lips, which uttered mischief against others, shall be the means of covering themselves with confusion, when out of their own mouths they shall be judged. Those tongues, which have contributed to set the world on fire, shall be tormented with the hot burning coals of eternal vengeance." (Horne)

c. **Let burning coals fall upon them**: David prayed that the same fire that wicked men poured out on others would be poured out on them. He prayed that this would destroy the wicked, and that they would be hunted by evil until they were overthrown.

i. "The *burning coals* and *pits* are probably metaphorical, the former for the searing words which they have loved to use…the latter for the traps and pitfalls they have made for others." (Kidner)

ii. "The Psalmist doubtless had before his mind's eye the picture of Sodom, where burning coals fell on the guilty cities, and where men stumbled into the fire, and when they tried to escape, fell into the deep slime pits, and perished." (Spurgeon)

d. **Let evil hunt the violent man**: These evil men hunted David (verses 4-6). David prayed that the same would be returned to them – that the hunters would be hunted by their very **evil**.

i. "God's judgments against sinners are feathered from themselves, as a fowl shot with an arrow feathered from her own body." (Trapp)

ii. "Evil speakers and false accusers shall gain no lasting establishment, but punishment shall hunt sin through all its doubles, and seize it at last as its legal prey." (Horne)

3. (12-13) Confidence in God's victory.

I know that the LORD will maintain
The cause of the afflicted,
And justice for the poor.
Surely the righteous shall give thanks to Your name;
The upright shall dwell in Your presence.

a. **I know that the LORD will maintain the cause of the afflicted**: David remained confident that God would defend His **afflicted** people. This would mean **justice for the poor** and others who suffer from the words and works of wicked men.

i. VanGemeren remarked that the verb form of **I know** is "…expressive of a present condition…a victory cry."

ii. "**I know,** both by God's word, which hath promised it, and by my own experience of it in the course of God's providence." (Poole)

iii. "The final movement (vv. Psalm 140:11-13) is an affirmation of faith. The singer is confident that in the government of Jehovah evil men cannot continue. The afflicted will be delivered, and the righteous and upright will be perfectly vindicated." (Morgan)

iv. "That unjust and oppressive men shall, in the end, suffer proportionably…we are assured from this consideration, namely, that the Almighty is the patron of the injured and oppressed." (Horne)

v. "Many talk as if the poor had no rights worth noticing, but they will sooner or later find out their mistake when the judge of all the earth begins to plead with them." (Spurgeon)

vi. "Every person who is *persecuted* for righteousness' sake has God for his *peculiar help* and *refuge*; and the *persecutor* has the same God for his *especial enemy.*" (Clarke)

b. **Surely the righteous shall give thanks to Your name**: This psalm ends on a note of confidence. Though assaulted by the wicked, David put his trust in the Lord, and gave all his desire for retribution unto Him. David believed that in the end, **the righteous** would be thankful and **the upright** would **dwell in Your presence** – the best reward of all.

i. "At the time of the intervention and vindication, 'the righteous'… will alter their prayers for deliverance…to songs of triumph." (VanGemeren)

ii. "The last line is wholly positive. His heart is free to find its true home, and his last words match the climax to which the whole of Scripture moves: 'His servants shall serve him: and they shall see his face' (Rev. 22:3f.)." (Kidner)

iii. G. Campbell Morgan noted that Psalm 140 begins in great trouble and sorrow, but ends in praise and triumph. "If sorrow is a certainty, so also is the action of Jehovah…. Sorrow and darkness come to all men, but only those who know God and are sure of Him, make suffering, and the night, occasions of triumphant psalmody."

Psalm 141 – No Compromise

This psalm has the title **A Psalm of David**. *It shows David as a man of tender conscience, who asked God to deal with his own sin and weakness before addressing the wicked men who fought against him. It shows that David was even more concerned about evil inside himself than he was about evil from others.*

"The colourful Hebrew of the middle verses is difficult, but the thrust of the psalm is plain: a prayer against insincerity and compromise, and a plea for survival under the savage attacks which such an attitude has invited." (Derek Kidner)

According to John Trapp, the great preacher of the early church John Chrysostom said this psalm was used in his era (A.D. 349-407) as part of the evening liturgy in the Greek Church, due to the reference in verse 2 to the evening sacrifice.

A. The nature of David's prayer.

1. (1-2) A prayer like incense.

Lord, I cry out to You;
Make haste to me!
Give ear to my voice when I cry out to You.
Let my prayer be set before You *as* incense,
The lifting up of my hands *as* the evening sacrifice.

a. **Lord, I cry out to You; make haste to me**: David's need was urgent, so he directed his prayer to the true God (Yahweh, the **Lord**) and begged him to help with **haste**.

i. "I have cried unto thee, I still cry to thee, and I always mean to cry to thee. To whom else could I go? What else can I do? Others trust to themselves, but I cry unto thee." (Spurgeon)

b. **Give ear to my voice**: When a child cries out to a parent, the parent hears not only the words but the **voice** of the cry. The Lord can hear the **voice** of His people when they **cry out** to Him, and it moves Him to action.

c. **Let my prayer be set before You as incense**: David used the smoke and smell of **incense** as a representation of his **prayer** to God. His posture of prayer (**the lifting up of my hands**) was a gift to God even as **the evening sacrifice** was a gift to God. Revelation 5:8 says that the prayers of God's people are like incense, and Hebrews 13:15 describes praise as a sacrifice unto God.

- Prayer rises to heaven even as the smoke of incense rises upward.

- Prayer pleases God even as incense has a pleasing smell.

- Prayer needs some "fire" to be effective (James 5:16 speaks of "…the effective, fervent prayer"), and incense is activated with fire.

  i. If David wrote this psalm while a fugitive from King Saul, then the ideas of **incense** and the **evening sacrifice** held special meaning, because he was not free to publically go to the tabernacle and share in these acts of worship. When necessity kept him from the tabernacle, prayer would replace the offering of incense and sacrifice.

  ii. "Incense was offered every morning and evening before the Lord, on the golden altar, before the veil of the sanctuary. Exodus 29:39, and Numbers 28:4." (Clarke)

  iii. **Incense** connected with the tabernacle and temple rituals needed to be pure and it needed to be prepared. David intended to offer pure and prepared prayers unto God.

  iv. "The raising up of one's hands was symbolic of dependence on and praise of the Lord." (VanGemeren)

2. (3-4) A prayer to be kept from evil.

Set a guard, O Lord, over my mouth;
Keep watch over the door of my lips.
Do not incline my heart to any evil thing,
To practice wicked works
With men who work iniquity;
And do not let me eat of their delicacies.

a. **Set a guard, O Lord, over my mouth**: David didn't want the same mouth that prayed as if it were incense to be used for lies or any **evil thing**. He asked God to **keep watch over the door of my lips**, so that he would not say evil or foolish things.

  i. **Keep watch over the door of my lips**: "That it move not creaking, and complaining, as on rusty hinges, for want of the oil of joy and gladness." (Trapp)

ii. "If the house of God needed its guards and doorkeepers, how much more the man of God!" (Kidner)

iii. "Nature having made my lips to be a door to my words, let grace keep that door, that no word may be suffered to go out which may any way tend to the dishonour of God, or the hurt of others." (Henry, cited in Spurgeon)

b. **Do not incline my heart to any evil thing**: David knew that it was more than his lips that needed protection; his **heart** could also be affected by some **evil thing**, resulting in **wicked works**. This was David's way of praying what Jesus later taught, *do not lead us into temptation* (Matthew 6:13).

i. "The way the heart inclines the life soon tends: evil things desired bring forth wicked things practised. Unless the fountain of life is kept pure the streams of life will soon be polluted." (Spurgeon)

ii. "The psalmist is not suffering from the hostility of the workers of iniquity, but dreads becoming infected with their sin." (Maclaren)

iii. "David is not too good for evil people; he is too much like them and therefore likely to be swept away by their wickedness if in their company." (Boice)

c. **Do not let me eat of their delicacies**: David didn't want to walk in the ways of **men who work iniquity**, so he didn't want to eat at their table either. This may have been a literal situation for David, but the principle of not enjoying all the luxuries that the wicked partake of is always relevant to God's people.

i. **Men who work iniquity**: "The word 'men'...denotes men of land, rank, and status within the community. However, these members of the aristocracy were nevertheless 'evildoers' who practiced 'wicked deeds' (cf. Psalm 28:3).... Removal of oneself from their influence and from the enjoyment of their material benefits was the second step away from temptation; dependency on the Lord was the first." (VanGemeren)

ii. Sometimes there are many advantages in an evil, wicked way. The godly man or woman knows to avoid such advantages. "My afflictions are more desirable than such prosperity." (Poole)

iii. "Instead of slander and violence, they are seeking to seduce him from his loyalty to truth and uprightness, The reference to 'their dainties' [**delicacies**] would seem to suggest that they were endeavouring to show him the advantages which he would enjoy if he would throw in his lot with theirs." (Morgan)

iv. "A Christian living among the unbelievers and sensualists in the world, hath abundant reason to put up the same prayers, and to use the same precautions." (Horne)

3. (5) A prayer to be corrected by the righteous.

Let the righteous strike me;
***It shall be* a kindness.**
And let him rebuke me;
***It shall be* as excellent oil;**
Let my head not refuse it.

a. **Let the righteous strike me**: David rejected the *delicacies* of the wicked, but embraced the correction that came from **the righteous**. He recognized that it would be **a kindness** (*hesed*) to him.

i. "In case I do offend in word or deed, let me never [lack] a faithful reprover, who may smite me as with a hammer (so the word signifieth), reprove me sharply." (Trapp)

ii. "When the ungodly smile upon us their flattery is cruel; when the righteous smite us their faithfulness is kind." (Spurgeon)

iii. "Depend upon it, the man who will tell you your faults is your best friend. It may not be a pleasant thing for him to do it, and he knows that he is running the risk of losing your friendship; but he is a true and sincere friend, therefore thank him for his reproof, and learn how you may improve by what he tells you." (Spurgeon)

b. **It shall be as excellent oil**: The **rebuke** of a good man could be as healing and helpful to David as **excellent oil** upon his **head**. Like a kind anointing from a friend, he would not **refuse** such rebuke or correction – even if it were as severe as a **strike** upon him.

i. **Excellent oil**: "[In] Hebrew a head oil, such as they poured on their friends' heads; and that was of the best." (Trapp)

ii. You may want a fresh anointing, yet miss it because it comes to you as correction from a righteous man or woman. "The fresh anointing which you seek in the morning may come not in rapt emotional experiences, but in the straight dealing of some fellow-disciple. Whenever anything is said which finds fault with you and blames you, receive it humbly and tenderly, asking whether it may not contain a message from your Father." (Meyer)

B. A prayer for preservation against the wicked.

1. (5b-7) The wicked and their work.

For still my prayer *is* against the deeds of the wicked.
Their judges are overthrown by the sides of the cliff,
And they hear my words, for they are sweet.
Our bones are scattered at the mouth of the grave,
As when one plows and breaks up the earth.

a. **Still my prayer is against the deeds of the wicked**: The previous lines described David as grateful for correction from the righteous. Still, he prayed for God's work **against the deeds of the wicked**. For example, he wanted to see wicked **judges** be **overthrown by the sides of the cliff** – a severe but fitting judgment for those who improperly take sides, ignoring David's righteous **words** (as he prayed for in verses 3-4).

i. This section of the psalm is a great challenge for the translator and the interpreter. Alexander Maclaren wrote of the phrase, **still my prayer is against the deeds of the wicked**: "But what is the meaning and bearing of the last clause of Psalm 141:5? No wholly satisfactory answer has been given."

ii. The meaning of **their judges are overthrown by the sides of the cliff** is difficult to understand from the original Hebrew. George Horne said of verse 6, "Of this verse, as it stands in our translation, I know not what can be made." Perhaps David meant King Saul, his chief enemy, yet would not name him out of a desire to avoid attacking God's chosen king.

iii. "The psalmist prays that they may die a cruel death, being thrown down the cliffs (cf. 2 Chronicles 25:12; Luke 4:29). The shock of God's judgment on their despotic regime will affect their followers and may bring them to their senses." (VanGemeren)

iv. **They hear my words, for they are sweet**: "And so they did: the death of Saul made all the best of the nation look to the son of Jesse as the Lord's anointed; his words became sweet to them." (Spurgeon)

b. **Our bones are scattered at the mouth of the grave**: This is another phrase difficult to understand from the original. Perhaps David used this word picture to describe how ruined he felt he and his righteous companions were at the **deeds of the wicked**. Those so ruined could only cry out to God for help.

i. "Our case is almost as hopeless as of those who are dead, and whose bones are scattered in several places." (Poole)

ii. "The point of the figure lies in the resemblance of the bones strewn at the mouth of Sheol to broken clods turned up by a plough. Sheol seems here to waver between the meanings of the unseen world of souls and the grave." (Maclaren)

iii. "To the Jews such a spectacle must have been very dreadful, as the want of burial was esteemed one of the greatest calamities which could befall them." (Burder, cited in Spurgeon)

2. (8-10) A prayer to find safety in the LORD.

But my eyes *are* upon You, O GOD the Lord;
In You I take refuge;
Do not leave my soul destitute.
Keep me from the snares they have laid for me,
And from the traps of the workers of iniquity.
Let the wicked fall into their own nets,
While I escape safely.

a. **But my eyes are upon You**: Even in such a terrible condition (described in the previous lines), David deliberately set his **eyes** upon the Lord. Because God Himself was his **refuge**, David prayed **do not leave my soul destitute**. Without God's protection, he was at the mercy of his wicked enemies.

i. **But my eyes are upon You**: "In all times, in all places, on all occasions, I will cleave unto the Lord, and put my whole confidence in him." (Clarke)

ii. "That he is able to say, 'Mine eyes are unto Thee, O God the Lord,' is a revelation of the fact that his anchor still holds, not only against the fierce onslaught of enemies, but also against the insidious temptation to turn aside from the path of rectitude in order to escape the vindictive opposition of his enemies." (Morgan)

iii. Remember what David said to Saul in 1 Samuel 26:19: *If the LORD has stirred you up against me, let Him accept an offering. But if it is the children of men, may they be cursed before the LORD, for they have driven me out this day from sharing in the inheritance of the LORD, saying, "Go, serve other gods."* This shows that David knew that many others lied about him to Saul, hoping to slay him with their slander. It also shows that when David was a fugitive, his enemies hoped to entice him to idolatry saying, *Go, serve other gods.* David would not; in the LORD alone he took **refuge**.

b. **Keep me from the snares they have laid for me**: The enemies of David were determined to destroy him, and so they set many **snares**, **traps**, and **nets** for him. David's prayer was that they would **fall into their own**

nets, even as he would **escape safely**. David's trust in God was repeatedly vindicated as those who sought to destroy him were themselves destroyed.

i. **Keep me from the snares**: "It is hard to keep out of snares which you cannot see, and to escape [snares] which you cannot discover. Well might the much-hunted Psalmist cry, 'Keep me.'" (Spurgeon)

ii. **While I escape safely**: "The last line ('while, as for me – I pass right on!') has a buoyancy worthy of the man who has slipped through many a net with the help of God, and is sure that his journey is by no means over." (Kidner)

iii. "What is uppermost in the psalmist's mind is, in any case, not the destruction of his enemies, but their being made powerless to prevent his "passing by" their snares uncaptured." (Maclaren)

iv. This prayer was answered. "From the sequel of the history we find that the hope and assurance here expressed by the Psalmist were not vain. He escaped all the snares that were laid for him on every side." (Horne)

Psalm 142 – My Only Refuge

Psalm 142 is titled **A Contemplation of David. A Prayer when he was in the cave.**

The Hebrew word for **Contemplation** (maskil) *could be better translated as* instruction. *"He calls this prayer Maschil, 'a Psalm of instruction,' because of the good lessons he had himself learned in the cave, learned on his knees, and so learned that he desired to teach others." (Matthew Henry, cited in Charles Spurgeon)*

The **cave** *was probably Adullam cave, mentioned in 1 Samuel 22:1, though the caves of En Gedi (1 Samuel 24:1) are also a possibility. Adullam seems to be the best fit, which would suggest that Psalms 34 and 57 are also associated with this period of David's life.*

"There are two notes running side by side throughout the song. The first is that of this terrible sense of helplessness and hopelessness so far as man is concerned. The other is that of the determined application of the helpless soul to Jehovah." (G. Campbell Morgan)

A. The preface to David's prayer.

1. (1) David's cry to the LORD.

I cry out to the LORD with my voice;
With my voice to the LORD I make my supplication.

> a. **I cry out to the LORD:** This was more than David's appeal for help. It was also his declaration of allegiance to Yahweh, the God of Israel. David knew about the pagan gods worshiped by the surrounding Gentiles, but he determined that he would never **cry out** to them – only to the LORD.

> > i. "Trouble and lack of human sympathy or help have done their best work on him, since they have driven him to God's breast. He has cried in vain to man; and now he has gathered himself up in a firm resolve to cast himself upon God." (Maclaren)

ii. "Caves make good closets for prayer; their gloom and solitude are helpful to the exercise of devotion. Had David prayed as much in his palace as he did in his cave, he might never have fallen into the act which brought such misery upon his later days." (Spurgeon)

b. **With my voice; with my voice to the Lord**: As a man of deep spiritual experience, David knew that there were many ways to **cry out to the Lord** – in thought, in feeling, in action. Here David cried out to God with his **voice**, feeling that silent feelings were not enough for his present need.

i. "David, like Bartimaeus in the Gospels, knows the value of refusing to relapse into silence. That way lies despair." (Kidner)

ii. "The state of David in the cave of Adullam was a state of utter destitution. Persecuted by his own countrymen, dismissed by Achish, and not yet joined by his own relations, or any other attendants, he took refuge in the cave, and was there alone." (Horne)

2. (2) David's complaint to the Lord.

I pour out my complaint before Him;
I declare before Him my trouble.

a. **I pour out my complaint before Him**: David had a **complaint** to bring before God. As this psalm develops, David asks for God's help in the face of enemies who hoped to trap him, so this **complaint** is likely against his enemies. Whatever the source, David did the right thing with his **complaint**; he brought it before the Lord.

i. "*My complaint* is not as petulant a word as in English, but might be rendered 'my troubled thoughts'." (Kidner)

ii. "The outpouring of complaint is not meant to tell Jehovah what He does not know. It is for the complainer's relief, not for God's information." (Maclaren)

iii. **I pour out**: "Those words teach us that in prayer we should not try to keep anything back from God, but should show him all that is in our hearts, and that in his presence in our closet, with the door shut, but not before men." (Neale and Littledale, cited in Spurgeon)

b. **I declare before Him my trouble**: David had the heart later expressed by the Apostle Paul in Philippians 4:6: *Be anxious for nothing, but in everything by prayer and supplication, with thanksgiving, let your requests be made known to God.*

i. "David had no provisions, no followers, and no place to turn.... David then went to Gath, the Philistine city, but this proved to be both dangerous and unworkable, and David eventually escaped into the wilderness again and hid in the cave of Adullam." (Boice)

ii. "it is not merely words that you have to utter, you have to lay all your trouble before God. As a child tells its mother its griefs, tell the Lord all your griefs, your complaints, your miseries, your fears. Tell them all out, and great relief will come to your spirit." (Spurgeon)

B. David's prayer.

1. (3-4) God's care for the lonely saint.

When my spirit was overwhelmed within me,
Then You knew my path.
In the way in which I walk
They have secretly set a snare for me.
Look on *my* right hand and see,
For *there is* no one who acknowledges me;
Refuge has failed me;
No one cares for my soul.

a. **When my spirit was overwhelmed within me, then You knew my path**: Any time David felt **overwhelmed**, he found confidence in knowing that God **knew** his journey and his walk. God knows our **path** and our **walk** in all of its good and all of its bad.

i. **Overwhelmed**: "David was a hero, and yet his spirit sank: he could smite a giant down, but he could not keep himself up. He did not know his own path, nor feel able to bear his own burden." (Spurgeon)

ii. **You knew my path**: "Then it is an infinite solace to look up into the face of the Father, and say: Before I was born, or took the first steps on this path, or essayed to meet its manifold vicissitudes, Thou knewest it; and Thou must have known that it was not too hard, and that there were resources of strength in Thyself sufficient for my day, which the emergency would bring out in a clearer manifestation." (Meyer)

b. **They have secretly set a snare for me**: David didn't know where the snares were, but he knew they were out there. David also knew that as He depended upon Him, God could preserve him from secret snares.

i. "The use of concealed traps is disgraceful to our enemies, but they care little to what tricks they resort for their evil purposes. Wicked men must find some exercise for their malice, and therefore when they dare not openly assail they will privately ensnare." (Spurgeon)

c. **There is no one who acknowledges me...no one cares for my soul**: David felt alone and forsaken, yet this very cry to God declares that David knew that even if he were forsaken by men, God had not forsaken him. Even if every other **refuge has failed**, David found in God an ear for the voice of his cry.

> i. **Look on my right hand and see**: "The 'right hand' is the place for a champion or helper, but this lonely sufferer's is unguarded, and there is none who knows him, in the sense of recognising him as one to be helped." (Maclaren)

> ii. "The 'right' signifies the place where one's witness or legal council stood (cf. Psalms 16:8; 109:31; 110:5; 121:5). He has no one to defend him against the adversaries." (VanGemeren)

> iii. "We have companions in joy; sorrow we have to face by ourselves. Unless we have Jesus with us in the darkness, we have no one." (Maclaren)

> iv. "In the event, it seems that God answered abundantly, soon sending David's 'brothers and all his father's house' to join him in his cave, and then by degrees a company that would become the nucleus of his kingdom (1 Sam. 22:1f.). This low ebb in his fortunes proved in fact to be a turning point." (Kidner)

> v. **No one cares for my soul**: "When danger besetteth us around, and fear is on every side, let us follow the example of David, and that of a greater than David, who, when Jews and Gentiles conspired against him, and he was left all alone, in the garden, and on the cross, gave himself unto prayer." (Horne)

2. (5) David's trust in God alone.

I cried out to You, O LORD:
I said, "You *are* my refuge,
My portion in the land of the living.

a. **You are my refuge**: Among men, David had no refuge (verse 4). Yet as he **cried out to** God, David could confidently proclaim that God was indeed his **refuge**. The cities of refuge were, in the Old Testament times, for the protection of an Israelite in special circumstances; and David found his place of **refuge** not in a place or in a particular circumstance, but in the LORD Himself.

> i. **I said**: "If David had not *cried* he would not have *said;* and if the Lord had not been his *refuge* he would never have been his *portion.* The lower step is as needful as the higher." (Spurgeon)

b. **My portion in the land of the living**: Many times in David's seasons as a fugitive, he had reason to believe that all his inheritance in this world was gone. In such times he had the confidence that God Himself was his **portion**, his inheritance. David also knew that he would benefit from this **portion in the land of the living**, in the here and now, not only in the age to come.

    i. **My portion**: "To say '*my portion*' goes as far beyond this as love goes beyond fear. [The Good News Bible] brings out the great force of this word by the phrase 'you are all I want'." (Kidner)

3. (6-7) David's prayer for deliverance.

Attend to my cry,
For I am brought very low;
Deliver me from my persecutors,
For they are stronger than I.
Bring my soul out of prison,
That I may praise Your name;
The righteous shall surround me,
For You shall deal bountifully with me."

    a. **Attend to my cry, for I am brought very low**: David once again brought his **cry** to the LORD, honestly confessing his **low** circumstances. David didn't feel a need to pretend that everything was fine or that he wasn't weak; he could come to God for help even when **brought very low** by **persecutors** who were **stronger** than him.

    i. "The song ends with an earnest cry for deliverance, and an affirmation of confidence that the cry will be heard and answered." (Morgan)

    b. **They are stronger than I**: This means that David well understood his present weakness. The one who killed Goliath felt himself to be very weak – and actually, that was a good place for David to be. God's strength would soon flood his life.

    i. "You always hear about Jacob's wrestling. Well, I dare say he did; but it was not Jacob who was the principal wrestler.... The wrestling was to take all his strength out of him; and when his strength was gone, then God called him a prince. Now, David was to be king over all Israel. What was the way to Jerusalem for David? What was the way to the throne? Well, it was round by the cave of Adullam." (Spurgeon)

    c. **Bring my soul out of prison**: This was likely a figure of speech, yet David felt constrained and bound in his **soul**. He longed to be free from this sense, so that he could **praise** God's **name**.

    i. "'My soul' is frequently a longer way of saying 'me'." (Kidner)

ii. "'Prison' may denote actual imprisonment but may also be a metaphor for his desperate condition in the light of the allusions to adversity and isolation (cf. Psalm 107:10; Isaiah 42:7)." (VanGemeren)

d. **That I may praise Your name**: Though his cry came from a great sense of humility and weakness, David ended this psalm with great confidence.

- David began the song with *complaint* (verse 2); he closes confident of **praise** to come.

- David began the song with a great sense of isolation (verse 4); he closes with confidence in coming companionship and support from the **righteous**.

- David began with the sense of being low and weak (verse 6); he closes confident in God's future goodness, knowing that God would **deal bountifully** with him.

  i. "This prayer of David was heard and answered; he was delivered from his persecutors, enlarged from his distress, exalted to the throne, and joined by all the tribes of Israel." (Horne)

  ii. "In spite of all the opposition of men he realized that his God would deal bountifully with him, therefore instead of his foes, he would find himself surrounded by the righteous." (Morgan)

  iii. **The righteous shall surround me**: "[In] Hebrew, shall crown me; that is, shall encircle me, as wondering at thy goodness in my deliverance; or they shall set the crown on mine head." (Trapp)

  iv. "Perhaps when he wrote the song he already began to realize that the crowd of men in debt, in danger, and discontented, who were coming to him, would presently bring him into his kingdom." (Morgan)

Psalm 143 – Hope for the Persecuted Soul

The title of this psalm is simply **A Psalm of David**. *It is another cry to God from a time of crisis and affliction because of David's many enemies. It is numbered among the seven Penitential Psalms – songs of confession and humility before God. It was a custom in the early church to sing these psalms on Ash Wednesday, the Wednesday six weeks before Easter. Psalm 143 does not seem to belong to this group as much as the others do (Psalms 6, 32, 38, 51, 102, and 130), but 143:2 is a strong and clear statement about the unrighteousness of mankind.*

A. Pleading for God's help in a time of crisis.

1. (1-2) Pleading for God to hear.

Hear my prayer, O LORD,
Give ear to my supplications!
In Your faithfulness answer me,
***And* in Your righteousness.**
Do not enter into judgment with Your servant,
For in Your sight no one living is righteous.

a. **Hear my prayer, O LORD:** This psalm describes David in another crisis. Because his life was filled with so much activity and danger, it is impossible to link this psalm to any one particular point of crisis. It could be from the time before David was recognized as king, living as a fugitive from King Saul, or it could be from David's time as king, particularly when his son Absalom led a rebellion against him.

i. In this crisis, David knew that he must cry out to God and that God must **hear** him, or he would be lost. For David, prayer was not merely a self-improvement exercise that was good for him whether God heard him or not; prayer was a real plea made to a real God who could be appealed unto to **hear**, to answer, and to help.

b. **Give ear to my supplications**: This is the same idea as **hear my prayer** in the previous line. David used the familiar Hebrew poetic form of parallelism, repeating the same idea in different words for the purpose of emphasis.

c. **In Your faithfulness answer me, and in Your righteousness**: David appealed to the **faithfulness** and **righteousness** of God in his request. He asked God to act consistently with those attributes and to **answer** David.

i. David knew something of the character and nature of God, and this shaped his prayer life. He could never ask God to be unfaithful or unrighteous. Yet he could ask God to act according to His character, and David did boldly make his request on that basis.

ii. **In Your righteousness**: "Even the sterner attributes of God are upon the side of the man who humbly trusts, and turns his trust into prayer." (Spurgeon)

d. **Do not enter into judgment with Your servant, for in Your sight no one living is righteous**: David understood that if God were to deal with *him* only on the basis of His righteousness, it could mean **judgment** and ruin for David. So he asked God to deal with him on the basis of mercy (**do not enter into judgment**) and understood that he appealed to God because the LORD is righteous, not because David was **righteous**.

i. We may consider David's thoughts as such: "LORD, I know that You are righteous and I am not. Yet I come to You as **Your servant**, asking You to act on my behalf because of Your mercy and Your righteousness, not on my supposed righteousness."

ii. In saying **in Your sight no one living is righteous**, David seemed to anticipate the Apostle Paul in Romans 3:10 (quoting Isaiah), *There is none righteous, no not one;* and Romans 3:23, *for all have sinned and fall short of the glory of God.* "Luther called this psalm one of the 'Pauline Psalms' (see also 32; 51; 130)." (VanGemeren)

iii. When David said this, he wasn't thinking of *others*, as in "LORD, they – the whole world – are unrighteous." Instead he thought about *himself*, as in "LORD, **no one living in righteous**, and I am certainly numbered among them."

iv. "How contrary is this spirit to the confession of innocence in several psalms (7:3-5)! Both expressions are valid, depending on the context in which one finds himself. The confession of innocence is appropriate when one is insulted and persecuted for righteousness's sake, and the confession of guilt is proper when confronted with one's own frailties." (VanGemeren)

v. "His peril has forced home the penitent conviction of his sin, and therefore he must first have matters set right between him and God by Divine forgiveness." (Maclaren)

2. (3-4) The nature of the crisis.

For the enemy has persecuted my soul;
He has crushed my life to the ground;
He has made me dwell in darkness,
Like those who have long been dead.
Therefore my spirit is overwhelmed within me;
My heart within me is distressed.

a. **For the enemy has persecuted my soul**: In his wide and amazing life, David knew suffering of many kinds. Here he spoke of the persecution and suffering of his **soul**. Perhaps there was also a physical or material aspect to his misery, but that is not in view. David ached and cried out to God out of **soul**-misery.

b. **He has crushed my life to the ground**: David went on to describe his sense of soul-misery.

- His life felt **crushed...to the ground**.
- He felt that he lived **in darkness** as would be true of those **long... dead**.
- He felt his **spirit** to be **overwhelmed within** himself.
- He felt his **heart** to be **distressed**.

  i. Collectively, this is a powerful picture of the deep misery of a soul. Worse for David, he felt this was *pressed upon him* by his **enemy**. This wasn't because David was of a melancholy or depressive nature; such misery is of its own character. This was something brought upon David by his adversary.

  ii. This makes us think of the times when others caused great misery for David, misery that surely extended to the depths of his soul. For many years he lived as a fugitive from King Saul, having to forsake all because a wicked man persecuted him without cause. David also experienced deep misery when his son Absalom rebelled and deposed him as king. David knew what it was like to have great soul-misery inflicted upon him by another person.

  iii. **Dwell in darkness**: "Literally, *in dark places*. This may be understood of David's taking refuge in *caves* and *dens* of the earth." (Clarke)

c. **Therefore my spirit is overwhelmed within me; my heart within me is distressed**: David spoke long before the greater Son of David, but these words could also be in the mouth of Jesus, especially in His Gethsemane agony. In Gethsemane, before His betrayal and crucifixion, Jesus said: *My soul is exceedingly sorrowful, even to death* (Matthew 26:38).

> i. "Such words our Lord Jesus might have used: in this the Head is like the members, and the members are as the Head." (Spurgeon)

3. (5-6) The workings of the soul.

I remember the days of old;
I meditate on all Your works;
I muse on the work of Your hands.
I spread out my hands to You;
My soul *longs* for You like a thirsty land. Selah

a. **I remember the days of old**: In this dark season of his soul, David considered the days of old when things were not so bad. He probably thought of early days of innocence and freshness in his life and his life with God.

> i. There were probably mixed emotions within David as he remembered the **days of old**. If he thought of the joy, the simplicity, and the goodness of how God met him and blessed him as an anonymous (even somewhat despised) shepherd boy, it would bring a warm smile to his face. Yet it would also cause him some pain to consider how far away all that seemed in his present misery of soul.

> ii. There are times when it is good for us to **remember the days of old**. We can remember the sweet and good times of our early life with God, and it blesses us. We can also remember **the days of old** before our own time, thinking of the great things God has done among His people in days past. Even if remembering **the days of old** fills us with a measure of sadness to think of how distant those better days may seem, we can use those memories to restore our hope.

> iii. "When we see nothing new which can cheer us, let us think upon old things. We once had merry days, days of deliverance, and joy and thanksgiving; why not again?" (Spurgeon)

b. **I meditate on all Your works; I muse on the work of Your hands**: David's consideration of **the days of old** was not only a nostalgic longing for the past. It was a remembrance of God's great **works**. David didn't remember *his* past as much as he remembered *the LORD's* past works.

> i. For David, what made the past worth remembering was the work of the LORD. He thought *carefully* about what God had done; **meditate** and **muse** are words that speak of *deep thought*.

c. **I spread out my hands to You**: Thinking deeply about what God did with His hands made David respond with *his* **hands**, spreading them out before God in prayer and praise. David praised God for what He had done in **the days of old**, and he prayed that God might draw close to him now.

i. This posture of prayer and praise was genuine hope for David in the midst of his misery of soul. *"I stretch forth my hands unto thee,'* as if I were in hope thou wouldst take me by the hand and draw me to thee." (Baker, cited in Spurgeon)

d. **My soul longs for You like a thirsty land**: Thankfully, the ache in David's soul did not drive him away from God. It drove David to God in prayer, praise, and deep longing. His persecuted soul (psalm 3) sought after God with the intensity of thirst.

i. "While we recite this verse, let us not be unmindful of Him whose hands were often stretched forth in prayer for his people, and whose soul thirsted after our salvation, even then, when he felt extremity of bodily thirst on the cross." (Horne)

B. The plea presented again

1. (7) The need for a quick answer.

Answer me speedily, O LORD;
My spirit fails!
Do not hide Your face from me,
Lest I be like those who go down into the pit.

a. **Answer me speedily**: David felt that his failing **spirit** could not last long without God's **answer** and intervention. Many a saint has felt as David did, feeling an *urgency* to hear God's answer.

i. Experience had taught David that God always did things at just the right time, but the present crisis made him cry out, "**Answer me speedily, O LORD.**"

b. **Do not hide Your face from me**: David knew what it was like to enjoy the sense of God's favor and blessing. To feel that God might **hide** His face drove David into despair, so he pleaded to see the light of God's countenance.

i. Much later, the Apostle Paul wrote: *If God is for us, who can be against us?* (Romans 8:31). When we live with the belief that God is for us, we are confident in the face of any adversary. Yet if we sense that God may **hide** His **face from** us, we feel weak before any adversary.

ii. Sadly, David's words do not connect with the daily experience of many who think of themselves as followers of God. The spiritually insensitive man cares little about God's favor and blessing. He lives only occasionally aware of a break in communion with God. David was not such a man.

c. **Lest I be like those who go down into the pit**: David considered this to be the worst imaginable fate: to leave the land of the living and go to the pit of the grave. He felt that he could not go on without a continued sense of the favor and blessing of God.

2. (8) The need for loving guidance.

Cause me to hear Your lovingkindness in the morning,
For in You do I trust;
Cause me to know the way in which I should walk,
For I lift up my soul to You.

a. **Cause me to hear**: David needed to hear a good word from God, and asked that he would be **caused** to hear it. Perhaps David wondered if God was speaking and he somehow failed to hear, so he prayed, "**Cause me to hear**." This is a good prayer for all to pray.

i. "He who made the ear will cause us to hear, he who is love itself will have the kindness to bring his lovingkindness before our minds." (Spurgeon)

b. **Your lovingkindness in the morning**: David needed to hear something of God's great mercy, His **lovingkindness** – His *hesed*. He needed to hear this early in the day, **in the morning**, so we would have assurance and know how to walk during the day.

i. The ancient Hebrew word here translated **lovingkindness** is *hesed*. For centuries it was translated with words like *mercy, kindness,* and *love*. In 1927, a scholar named Nelson Glueck (among others) argued that the real idea behind *hesed* was "covenant loyalty" and not so much love or mercy. However, many disagreed and there is no good reason for changing the long-held understanding of *hesed* and taking it as a word that mainly emphasizes covenant loyalty (see R. Laird Harris on *hesed* in the *Theological Wordbook of the Old Testament*).

ii. Spurgeon on **lovingkindness** (*hesed*): "Lovingkindness is one of the sweetest words in our language. Kindness has much in it that is most precious, but lovingkindness is doubly dear; it is the cream of kindness."

iii. "He is beginning to look ahead and seek direction. The phrase, *in the morning*, is already a token of this by its admission that the night is not endless." (Kidner)

c. **Cause me to know the way in which I should walk**: David confessed that he didn't **know the way**, and that he needed God to **cause** him to **know the way**. He didn't only need the love of God – he also needed the guidance of God. **Cause me to know the way in which I should walk** is a wonderful prayer for all to pray.

d. **For in You do I trust...for I lift up my soul to You**: David appealed to God on the basis of his trust and surrender to God. It was as if David prayed, "LORD, I am genuinely depending on you. Please don't let me down; speak to me and guide me."

> i. "If the soul will not rise of itself we must lift it, lift it up unto God." (Spurgeon)

3. (9) The need for deliverance from wicked men.

Deliver me, O LORD, from my enemies;
In You I take shelter.

a. **Deliver me, O LORD, from my enemies**: David's enemies had persecuted his soul (verse 3). He prayed not only for God's encouragement, but also for His defense against these **enemies**.

b. **In You I take shelter**: This was a beautiful statement of faith. David would not take **shelter** in sinful pleasures, in the distractions of entertainment, in positive thinking, in self-reliance, in bitterness, or in vengeance. David was determined to **take shelter** in the LORD.

> i. "The blessedness of contrite trust is that it nestles the closer to God, the more it feels its unworthiness. The child hides its face on the mother's bosom when it has done wrong." (Maclaren)

4. (10) The need to do God's good will.

Teach me to do Your will,
For You *are* my God;
Your Spirit *is* good.
Lead me in the land of uprightness.

a. **Teach me to do Your will**: David could say, "*Cause me to hear Your lovingkindness*" and "*Cause me to know the way in which I should walk*" (verse 8). Yet he did not say, "*Cause me to do Your will.*" In all his reliance upon God, he knew that God would not obey *for him*. Rather, the loving God would **teach** David to do His will. He would **lead** David **in the land of uprightness**.

> i. "The psalmist does not say, 'Lord, help me to talk about thy will,' though it is a very proper thing to talk about, and a very profitable thing to hear about. But still doing is better than talking." (Spurgeon)

ii. Spurgeon also described *how* the believer should **do** the **will** of God: thoughtfully, immediately, cheerfully, constantly, universally, spiritually, and intensely.

iii. The next line, **Your Spirit is good**, connects this teaching work of God with the presence of His **Spirit**. "Moreover the Lord has a way of teaching us by his own Spirit. The Holy Spirit speaks in secret whispers to those who are able to hear him. It is not every professing Christian that has the visitations of the Spirit of God in personal monitions, but there are saints who hear a voice behind them saying, 'This is the way, walk ye in it.' God guides us with his eye as well as by his word." (Spurgeon)

b. **For You are my God**: It was appropriate for David to expect **God** to teach him. The God of Abraham, Isaac, and Jacob will teach the willing servant to do His will, a demonstration of the goodness of God's **Spirit**.

i. We should know what David knew – that **Your Spirit is good**. We should know it even more than David did, in light of the outpouring of the Holy Spirit that is part of the New Covenant. A believer has no reason to fail to yield to the presence and the power of the Holy Spirit.

ii. John Trapp noted this from Cyril of Alexandria (A.D. 378-444): "Cyril gathereth from this text, that the good Spirit is God, because none is good but God."

5. (11-12) The need for revival and rescue.

Revive me, O LORD, for Your name's sake!
For Your righteousness' sake bring my soul out of trouble.
In Your mercy cut off my enemies,
And destroy all those who afflict my soul;
For I *am* Your servant.

a. **Revive me, O LORD**: David prayed for *revival*, for a renewal of life and vitality. Yet he prayed this not for his own benefit or reputation, but **for Your name's sake** – the sake of the LORD's name and reputation.

i. A genuine concern for the sake of God's name is a necessary aspect of true revival – and not for the name or the advancement of any man or woman of God. Many prayers for revival are actually self-interested, praying "Lord, let *me* be known for a great work of revival."

b. **For Your righteousness' sake bring my soul out of trouble**: David knew that his rescue would bring glory to God, so he could pray for deliverance on that basis. He could ask God to **destroy all those who afflict my soul**, leaving vengeance to God against those who persecuted his soul.

i. **Bring my soul out of trouble**: "I can bring it in, but thou only canst bring it out." (Trapp)

c. **In Your mercy cut off my enemies...for I am Your servant**: David appealed to God on the basis of His name, His righteousness, and His **mercy** – yet also on the basis of his relationship with God as His **servant**. David understood that the servant has obligations to the Master; yet, the Master also has obligations to the **servant**.

i. "For God is pledged to His servant as surely as His servant is pledged to Him." (Kidner)

ii. David asked God to deal with his enemies; but before that, he asked God to deal with *him*. He knew that his own low or uninspired or undirected walk with God was a greater danger than any enemy.

Psalm 144 – War and Peace

This psalm has the title **A Psalm of David**. *It is believed to have been written near the time David came to be recognized as the king over all the tribes of Israel, and the psalm expresses David's heart for the nation in both war and peace.*

"It appears from verse 2 and verse 10 of this psalm, that it was composed after David's accession to the throne. And it is evident, from verse 5, etc. that he had more enemies still to conquer, such as the Philistines, etc." (George Horne)

A. Prayer and worship regarding seasons of war.

1. (1-2) Praising God who blessed and helped David in battle.

Blessed *be* **the LORD my Rock,**
Who trains my hands for war,
And **my fingers for battle—**
My lovingkindness and my fortress,
My high tower and my deliverer,
My shield and *the One* **in whom I take refuge,**
Who subdues my people under me.

> a. **Blessed be the LORD my Rock, who trains my hands for war**: David was a remarkable warrior, who in today's terms would be an elite special forces soldier. David killed many men in hand-to-hand combat, as described in 1 Samuel 17:48-50 and 18:26-27. Training is an essential part of success as a soldier, and David understood that it was the **LORD** who had trained his **hands for war** and his **fingers for battle**.

> > i. In his youth, David's **hands** and **fingers** were familiar with "…the [shepherd's] hook and [musician's] harp, and not to the sword and spear; but God hath apted and abled them to feats of arms, and warlike exploits." (Trapp)

ii. Adam Clarke listed the weapons he thought David intended: "...
to use the *sword, battle-axe,* or *spear*...to use the *bow and arrows,* and
the *sling.*"

iii. **Who trains my hands for war**: If a man or woman feels that God
is training him or her to use spiritual weapons – such as the sword of
the Spirit, the word of God – then training must always continue. It is
never "who trained my hands for war," but always in the present: **who
trains my hands for war**.

iv. Spurgeon wrote of the danger of using some weapons without
adequate training – a danger in both the natural and spiritual realms:
"Untrained force is often an injury to the man who possesses it, and
it even becomes a danger to those who are round about him; and
therefore the psalmist blesses the Lord as much for teaching as for
strength."

b. **My lovingkindness and my fortress, my high tower and my deliverer**:
David poured out names and titles for God, each representing some aspect
of God's character or help that had been of use in battle. David knew God's
help and presence in many ways, not just one or two.

i. Of all the names and titles, we note that David began with **my
lovingkindness** (*hesed*, the great word for God's loyal and covenant
love). He loved and valued God for being his **fortress**, his **high tower**,
his **deliverer**, his **shield**, his **refuge**, and his conquering victory. Yet first
among all those was the gift from God of love, mercy, and faithfulness.

ii. "In Psalm 144 David is extremely personal as he confesses who
he had found God to be. He says '*my* Rock,' '*my* loving God,' '*my*
fortress,' '*my* stronghold,' '*my* deliverer,' and '*my* shield'." (Boice)

c. **Who subdues my people under me**: David likely wrote this after he
was received as king over all the tribes of Israel (2 Samuel 5:1-5). If this
psalm comes from an earlier period, he may have meant the subduing of
the *mighty men* under his authority (as in 1 Samuel 22:1-2).

i. "Men who rule others should thank God if they succeed in the task.
Such strange creatures are human beings, that if a number of them
are kept in peaceful association under the leadership of any one of the
Lord's servants, he is bound to bless God every day for the wonderful
fact." (Spurgeon)

2. (3-4) The unexpected love and care of God for humanity.

L<small>ORD</small>, what *is* man, that You take knowledge of him?
***Or* the son of man, that You are mindful of him?**

Man is like a breath;
His days *are* like a passing shadow.

> a. **LORD, what is man, that You take knowledge of him?** In the previous lines David exalted God's great strength and victory. In light of that, it amazed David that God would have an interest in him, or in humanity in general.

> > i. Psalm 8:4 asks the same questions from a slightly different perspective. Here the emphasis is on the LORD as a warrior that none can oppose. In Psalm 8:4 the emphasis is on the power of God as Creator and sustainer of the universe.

> > ii. "The Lord thinks much of man, and in connection with redeeming love makes a great figure of him: this can be believed, but it cannot be explained." (Spurgeon)

> b. **Or the son of man, that You are mindful of him?** David used the common method of repetition to bring emphasis to the concept of God's unusual and even unexpected care for humanity.

> > i. "Though I am king over my people, yet, alas, I am but a man. a base, sinful, mortal, and miserable creature; if compared with thee, less than nothing and vanity." (Poole)

> c. **Man is like a breath**: Having been responsible for the death of so many men, and having been so near to death himself, David knew how temporary human life was. It was as fleeting as a **breath** or **a passing shadow**.

> > i. "The psalmist does not present his petition before the Lord timidly but with boldness. He knows his God; and despite human shortcomings, he is convinced that the Lord does 'care for him' and 'think of him.'" (VanGemeren)

3. (5-8) A plea for rescue from the great God.

Bow down Your heavens, O LORD, and come down;
Touch the mountains, and they shall smoke.
Flash forth lightning and scatter them;
Shoot out Your arrows and destroy them.
Stretch out Your hand from above;
Rescue me and deliver me out of great waters,
From the hand of foreigners,
Whose mouth speaks lying words,
And whose right hand *is* a right hand of falsehood.

a. **Bow down Your heavens, O Lord, and come down**: David used phrases and images from God's appearance on Mount Sinai (Exodus 19:16-20) to give the sense of awe and even terror connected with God's presence.

i. "He wants God to be as present in his day as he was when he revealed himself at Sinai." (Boice)

ii. "In like manner, the church, or mystical body of Christ, is instant in prayer for the final completion of all her hope. She wisheth for the glorious day, when her God and Saviour shall bow the heavens, and come down to judgment, causing the mountains to smoke, and flame, and dissolve, and flow down before him; when his lightnings, those arrows of his indignation, and ministers of his vengeance, shall scatter the host of darkness, and destroy the anti-christian powers; when we shall be delivered from every enemy, and from all that hate us." (Horne)

b. **Rescue me and deliver me out of great waters**: David asked that the same God of majestic awe would fight for him, sending forth **lightning** like **arrows** against the **foreigners** who fought against David with lies and **falsehood**.

i. During David's days as a fugitive from Saul, he had many men who informed against him so they might gain favor with King Saul (1 Samuel 22:6-10, 23:19-20). David also likely faced whisperers and liars against his character when he was king. Like the greater Son of David, he was often lied about and slandered.

ii. When David spoke against these **foreigners**, it was not because of their nationality. By their actions they proved that they were truly **foreigners** from the people of God and rejected Yahweh, the God of Israel.

iii. "Those against whom he pleaded were out of covenant with God; they were Philistines and Edomites; or else they were men of his own nation of black heart and traitorous spirit, who were real strangers, though they bore the name of Israel!" (Spurgeon)

B. Praise and prayer to God for the blessing of peace.

1. (9-10) Praise to the God who rescues.

I will sing a new song to You, O God;
On a harp of ten strings I will sing praises to You,
***The One* who gives salvation to kings,**
Who delivers David His servant
From the deadly sword.

a. **I will sing a new song to You, O God**: New victories and new deliverance required a **new song**. God's love and help for David were always fresh and new, so his praise would also be.

i. **I will sing a new song**: "Upon the receipt of any new mercy, like as in a lottery, at every new prize drawn the trumpet soundeth." (Trapp)

b. **On a harp of ten strings I will sing praises to You**: David was a skilled musician (1 Samuel 16:18), and he played his **harp of ten strings** as he sang praises to God.

c. **The One who gives salvation to kings**: David had felt God's help many times as a humble shepherd boy (1 Samuel 17:34-36) and as a despised fugitive (1 Samuel 23:24-29). We sense that David was almost surprised that God would *also* help him as king, rescuing him **from the deadly sword**.

2. (11-15) Praying that the enemy be defeated so that God's people would prosper.

Rescue me and deliver me from the hand of foreigners,
Whose mouth speaks lying words,
And whose right hand *is* a right hand of falsehood—
That our sons *may be* as plants grown up in their youth;
***That* our daughters *may be* as pillars,**
Sculptured in palace style;
***That* our barns *may be* full,**
Supplying all kinds of produce;
***That* our sheep may bring forth thousands**
And ten thousands in our fields;
***That* our oxen *may be* well laden;**
***That there be* no breaking in or going out;**
***That there be* no outcry in our streets.**
Happy *are* the people who are in such a state;
Happy *are* the people whose God *is* the LORD!

a. **Rescue me and deliver me from the hand of foreigners**: David here repeated the idea from earlier in the psalm (verses 7-8). The presence and destructive work of these foreign liars and false speakers were of great concern to him, and he pleaded with God to **rescue** him.

b. **That our sons may be as plants grown up in their youth**: David prayed for a series of blessings that would come among God's people when God dealt with the evil speakers in their midst. The list of blessings focuses on the concerns of everyday people in farming societies:

- Blessed with children in the home; well-rooted and flourishing **sons**, and stable and stately **daughters**.

- Blessed in the work of their hands, with **barns** full, **ten thousands** of **sheep**, and **oxen** burdened with heavy harvests.

- Blessed with safety and peace in the community, with no violence (**breaking in or going out**) or riot over injustice (**outcry in our streets**).

    i. "The Lord had promised to bless his people with stalwart youth, productivity, and prosperity, and to protect them from enemy attacks and humiliation (cf. Leviticus 26:1-13; Deuteronomy 28:1-14; Psalm 132:13-18)." (VanGemeren)

    ii. **Daughters may be as pillars**: "…the daughters as the very picture of statuesque elegance and strength, 'like sculptured pillars at the corners of a palace' (New English Bible). There has been nothing slipshod in their upbringing." (Kidner)

    iii. "We desire a blessing for our whole family, daughters as well as sons. For the girls to be left out of the circle of blessing would be unhappy indeed." (Spurgeon)

    iv. **No breaking in or going out**: "So well ordered is the *police* of the kingdom, that there are no depredations, no robbers, house-breakers, or marauding parties, in the land; no sudden incursions of neighbouring tribes or banditti breaking into fields or houses, carrying away property, and taking with them the people to sell them into captivity: there is no such *breaking in*, and no such *going out*, in the nation." (Clarke)

c. **Happy are the people who are in such a state**: David prayed as a wise and caring king, asking God for blessing upon his **people** in their common, everyday lives.

    i. "This mercy I beg, not only for my own sake, but for the sake of thy people, that thine and our enemies being subdued, and peace established in the land, thy people may enjoy those blessings which thou hast promised to them." (Poole)

    ii. "These verses may with a little accommodation be applied to a prosperous church, where the converts are growing and beautiful, the gospel stores abundant, and the spiritual increase most cheering. There ministers and workers are in full vigour, and the people are happy and united. The Lord make it so in all our churches evermore." (Spurgeon)

d. **Happy are the people whose God is the** LORD: Yet such blessings could only come to God's covenant people when they were loyal to God as they had promised to be loyal (Exodus 24:3-8). When they looked to Yahweh as their only God and Master, rejecting all the idols of the nations, the promised blessings were granted – and God's people were **happy**.

i. What was true for David and Israel under the Old Covenant is even truer for the believer in Jesus under the New Covenant. It should be said of believers, **Happy are the people whose God is the** LORD. This is our promise and heritage as believers, followers of Jesus Christ.

ii. "Those who worship the happy God become a happy people." (Spurgeon)

iii. "The prayer ends at the source of the harmony it has visualized. For while it treasures the gifts, it reserves its final beatitude for the relationship behind them: that of being the people who know the Lord as their own." (Kidner)

Psalm 145 – Praising God for Who He Is and What He Does

This psalm is titled **A Praise of David**. *Though Psalms 17 and 86 were also called A Prayer of David, this is the only one titled* **A Praise of David**, *and it is a high point of praise. "Psalm 145 is indeed a monumental praise psalm, a fit summary of all David had learned about God during a long lifetime of following hard after the Almighty." (James Montgomery Boice)*

Psalm 145 is the last psalm attributed to David in the collection of psalms, and it is the last of the nine psalms using some kind of acrostic pattern (9, 10, 25, 34, 37, 111, 112, 119, and 145). Five of these acrostic psalms are attributed to David.

"In Jewish practice this psalm was recited twice in the morning and once in the evening service. The Talmud commends all who repeat it three times a day as having a share in the world to come." (Willem VanGemeren)

A. Learning to praise God.

1. (1-3) Learning from David's example of a heart fully given to praise.

I will extol You, my God, O King;
And I will bless Your name forever and ever.
Every day I will bless You,
And I will praise Your name forever and ever.
Great *is* the LORD, and greatly to be praised;
And His greatness *is* unsearchable.

> a. **I will extol You, my God, O King**: To **extol** is to praise, to lift high, to exalt. David honored and promoted the name of God in the most personal of ways:
>
> - He did it with a direct address (**You**).
>
> - He did it with a personal reference (**my God**).
>
> - He did it with a surrendered heart (**O King**).

- He did it unendingly (**forever and ever...every day**).

    i. "In the opening sentences He is addressed as 'My Elohim, O King,' and afterwards always as Jehovah (nine times)." (Morgan)

    ii. **O King**: "This is a significant statement from the mouth of Israel's king, for it acknowledges that although David may have been king of the elect nation of Israel, God is nevertheless the King of kings and therefore David's king too." (Boice)

    iii. **Every day I will bless You**: "To bless God is to praise him with a personal affection for him, and a wishing well to him; this is a growingly easy exercise as we advance in experience and grow in grace." (Spurgeon)

    iv. "Observe that David is firmly resolved to praise God. My text has four 'I wills' in it. Frequently it is foolish for us poor mortals to say 'I will,' because our will is so feeble and fickle; but when we resolve upon the praise of God, we may say, 'I will,' and 'I will,' and 'I will,' and 'I will.'" (Spurgeon)

  b. **Great is the Lord, and greatly to be praised**: David piled praise upon praise, declaring God's greatness and great *worthiness* **to be praised**. We get the feeling that David felt it would be dishonorable to withhold his praise to God or to give Him half-hearted praise.

2. (4-7) Passing the praise of God from one generation to another.

One generation shall praise Your works to another,
And shall declare Your mighty acts.
I will meditate on the glorious splendor of Your majesty,
And on Your wondrous works.
***Men* shall speak of the might of Your awesome acts,**
And I will declare Your greatness.
They shall utter the memory of Your great goodness,
And shall sing of Your righteousness.

  a. **One generation shall praise Your works to another**: David looked for God's people to encourage each other in praise. An older **generation** might inspire a younger generation to praise by remembering God's **mighty acts** in the past. A young **generation** might stir praise in an older generation by declaring the fresh and new things God was doing.

    i. "God's praises are many, and man's life short, and one generation succeedeth another: let them relate God's wonderful works one to another, and so perpetuate his praises to all posterity." (Trapp)

ii. "The generations shall herein unite: together they shall make up an extraordinary history. Each generation shall contribute its chapter, and all the generations together shall compose a volume of matchless character." (Spurgeon)

b. **I will meditate on the glorious splendor of Your majesty, and on Your wondrous works**: Praise comes not only from emotion, but from careful thought – from careful meditation. David meditated not only on the great things God did (His **wondrous works**), but he also paid attention to God's **glorious splendor**. The idea is of the glory and wonder of who God actually is.

i. "It seems, then, dear friends, that David studied the character and doings of God, and thus praised him; knowledge should lead our song. The more we know of God the more acceptably shall we bless him through Jesus Christ." (Spurgeon)

ii. When we think of the aspects of God's **glorious splendor** – His majesty, His wisdom, His constant presence, His complete knowledge, His unlimited power, His loving and wise plan and purpose – all this should stir up praise within us.

iii. When we think of God's **wondrous works** – His works of planning, His works of creation, His works of providence, His works of rescue, His works of salvation now and in the age to come – all this should stir up praise within us.

iv. "Here are [assorted] words heaped together, to intimate that no words were sufficient to express it." (Poole)

v. **The glorious splendor of Your majesty**: "The flashing brightness with which, when gathered, as it were, in a radiant mass, they shine out, like a great globe of fire." (Maclaren)

c. **Men shall speak of the might of Your awesome acts, and I will declare Your greatness**: To give emphasis, David repeated the idea of praising God for *who He is* and for *what He has done*. Repeating the idea a third time, we remember the demonstration of God's **great goodness** in what He does, and we declare that He Himself is full of **righteousness** in who He is.

i. "The psalmist enjoins all God's people to share in the extension of God's kingdom by private meditation, discussion, and public speaking about God's mighty acts." (VanGemeren)

ii. **I will declare Your greatness**: "All men are enamoured of greatness. Then they must seek it in God, and get it *from* God. David did both. All history shows the creature aspiring after this glory. Ahasuerus, Astyages, Cyrus, Cambyses, Nebuchadnezzar, were all called *the great*.

Alexander the Great, when he came to the Ganges, ordered his statue to be made of more than life size, that posterity might believe him to have been of nobler stature. In Christ alone does man attain the greatness his heart yearns for – the glory of perfect goodness." (Le Blanc, cited in Spurgeon)

iii. **They shall utter the memory**: "The Hebrew word has something to do with bubbling up: it means they shall overflow, they shall gush with the memory of thy great goodness." (Spurgeon)

B. Declaring and praising the greatness of God.

1. (8-9) The memory and present experience of God's goodness.

The LORD is gracious and full of compassion,
Slow to anger and great in mercy.
The LORD is good to all,
And His tender mercies *are* over all His works.

a. **The LORD is gracious and full of compassion**: David echoed the self-description of Yahweh to Moses: *The LORD, the LORD God, merciful and gracious, longsuffering, and abounding in goodness and truth* (Exodus 34:6).

i. "But greatness, majesty, splendour, are not the Divinest parts of the Divine nature, as this singer had learned. These are but the fringes of the central glory. Therefore the song rises from greatness to celebrate better things, the moral attributes of Jehovah." (Maclaren)

b. **The LORD is good to all**: David expressed the idea sometimes called *common grace* – that God spreads some of His goodness to all humanity. Jesus said, *He makes His sun rise on the evil and on the good, and sends rain on the just and on the unjust* (Matthew 5:45).

i. **Is good to all**: "…not to Israel only, but to all mankind, whose hearts he fills with food and gladness, as it is said, Acts 14:17." (Poole)

c. **His tender mercies are over all His works**: David saw the beautiful care of God pressed upon all that He did. All creation and all the wise plan of God were demonstrations of the greatness and goodness of God.

i. "The original word for 'his tender mercies'...signifies the 'womb.' The 'mercies' of God toward men are, therefore, represented by this word, to be like those of a mother towards the child of her 'womb.'" (Horne)

2. (10-13) All creation declares God's praise.

All Your works shall praise You, O LORD,
And Your saints shall bless You.
They shall speak of the glory of Your kingdom,

And talk of Your power,
To make known to the sons of men His mighty acts,
And the glorious majesty of His kingdom.
Your kingdom *is* an everlasting kingdom,
And Your dominion *endures* throughout all generations.

a. **All Your works shall praise You, O** Lord: Creation itself praises God, and does so out of grateful duty. Yet even more than the rivers and hills praising God (Psalm 98:8), God's people (**Your saints**) shoud gratefully praise and **bless** the Lord.

b. **They shall speak of the glory of Your kingdom**: This is a wonderful subject for the speech of God's people. There are many things we talk about, but all too little do we **speak of the glory** of God's kingdom and of His great **power**.

   i. **And talk of Your power**: "The recipients of His grace should be the messengers of His grace." (Maclaren)

c. **To make known to the sons of men His mighty acts, and the glorious majesty of His kingdom**: David again sensed the responsibility of God's people to tell the wider world the greatness of what God has done (**His mighty acts**) and who our King is (**the glorious majesty of His kingdom**).

   i. "As the State cannot teach these holy histories the people of God must take care to do it themselves. The work must be done for every age, for men have short memories in reference to their God, and the doings of his power." (Spurgeon)

   ii. "I consider that one of the great lacks of the Church, nowadays, is not so much Christian preaching as Christian talking – not so much Christian prayer in the prayer-meeting, as Christian conversation in the parlor. How little do we hear concerning Christ!" (Spurgeon)

d. **Your kingdom is an everlasting kingdom**: One reason why praise should continue forever (as in verse 2) is because God's **kingdom** will last forever. His **dominion** is unending, lasting **throughout all generations**.

   i. "Men come and go like shadows on the wall, but God reigneth eternally. We distinguish kings as they succeed each other by calling them first and second; but this King is Jehovah, the First and the Last." (Spurgeon)

   ii. **Your kingdom is an everlasting kingdom**: "These words are engraven on the door of a mosque in Damascus, which was formerly a Christian church. Originally they were plastered over by stucco; but this has dropped away, and the words stand out clearly defined. They seem to be contradicted by centuries of Mohammedanism; but they are essentially true." (Meyer)

iii. Derek Kidner noted that in the acrostic arrangement of this psalm, "One letter of the alphabet (*nun*) is lacking from the standard Hebrew text; but most of the ancient translations and now a text from Qumran (11Q Ps) supply the missing verse, which [the Revised Standard Version] and subsequent translations include at the end of verse 13."

3. (14-16) The kindness of God to those in need.

The LORD upholds all who fall,
And raises up all *who are* bowed down.
The eyes of all look expectantly to You,
And You give them their food in due season.
You open Your hand
And satisfy the desire of every living thing.

a. **The LORD upholds all who fall**: God's compassion is especially evident toward those who **fall** and fail. He does not despise or reject them; there is a sense in which He specially draws near them to hold them up. If they allow their **fall** to rightly humble them, God will draw near and uphold them.

i. **The LORD upholds all who fall**: "The phrase, *all who are falling*, is unusually expressive; and this timely help at an early stage is coupled with God's power to revive lost hope and failed abilities: cf. New English Bible, 'and straightens backs which are bent'." (Kidner)

ii. "Many are despondent, and cannot lift up their heads in courage, or their hearts with comfort; but these he cheers. Some are bent with their daily load, and these he strengthens." (Spurgeon)

iii. "The last portion of the psalm is marked by a frequent repetition of 'all,' which occurs eleven times in these verses. The singer seems to delight in the very sound of the word, which suggests to him boundless visions of the wide sweep of God's universal mercy, and of the numberless crowd of dependents who wait on and are satisfied by Him." (Maclaren)

b. **They eyes of all look expectantly to You, and You give them their food in due season**: The humble put their expectation on God, looking to Him for their needs. They pray, *give us this day our daily bread* (Matthew 6:11), and God answers their prayer **in due season**.

i. Most commentators connect this with the words **every living thing** that follow, and see that *all* creation is in view. "What a fine figure! The *young* of all animals look up to *their parents for food*. God is here represented as the *universal Father*, providing food for every living creature." (Clarke)

ii. "He condescends to the needs of his creatures…[this shows] the beauty of Yahweh's condescension to the needs of his people." (VanGemeren)

c. **You open Your hand and satisfy the desire of every living thing**: God's care for creation extends beyond His provision for men and women. As Jesus would later say, God also cares for the birds and the grass of the field (Matthew 6:26-30). God does this with a wonderfully **open** hand and heart to His creation.

i. As we take in David's amazing description of God, we see how different Yahweh (the true and living God) is compared to the idols of the nations. Those supposed gods were often angry and petulant, caring little for either humanity or creation. We are surprised and grateful for the love and care from the God who is really there.

4. (17-21) The love and righteousness of the LORD.

The LORD is righteous in all His ways,
Gracious in all His works.
The LORD is near to all who call upon Him,
To all who call upon Him in truth.
He will fulfill the desire of those who fear Him;
He also will hear their cry and save them.
The LORD preserves all who love Him,
But all the wicked He will destroy.
My mouth shall speak the praise of the LORD,
And all flesh shall bless His holy name
Forever and ever.

a. **The LORD is righteous in all His ways, gracious in all His works**: Throughout this psalm David has spoken much about how we should praise God for who He is and what He has done. Here again David gives us a reason to praise the LORD, recognizing the incomparable combination of being **righteous** and **gracious**.

i. Later the Apostle Paul would write about this idea, how in the person and work of Jesus, God did *demonstrate at the present time His righteousness, that He might be just and the justifier of the one who has faith in Jesus* (Romans 3:26). The combination of being both *just* and the *justifier* is much the same as being both **righteous** and **gracious**.

b. **The LORD is near to all who call upon Him**: God's responsiveness to His praying people demonstrates the graciousness mentioned in the previous lines. **He will fulfill the desire** and **hear** the **cry** of His people.

i. "Since the Lord is so good to his creation, how much more does he care for his covenant people! This is essentially what Jesus taught in the Sermon on the Mount (Matt 6:25-34)." (VanGemeren)

ii. **To all who call upon him in truth**: "…because there is a counterfeit and false sort of worshipping, and calling upon God, which is debarred from the benefit of this promise." (Dickson, cited in Spurgeon)

iii. **He will fulfill the desires of those who fear Him**: In his commenatary on this line of the psalm, John Trapp noted that Martin Luther prayed to God, "Let my will be done." Trapp added that Luther could pray this because he also said to God, "Because my will is for Your will to be done, and nothing else."

iv. "They who long for God will always have as much of God as they long for and are capable of receiving." (Maclaren)

c. **The LORD preserves all who love Him, but all the wicked He will destroy**: David gave a further example of God's graciousness in action (preserving **all who love Him**), along with His righteousness in action (**all the wicked He will destroy**).

i. "*Preserves* may be a little misleading, as though it promised the godly a charmed life. 'Watches over' (New English Bible) is better; see again Luke 21:16-18." (Kidner)

d. **My mouth shall…bless His holy name forever and ever**: We sense that David meant this as a declaration. Having written so eloquently about who God is and what He has done for His people, David's firm decision was to use his **mouth** to praise and **bless** God again and again.

i. "Whatever others may do, I will not be silent in the praise of the Lord, whatever others may speak upon, my topic is fixed once for all: I will speak the praise of Jehovah. I am doing it, and I will do it as long as I breathe." (Spurgeon)

ii. "So ends David's contribution to the Psalter, on a note of praise which is wholly his own (21a), yet as wide as mankind and as unfading as eternity." (Kidner)

iii. "The last verse of Psalm 145 is the last word we have from David in the Bible. It is his last will and testament. If he had said nothing else in his long life, these words would be a fine legacy for future generations. In it he praises God and invites others to praise God also." (Boice)

Psalm 146 – Praise to the LORD, Worthy of Our Trust

Psalm 146 begins a series of five final songs in the Book of Psalms, and the five are known as the Hallelujah Psalms. "In the earlier psalms, we have studied the writers' griefs, shames, sins, doubts, and fears. We have witnessed the people of God in their defeats and victories, their ups and downs in life. We have encountered rebellious words and struggling faith. All this is behind us now. In these final psalms every word is praise." (James Montgomery Boice)

A. The happiness of trusting in the LORD.

1. (1-2) A declaration of praise to Yahweh.

Praise the LORD!
Praise the LORD, O my soul!
While I live I will praise the LORD;
I will sing praises to my God while I have my being.

a. **Praise the LORD**: The psalmist meant this (*Hallelujah!*) as both a declaration of his own praise to God and as an exhortation to praise. He called upon his own **soul** to give Yahweh praise, and others to give praise as well.

i. "Hallelujah is a compound word made up of two Hebrew words: *hallel* (an imperative verb meaning 'praise') and *jah* (a contraction of the name for God, Jehovah). So hallelujah means 'Praise the Lord (or Jehovah).'" (Boice)

b. **While I live I will praise the LORD**: This is much the same as Psalm 104:33, declaring a determination to praise God with one's entire life and **being**.

i. "No sooner is one hallelujah ended, but another begins." (Horne)

ii. **While I have my being**: "...in my continuance, in my progression, my eternal existence. This is very expressive." (Clarke)

iii. "We cannot be too firm in the holy resolve to praise God, for it is the chief end of our living and being that we should glorify God and enjoy him for ever." (Spurgeon)

iv. "*George Carpenter,* the Bavarian martyr, being desired by some godly brethren, that when he was burning in the fire he would give them some sign of his constancy, answered, 'Let this be a sure sign unto you of my faith and perseverance in the truth, that so long as I am able to hold open my mouth, or to whisper, I will never cease to praise God, and to profess his truth'; the which also he did, saith mine author; and so did many other martyrs besides." (Trapp)

2. (3-4) A caution against confidence in man.

Do not put your trust in princes,
***Nor* in a son of man, in whom *there is* no help.**
His spirit departs, he returns to his earth;
In that very day his plans perish.

a. **Do not put your trust in princes**: Yahweh is to be praised, but man is to be questioned. Even the highest among men – **princes** – are not worthy of our confidence. We are sure to be disappointed when we put our trust **in whom there is no help**.

i. **Do not put your trust in princes**: "…in men of greatest wealth and power, in whose favour men are very prone to trust." (Poole)

ii. "The word *princes* may seem to remove this advice from the plane of ordinary folk and their needs; but a modern equivalent would be 'the influential', whose backing may well seem more solid and practical than God's." (Kidner)

iii. **In whom there is no help**: "However high his state, he is but a 'son of Adam' (the earth born), and inherits the feebleness and fleetingness which deprive him of ability to help. 'He has no salvation' is the literal rendering of the last words of Psalm 146:3b." (Maclaren)

b. **His spirit departs, he returns to his earth**: The greatest among men are only men, and subject to death. Ashes turn to ashes and dust to dust, and even the brilliant plans of man **perish**. These are reasons to set our confidence in God and not in man.

i. **Spirit** could also be understood as *breath*. "High as he stood, the want of a little air brings him down to the ground, and lays him under it." (Spurgeon)

ii. "Verses 3 and 4 make these points by two plays on Hebrew words. In Hebrew *adam*, meaning 'man,' is the same word for 'earth' or 'ground.' So dirt goes to dirt." (Boice)

iii. "Earthly princes, if they have the will, often want the power, even to protect their friends. And should they want neither will nor power to advance them, yet still all depends upon the breath in their nostrils." (Horne)

iv. **His plans perish**: "As soon as ever he is dead, his thoughts perish; all his designs and endeavours, either for himself or for others." (Poole)

v. "This is the narrow estate of man, his breath, his earth, and his thoughts; and this is his threefold climax therein – his breath goeth forth, to his earth he returns, and his thoughts perish. Is this a being to be relied upon? Vanity of vanities, all is vanity. To trust it would be a still greater vanity." (Spurgeon)

3. (5-7) Happy confidence in a great God.

Happy *is he* who *has* the God of Jacob for his help,
Whose hope *is* in the LORD his God,
Who made heaven and earth,
The sea, and all that *is* in them;
Who keeps truth forever,
Who executes justice for the oppressed,
Who gives food to the hungry.
The LORD gives freedom to the prisoners.

a. **Happy is he who has the God of Jacob for his help**: Princes among men often fail, but God never disappoints the one who hopes in Him.

i. The psalmist has abruptly transitioned from negative to positive. "His negative teaching, if it stood alone, would be a gospel of despair, the reduction of life to a torturing cheat; but taken as the prelude to the revelation of One whom it is safe to trust, there is nothing sad in it." (Maclaren)

ii. "We have here a statement which we have personally tried and proved: resting in the Lord, we know a happiness which is beyond description, beyond comparison, beyond conception." (Spurgeon)

iii. **Whose hope is in the LORD his God**: "We never praise God better than by exercising faith in him! Quiet trust is among the sweetest music that reaches the heart of God; and when we put our trust in man, we rob God of his glory; we are giving to others the confidence which belongs alone to him." (Spurgeon)

b. **Who made heaven and earth**: The singer gives us more reasons for confidence in God. When we trust in the LORD as the Creator of all things, we realize He has power to help us and deliver us that even great men do not have.

> i. "The psalmist does not introduce anything new in this description of the Lord's mighty acts...but the manner in which he brings the various ways of divine sustenance together is most creative, including the conclusion." (VanGemeren)

c. **Who keeps truth forever**: God can also be trusted because He is a moral, upright God. Yahweh is unchangingly true. He champions **justice for the oppressed**. The God of such creating power would be a tyrant without His abundant passion for **truth** and **justice**.

> i. **Who keeps truth forever**: "And this 'for ever' is opposed to that mortality and mutability of earthly princes, Psalm 146:4." (Trapp)

> ii. "He is true to his own nature, true to the relationships which he has assumed, true to his covenant, true to his Word, true to his Son. He keeps true, and is the keeper of all that is true." (Spurgeon)

d. **Who gives food to the hungry**: God also cares for those who are in need. For the **hungry** He provides **food** and for **prisoners** He provides **freedom**. In all this we see a God of power, holiness, and love. This is a God who can be trusted with confidence.

> i. **Food to the hungry**: "The hungry hearts of men, who are all full of needs and longing, may turn to this mighty, faithful, righteous Jehovah, and be sure that He never sends mouths but He sends meat to fill them. All our various kinds of hunger are doors for God to come into our spirits." (Maclaren)

> ii. "Thus he completes the triple blessing: justice, bread, and liberty." (Spurgeon)

B. The helpfulness of the holy God.

1. (8-9) Declaring the power and loving care of God.

The LORD opens *the eyes of* the blind;
The LORD raises those who are bowed down;
The LORD loves the righteous.
The LORD watches over the strangers;
He relieves the fatherless and widow;
But the way of the wicked He turns upside down.

a. **The LORD opens the eyes of the blind**: The psalmist here continues a marvelous description of Yahweh as a God of power, care, justice, and compassion. The psalmist seems delighted to describe Yahweh in His great works of love and power.

i. "All these classes of afflicted persons are meant to be regarded literally, but all may have a wider meaning and be intended to hint at spiritual bondage, blindness, and abjectness." (Maclaren)

ii. We instantly connect this list with the work of Jesus the Messiah.

- Jesus opened **the eyes of the blind** (Matthew 9:27-29).
- Jesus raised **those who are bowed down** (Luke 13:11-13).
- Jesus loved **the righteous** (Matthew 13:43, 25:46).
- Jesus watched **over the strangers** (Matthew 8:5-10).
- Jesus blessed **the fatherless and widow** (Luke 7:12-15).
- Jesus turned **the way of the wicked...upside down** (Matthew 21:12).
- The logical conclusion is that Jesus is Yahweh, **the LORD**.

iii. "Like Father, like Son. For us, these lines may bring to mind the oracle of Isaiah 61 by which Jesus announced his mission, and the further clues to his identity which he sent back to John the Baptist (Luke 4:18f.; 7:21f.)." (Kidner)

b. **But the way of the wicked He turns upside down**: God shows great love and compassion to the poor, afflicted, and needy. Yet the Lord also brings justice against **the wicked**, and turns their way **upside down**.

i. **He turns upside down**: "He maketh them to lose their way; he not only frustrateth their plots and enterprises but turneth them against themselves." (Poole)

ii. "That aspect of God's government is lightly handled in one clause, as befits the purpose of the psalm. But it could not be left out. A true likeness must have shadows. God were not a God for men to rely on, unless the trend of His reign was to crush evil and thwart the designs of sinners." (Maclaren)

2. (10) Praising the God who reigns forever.

The LORD shall reign forever—
Your God, O Zion, to all generations.
Praise the LORD!

a. **The LORD shall reign forever**: The psalmist was happy to declare this, because God's power and might were expressed with such love and compassion. Through both might and right, **the LORD shall reign forever**, even **to all generations**.

i. **The LORD shall reign forever**: "Therefore he can never fail; and he is *thy God, O Zion*. Hitherto he has helped *you* and your *fathers*; and has extended that help from *generation to generation*. Therefore trust in him and bless the Lord." (Clarke)

ii. "However humbling the thought may be, and to whatever searching of heart it may drive us, it is certain that if, and when 'Hosannas languish on our tongues, and our devotion dies,' the reason is that we have lost our clear vision of God, our keen consciousness of what He is. To know Him is to praise Him, and that without ceasing." (Morgan)

b. **Praise the LORD**: Psalm 146 ends as it began – with a declaration of praise to Yahweh, the proclamation *Hallelujah!*

i. "Here endeth this gladsome Psalm. Here endeth *not* the praise of the Lord, which shall ascend for ever and ever." (Spurgeon)

Psalm 147 – Praising the God of Care and Creation

This is another of the last five psalms that have no title in the Hebrew text, but each of these last five begin and end with Hallelujah or Praise the LORD!

A. Praising God for His protection and preservation.

1. (1) The goodness of *hallelujah*.

Praise the LORD!
For *it is* good to sing praises to our God;
For *it is* pleasant, *and* praise is beautiful.

a. **Praise the LORD**: These words are both a declaration and an encouragement of praise to Yahweh. We are encouraged to **praise** Yahweh with the psalmist.

i. "There is no heaven, either in this world, or the world to come, for people who do not praise God. If you do not enter into the spirit and worship of heaven, how should the spirit and joy of heaven enter into you?" (Puslford, cited in Spurgeon)

b. **It is good to sing praises to our God**: It was right for the psalmist to tell himself and others to **praise the LORD**, and he assumed that God's people would do it with singing. The goodness of praise comes from the truth that it is, in itself, **pleasant** and **beautiful**.

i. Psalm 33:1 says *praise from the upright is beautiful*. True praise is **beautiful** to God, to His people as a community, and to the individual worshipper.

ii. Praise is **pleasant** and **beautiful** for humanity. "It is decent, befitting, and proper that every intelligent creature should acknowledge the Supreme Being: and as he does nothing *but good* to the children of men, so they should *speak good of his name*." (Clarke)

293

iii. Since **praise is beautiful**, "...an unthankful man is an ugly, ill-favoured spectacle." (Trapp)

2. (2-6) The care and power of God.

The LORD builds up Jerusalem;
He gathers together the outcasts of Israel.
He heals the brokenhearted
And binds up their wounds.
He counts the number of the stars;
He calls them all by name.
Great *is* our Lord, and mighty in power;
His understanding *is* infinite.
The LORD lifts up the humble;
He casts the wicked down to the ground.

a. **The LORD builds up Jerusalem, He gathers together the outcasts of Israel**: The psalmist describes the goodness and greatness of God so he and others would have *reasons* to praise God. The first reason is God's active care for **Jerusalem**, perhaps a reference to its restoration after the exile.

i. "The twelfth chapter of Nehemiah tells how the Levites were brought to the city to lead a grand celebration 'with songs of thanksgiving and with the music of cymbals, harps and lyres' (Nehemiah 12:27)." (Boice) It would have been fitting for them to sing this psalm, especially verses 2-3.

ii. In a sermon titled *Good Cheer for Outcasts*, Spurgeon considered the many kinds of **outcasts** that Jesus gathers and blesses today.

- Outcasts may be the very poorest and most despised among men.
- Outcasts may be those who have made themselves so by their wickedness.
- Outcasts may be those who judge themselves to be outcasts.
- Outcasts may be backsliders from the church.
- Outcasts may be those who have fallen into great depression of spirit.
- Outcasts may be those who suffer for righteousness' sake.

b. **He heals the brokenhearted**: God not only cares for communities, but also for individuals. Those who hurt – the **brokenhearted** and the wounded – are special objects of His care.

i. "Hearts are broken through disappointment. Hearts are broken through bereavement. Hearts are broken in ten thousand ways, for this is a heart-breaking world; and Christ is good at healing all manner of heartbreaks" (Spurgeon).

ii. Spurgeon described many reasons why Jesus is good at healing **the brokenhearted**.

- Jesus is educated for this work, having His own heart broken.
- Jesus is experienced in this work, having healed broken hearts for 2,000 years.
- Jesus is willing to take the worst patients, and has never yet lost a patient.
- Jesus heals broken hearts with medicine that He himself provides.

iii. "That God tells the number of the stars is only what we should expect of Him…. But that He should be able to bend over one broken heart and bind it with His sympathy and heal its flowing wounds, this is wonderful, amazing, divine." (Meyer)

c. **He counts the number of the stars; He calls them all by name**: The same God who cares for the lowly individual also knows and names all the **stars**. His majesty extends in both directions, from the span of the universe to the individual need.

i. The psalmist allowed us to the make the logical conclusion – that if God knows and names all the stars, He certainly knows me and names me.

ii. Apparently in the days of Matthew Poole (1624-79), astronomers numbered 1,025 stars. "He telleth the number of the stars, which no man can do, Genesis 22:17. For those thousand and twenty-five which astronomers number, are only such as are most distinctly visible to the eye, and most considerable for their influences." In the 21st century scientists estimate that there are 1 billion trillion stars in the observable universe. God knows the exact number.

iii. **He calls them all by name**: "Calling them all by names (lit., He calls names to them all) is not giving them designations, but summoning them as a captain reading the muster roll of his band. It may also imply full knowledge of each individual in their countless hosts." (Maclaren)

iv. "The 'stars' are not forces or deities as in the ancient Near East but created entities over which the Lord is sovereign." (VanGemeren)

d. **Great is our Lord, and mighty in power**: The psalmist again described God in the highest aspects of His majesty (**His understanding is infinite**) and in the lowest and most compassionate aspects of His majesty (**the LORD lifts up the humble**).

> i. "It turns upside down the familiar argument that in so great a universe our small affairs are too minute to notice." (Kidner)

> ii. **His understanding is infinite**: "There is no fathoming his wisdom, or measuring his knowledge. He is infinite in existence, in power, and in knowledge, as these three phrases plainly teach us." (Spurgeon)

e. **The LORD lifts up the humble; He casts the wicked down to the ground**: This is much like the phrase repeated throughout in the Scriptures – *God resists the proud, but gives grace to the humble* (as in Proverbs 3:34, James 4:6, 1 Peter 5:5).

> i. "He reverses the evil order of things. The meek are down, and he lifts them up; the wicked are exalted, and he hurls them down to the dust." (Spurgeon)

> ii. "As a man ranks himself in one or other of these two divisions, he may expect from heaven storm or sunshine, mercy or judgment." (Horne)

B. Praising God for His work in nature.

1. (7-9) Exhortation to sing praises.

Sing to the LORD with thanksgiving;
Sing praises on the harp to our God,
Who covers the heavens with clouds,
Who prepares rain for the earth,
Who makes grass to grow on the mountains.
He gives to the beast its food,
***And* to the young ravens that cry.**

a. **Sing to the LORD with thanksgiving**: As we understand God's majesty in both its heavenly and earthly expressions, it should create in us a natural response of praise. We bring our praise with song, with **thanksgiving**, and with music (**on the harp to our God**).

> i. **Our God**: "He is 'our God,' whether he be the God of other men or not. He is 'our God' by his choice of us, and by our choice of him; 'our God' by eternal covenant, to whom we also pledge ourselves." (Spurgeon)

b. **Who covers the heavens with clouds, who prepares rain for the earth**: God's power and loving care come together again in His work in nature. He brings **rain**, He **makes grass to grow**, and **He gives to the beast its food**.

i. **To the young ravens**: "…which he mentions, partly, because they were most contemptible, especially to the Jews, to whom they were unclean and forbidden for food; partly, because they are greedy and voracious; and partly, because they are not only neglected by men, but also forsaken by their [mothers] as soon as ever they can fly, and so are wholly left to the care and keeping of Divine Providence." (Poole)

ii. "The Lord is sovereign over and concerned with all his creation, not only the magnificent stars, but also the lowly creatures on earth. How different is the God of Israel from Baal, whose [supposed] powers of rain and fertility were nothing in comparison!" (VanGemeren)

2. (10-11) What delights the LORD.

He does not delight in the strength of the horse;
He takes no pleasure in the legs of a man.
The LORD takes pleasure in those who fear Him,
In those who hope in His mercy.

a. **He does not delight in the strength of a horse**: We take great interest in the power of God's creation, whether it is **the strength of a horse** or the strength **in the legs of a man**. God created these things, but they are not what fundamentally **delight** Him.

b. **The LORD takes pleasure in those who fear Him**: What God takes pleasure in is the reverence and trust of His people. Those who find their **hope in His mercy** delight God, because they honor Him with their trust.

i. **Mercy** here is the word *hesed*, which refers to the great love of God, especially in the context of loyalty to His promises and covenant. It pleases God when we hope in His loyal love, His loving kindness.

ii. **Those who fear Him…those who hope**: "Marks of new birth are fear and hope. They fear, for they are sinners; they hope, for God is merciful. They fear him, for he is great; they hope in him, for he is good. Their fear sobers their hope; their hope brightens their fear: God takes pleasure in them both in their trembling and in their rejoicing." (Spurgeon)

C. Praising God for His wisdom, power, and word.

1. (12-18) More praise for the God of great care and power.

Praise the LORD, O Jerusalem!
Praise your God, O Zion!
For He has strengthened the bars of your gates;
He has blessed your children within you.
He makes peace *in* your borders,

And fills you with the finest wheat.
He sends out His command *to the* earth;
His word runs very swiftly.
He gives snow like wool;
He scatters the frost like ashes;
He casts out His hail like morsels;
Who can stand before His cold?
He sends out His word and melts them;
He causes His wind to blow, *and* the waters flow.

a. **Praise the LORD, O Jerusalem**: The exhortation to praise comes again, with another *hallelujah*. The more we understand and explain the power and care of God, the more we should **praise** Him.

b. **He has strengthened the bars of your gates**: This begins a series of four great and compassionate acts God had done for His people. Each of these were a *reason* for praise. Our worship is not empty adoration; it is gratitude for specific goodness and the anticipation of future goodness.

- He gives security (strengthen **the bars of your gates**).

- He gives a future (bless **your children within you**).

- He gives peace (**peace in your borders**).

- He gives provision (**fills you with the finest wheat**).

  i. **He has strengthened the bars of your gates**: "The fortifications of Jerusalem are now complete, and their strength gives security to the people gathered into the city. Over all the land once devastated by war peace broods, and the fields that lay desolate now have yielded harvest." (Maclaren)

c. **He sends out His command to the earth**: This begins a series of short descriptions of God's presence and work in the natural world. God's work in the natural world begins with **His command to the earth**, with His **word** that **runs very swiftly**.

  i. The Apostle Paul asked for prayer in 2 Thessalonians 3:1, asking *that the word of the Lord may run swiftly and be glorified*. Paul probably had verse 15 of this psalm in mind when he wrote that.

  ii. **His word runs very swiftly**: "If God's word runs very swiftly, then it can even overtake those who run away from it. Not only can the Lord come quickly to those who seek him, but he can overtake those who hasten away from him." (Spurgeon)

  iii. **His command**: "…which is sufficient without any instruments to execute whatsoever pleaseth him, either in works of nature or of providence. His word runneth very swiftly; the thing is done without delay or difficulty." (Poole)

d. **He gives snow like wool**: The psalmist considered God's power as it is seen in cold weather. The **snow**, the **frost**, the **hail**, and the **cold** are all expressions of His power in nature. Then, when God **sends out His word and melts them**, it is another expression of His power.

i. Hebrews 1:3 describes Jesus as the one who is *upholding all things by the word of His power*. Verse 18 of this psalm reminds us that even the natural order of snow and melting and flowing waters happens as God **sends out His word**.

ii. **Sends out His word and melts them**: "He can as easily melt the hardest heart by his Word, made effectual to such a purpose by his Holy Spirit. If that wind does but blow, the waters of penitent tears will soon flow." (Trapp)

iii. **He causes His wind to blow**: Spain attempted to invade England in 1588. The first step of their plan was to defeat the English Navy at sea. They sent 130 ships against England's 90 ships, yet at a critical point of the long battle, a strong wind turned the Spanish armada away and more than half their fleet was lost. "The English victory was complete. The Spanish defeat was total. The English celebrated their deliverance by minting a new issue of coins, which bore the Latin inscription *Affavit Deus* ('God blew'), taken from Psalm 147:18: 'He stirs up his breezes, and the waters flow.' In those days there was at least one nation that knew how to praise God for its safety." (Boice)

2. (19-20) The presence and goodness of God's word to Israel.

He declares His word to Jacob,
His statutes and His judgments to Israel.
He has not dealt thus with any nation;
And *as for His* judgments, they have not known them.
Praise the LORD!

a. **He declares His word to Jacob**: The same God who orders and directs the natural world through His word has also brought the revelation of His heart and mind through His word to Israel. He has declared **His statutes and His judgments to Israel**.

i. The declaration of **His word** shows that God regards humanity as rational and capable of relationship. "So by addressing us, not programming us, God shows that he seeks a relationship, not simply a sequence of actions carried out." (Kidner)

ii. "The Jews were God's library keepers; and unto them (as a special favour) were committed those lively and life-giving oracles, Romans 3:2." (Trapp)

iii. "He who is the Creator is also the Revealer. We are to praise the Lord above all things for his manifesting himself to us." (Spurgeon)

b. **He has not dealt thus with any nation**: God uniquely chose Israel to be the receivers and guardians of His revealed word. He did not choose the Philistines or the Edomites or the Egyptians for this role. The other nations **have not known** the **judgments** of God (that is, His word).

i. As the Apostle Paul would later write, one of the chief advantages God gave to Israel is that He committed to them *the oracles of God* (Romans 3:2). Israel received this responsibility seriously, and took great care to copy, learn, and preserve the Hebrew Scriptures.

ii. "The psalmist is not rejoicing that other nations have not received these, but that Israel has. Its privilege is its responsibility. It has received them that it may obey them, and then that it may make them known." (Maclaren)

c. **Praise the LORD**: Understanding the greatness of God, His care for humanity and all of nature, and the remarkable power and nature of His word, should move us to **praise** Him all the more. *Hallelujah!*

Psalm 148 – Let Heaven and Earth Praise the LORD

Psalm 148 calls upon all creation to praise Yahweh. "What a wonderful song this is! Look over it again, and note the fact that there is no reference in it, from first to last, to the mercy, or pity, or compassion of God. But that is because there is no reference to evil in any form." (G. Campbell Morgan)

Alexander Maclaren wrote that Psalm 148 continues "…a line of thought which runs through Scripture from its first page to its last – namely, that, as man's sin subjected the creatures to 'vanity,' so his redemption shall be their glorifying."

This call to all creation to praise Yahweh is not an empty wish. Revelation 5:11-13 tells us specifically that it will be fulfilled. "O what a hymn of praise is here! It is a universal chorus! All created nature have a share, and all perform their respective parts." (Adam Clarke)

A. Praise from the heavens.

1. (1-4) Calling upon heavenly things to praise the LORD.

Praise the LORD!
Praise the LORD from the heavens;
Praise Him in the heights!
Praise Him, all His angels;
Praise Him, all His hosts!
Praise Him, sun and moon;
Praise Him, all you stars of light!
Praise Him, you heavens of heavens,
And you waters above the heavens!

> a. **Praise the LORD**: Like each of the last five psalms in the Book of Psalms, Psalm 148 begins and ends with *hallelujah*, which is both an exclamation of praise to Yahweh and an encouragement to praise Him.

> b. **Praise the LORD from the heavens**: The psalmist considered that all heavenly beings and bodies should give praise to Yahweh. The God of Israel

was not a local deity who only expected honor from Israel. He was and is God over all, and as such deserves such praise **in the heights**.

i. Psalm 19 told us that *the heavens declare the glory of God* by their very nature and being. Here the psalmist speaks to the heavens that they continue this praise.

ii. "As God in framing the world began above and wrought downward, so doth the psalmist in this his exhortation to all creatures to praise the Lord." (Trapp)

iii. **In the heights**: "The very 'heights above,' where God rules… together with outer space and the atmosphere of the earth, are invoked to join in Israel's praise." (VanGemeren)

c. **Praise Him, all His angels**: The psalmist called upon all angelic beings to give God praise. This is the constant occupation of the living creatures surrounding God's throne (Revelation 4:8). The company of faithful angels is like a great army (**all His hosts**).

i. Other angelic beings fell because they would not properly honor God (Isaiah 14:12-15).

ii. "Not only in Old Testament times but in the Christian era, men have been tempted to worship *angels* (Col. 2:18), who are our fellow servants (Rev. 22:8f.), and to treat the *stars* as arbiters of destiny. The psalm sweeps away such folly." (Kidner)

d. **Praise Him, sun and moon…all you stars of light**: Heavenly bodies should also praise God, shining in their radiance for His honor and moving according to His plan.

i. The idea of creation praising God is found in many places in the Scriptures (such as Psalm 98:7-8 and Isaiah 55:12). This is the only place where specifically it is said that the **sun and moon** and the **stars** should praise Him.

ii. "Though they have neither speech nor language, and [lack] the tongue of men, yet by their splendor and magnificence, their motions and their influences, all regulated and exerted according to the ordinance of their Maker, do, in a very intelligible and striking manner, declare the glory of God." (Horne)

iii. "In these starry depths obedience reigns; it is only on earth that a being lives who can and will break the merciful barriers of Jehovah's law." (Maclaren)

iv. **You stars of light**: "…the brightest and most luminous stars: probably the planets may be especially intended." (Clarke)

e. Praise Him, you heavens of heavens: In the mind of an ancient Hebrew, the blue sky, the night sky, and God's dwelling place could all be thought of as an aspect of the **heavens**. The singer here looks to the ultimate of heaven, and all the **heavens**, to praise God, including the clouds with their **waters**.

> i. **Heavens of heavens**: "Ye highest and most glorious heavens, the place of God's throne and glorious presence, as this phrase is used, Deuteronomy 10:14, 1 Kings 8:27, Nehemiah 9:6, Psalm 115:16. Or, ye starry heavens, which also may well be so called, because they are above the air, which is often called heaven in Scripture." (Poole)

> ii. Adam Clarke speculated that these **heavens of heavens** were of them being other planets or solar systems. "Heavens exceeding heavens. Systems of systems extending as far beyond the solar system."

> iii. "The *waters above the heavens* are a poetic or popular term for the rain clouds." (Kidner)

2. (5-6) Reasons why the heavens should praise the LORD.

Let them praise the name of the LORD,
For He commanded and they were created.
He also established them forever and ever;
He made a decree which shall not pass away.

a. For He commanded and they were created: All creatures or creations owe honor and praise to their Creator, especially things created by the simple command of their Creator. Such a mighty maker deserves praise.

> i. "Evolution may be atheistic; but the doctrine of creation logically demands worship; and hence, as the tree is known by its fruit, it proves itself to be true. Those who were created by command are under command to adore their Creator." (Spurgeon)

b. He also established them forever and ever: These heavenly things – angels, the sun, the moon, the stars, the sky itself – were not only *made* by God, but they also *continue* because of His word (**a decree**). Their continued establishment gives them reason to praise the God who decreed it.

> i. "Therefore ought the Lord to be praised because he is Preserver as well as Creator, Ruler as well as Maker." (Spurgeon)

B. Praise from the earth.

1. (7-12) Calling upon earthly things to praise the LORD.

Praise the LORD from the earth,
You great sea creatures and all the depths;

Fire and hail, snow and clouds;
Stormy wind, fulfilling His word;
Mountains and all hills;
Fruitful trees and all cedars;
Beasts and all cattle;
Creeping things and flying fowl;
Kings of the earth and all peoples;
Princes and all judges of the earth;
Both young men and maidens;
Old men and children.

a. **Praise the LORD from the earth**: The first part of this psalm called upon things in the heavens to give praise to Yahweh. **Earth** should also not fail to give its praise to God, and all the earth should join in this praise.

i. Modern men and women make the mistake of worshipping the creation rather than the Creator. "We worship it [nature] in place of God, attributing creative powers to nature and virtually deifying the dynamic within living things. In opposition to this sad pagan error, the psalmist reminds us that the animals themselves worship God." (Boice)

b. **You great sea creatures**: All things in the **sea** and all the phenomenon of weather (**fire and hail, snow, clouds, wind**) should praise God, **fulfilling His word**.

i. **Great sea creatures**: "…either, 1. Dragons and serpents, which abide in the deep caverns and holes of the earth; or, 2. Whales or other sea-monsters, which dwell in the depths of the sea, which are oft called by this name, as Job 7:12, Ezekiel 29:3, and elsewhere, as the word here rendered." (Poole)

ii. "Its enormous inhabitants, which are under the command of Jehovah, and of none but him." (Horne)

c. **Mountains and all hills**: Everything on the land, both fixed and moving – including all the animals of the land – should give praise to the LORD.

i. **Beasts**: "Those are worse than beasts who do not praise our God. More than brutish are those who are wilfully silent concerning their Maker." (Spurgeon)

ii. **Creeping things and flying fowl**: "The lowest worm that crawls and the light-winged bird that soars, these all have voices to praise God." (Maclaren)

d. **Kings of the earth and all peoples**: Yahweh's praise should be proclaimed by all who are made in His image. All humanity – **kings, princes, judges,**

young and **old** – all owe praise to the God who made them and sustains them.

i. "After the whole creation hath been called upon to praise Jehovah; man, for whom the whole was made; man, the last and more perfect work of God; man, that hath been since redeemed by the blood of the Son of God incarnate, is exhorted to join and fill up the universal chorus of heaven and earth." (Horne)

ii. "The young man's strong bass, the maiden's clear alto, the old man's quavering notes, the child's fresh treble, should blend in the song." (Maclaren)

iii. That *all* men and women will one day praise the LORD is certain: *That at the name of Jesus every knee should bow, of those in heaven, and of those on earth, and of those under the earth, and that every tongue should confess that Jesus Christ is Lord, to the glory of God the Father.* (Philippians 2:10-11)

2. (13-14) Reasons why the earth should praise the LORD.

Let them praise the name of the LORD,
For His name alone is exalted;
His glory *is* above the earth and heaven.
And He has exalted the horn of His people,
The praise of all His saints—
Of the children of Israel,
A people near to Him.
Praise the LORD!

a. **For His name alone is exalted**: Yahweh deserves such praise from all things on earth because He alone is God. There is no other being that deserves the worship, honor, and praise that God deserves.

i. **Let them praise**: VanGemeren points out that this is in the form of a command. "By the use of the jussive [command], the psalmist restates the universal obligation of all of God's creation to demonstrate their allegiance by praising him."

b. **His glory is above the earth and heaven**: Yahweh deserves such praise from all things on earth because He is immeasurably greater and more glorious than anything on earth. We should reserve our praise for only that which is truly greater and more glorious, not for the lesser things (such as the idols of men's hands).

i. "He is himself the crown of all things, the excellency of the creation. There is more glory in him personally than in all his works united. It is not possible for us to exceed and become extravagant in the Lord's praise: his own natural glory is infinitely greater than any glory which we can render to him." (Spurgeon)

c. **He has exalted the horn of His people**: Yahweh deserves such praise from all things on earth because He has rescued and established **His people**. Those who find their power (**the horn of His people**) established because of Yahweh owe Him praise.

> i. "God loves and cares for all his creation, but he has a special affinity for 'his people,' 'his saints'." (VanGemeren)

> ii. **Of the children of Israel**: "It is a nation of priests, having the privilege of access to His presence; and, in the consciousness of this dignity, 'comes forward in this psalm as the leader of all the creatures in their praise of God, and strikes up a hallelujah that is to be joined in by heaven and earth' (Delitzsch)." (Maclaren)

> iii. "His goodness to all his creatures does not prevent his having a special favour to his chosen nation: he is good to all, but he is God to his people." (Spurgeon)

d. **A people near to Him**: Yahweh deserves such praise from all things on earth because He has drawn **near** to His people. He is with and for His people, a blessing and a benefit greater than any other.

> i. **A people near to Him**: "And in that respect happy above all people on the earth, Deuteronomy 4:7; Deuteronomy 33:29, because in covenant with him and near allied to him, as the word here importeth." (Trapp)

e. **Praise the LORD**: The composer of Psalm 148 has persuaded us to do what we and all creation should do – give to Yahweh the praise due to Him. *Hallelujah!*

Psalm 149 – The High Praises of God and a Two-Edged Sword

This is another of the last five psalms that have no title in the Hebrew text, but each of these last five begin and end with Hallelujah or Praise the LORD!

A. The praise of God's people.

1. (1) Praising Yahweh with a new song.

Praise the LORD!
Sing to the LORD a new song,
***And* His praise in the assembly of saints.**

    a. **Praise the LORD:** The last five of the 150 collected psalms begin and end with this phrase. In many (or most) of the previous songs there was a trouble, crisis, or evil described and brought before the LORD. In these last psalms, it is all praise.

    b. **Sing to the LORD a new song:** God loves to receive the rejoicing and praise of His people expressed in **song**, especially the **new song**. The **new song** can come from an old saint as he or she gains fresh awareness of God's love and grace.

        i. "He is ever new in his manifestations; his mercies are new every morning; his deliverances are new in every night of sorrow; let your gratitude and thanksgivings be new also." (Spurgeon)

    c. **And His praise in the assembly of saints:** It is wonderful for the individual saint to offer praise to God; it is even better and greater to do so **in the assembly of saints**. The community of God's people makes praise all the richer, especially praise offered in **song**.

2. (2-4) The pleasure of true praise.

Let Israel rejoice in their Maker;
Let the children of Zion be joyful in their King.
Let them praise His name with the dance;

Let them sing praises to Him with the timbrel and harp.
For the LORD **takes pleasure in His people;**
He will beautify the humble with salvation.

a. **Let Israel rejoice in their Maker**: If one ever lacked for reasons to praise God, there is one great reason that is always at hand. It is always *right* and *honorable* for us to praise and **rejoice** in our Creator.

i. "The starting point for us creatures must be our acknowledgment of the Creator, since it is only when we have begun to know God as our Creator that we can appreciate what we owe him and understand how we have failed to praise and thank him properly." (Boice)

b. **Let the children of Zion be joyful in their King**: God is the **Maker** of all humanity, but is recognized as **King** only over His people. This recognition is a source of incomparable joy to His people, who realize they could never hope for a ruler greater in love, wisdom, and power.

i. It is common for people to be **joyful** over a political leader or a head of state. The visit of such a ruler is treated as a happy, special occasion. Believers regard it is a special and **joyful** thing to recognize and enjoy the presence of their **King**.

ii. "The true splendor of kings lies not in what their people do for them, but in what they do for their people: and herein our Lord excelleth all the princes that ever lived." (Spurgeon)

c. **Let them praise His name with the dance**: The joy among God's people in their Creator and King was evidenced by **dance**, song, and instrumental music. These were happy expressions of gratitude, and show that God approves of and encourages such happiness among His people.

i. Adam Clarke disagreed with most translations that the Hebrew word here translated **dance** (*mahol*) means a flute or musical pipe, not a dance. "I know no place in the Bible where *machol* and *machalath* mean *dance* of any kind; they constantly signify some kind of *pipe*."

d. **For the L**ORD **takes pleasure in His people**: If God is so rich in grace and mercy that He takes **pleasure in His people** – despite all their sin and weakness – it is cause for great rejoicing.

i. "It is the constant teaching of Scripture that we may please God. This was the testimony borne of Enoch before his translation, and the apostle [Paul] exhorts us to walk worthily of the Lord, unto all pleasing." (Meyer)

ii. "Such 'pleasure' the King of Zion taketh in his people, that he hath [chosen] to become like one of them; to partake of their flesh and blood." (Horne)

iii. "What is there in us in which the Lord can take pleasure? Nothing, unless he has put it there. If he sees any beauty in us, it must be the reflection of his own face. Yet still the text says so, and therefore it must be true: 'The Lord taketh pleasure in his people.'" (Spurgeon)

e. **He will beautify the humble with salvation**: Most of the great ones among men despise the **humble** and leave them in their low condition. God resists the proud, but gives grace to the **humble** (James 4:6, 1 Peter 5:5). He makes **the humble** beautiful with **salvation**.

i. "Not only does God take a personal interest in each step of the obedient soul, but He makes it beautiful, and leads it from victory to victory." (Meyer)

ii. "The qualification for receiving Jehovah's help is meekness, and the effect of that help on the lowly soul is to deck it with strange loveliness." (Maclaren)

iii. "God taketh pleasure in all his children as Jacob loved all his sons; but the meek are his Josephs, and upon these he puts the coat of many colours, beautifying them with peace, contentment, joy, holiness, and influence." (Spurgeon)

B. The power of God's people.

1. (5-6) Making ready for conflict.

Let the saints be joyful in glory;
Let them sing aloud on their beds.
Let **the high praises of God** *be* **in their mouth,**
And a two-edged sword in their hand,

a. **Let the saints be joyful in glory**: The spirit of the first part of this psalm continues. The saints are so happy in God's glory that they **sing aloud on their beds**. Waking hours do not give enough time to express all their praise and joy unto God, so they must continue it **on their beds**.

i. This reminds us that though songs of praise are especially wonderful among the assembly of God's people (verse 1), they should never be restricted to the assembly. It is a sacred and wonderful thing for the saints to **sing aloud on their beds**.

b. **Let the high praises of God be in their mouth, and a two-edged sword in their hand**: God's people are pictured as ready for battle, equipped with two mighty weapons.

- They bear **the high praises of God**; their worship indicates the allegiance and surrender to the God of every victory. In 2 Chronicles 20:20-21, a great victory was won for the people of God as they entered the battle with praise.

- They bear **a two-edged sword in their hand**, demonstrating both the use of practical weapons and means, and in a spiritual sense, reliance upon God's word, which is described as a **two-edged sword** (Revelation 19:15) as even sharper than any two-edged sword (Hebrews 4:12), and as the **sword** of the Spirit (Ephesians 6:17).

    i. "Their praise is not merely to be that of the chanting of words. It is also to be in the doing of His will. While the high praises of God are in their mouth, a two-edged sword is to be in their hand, with which they carry out His purposes among the peoples, the kings, and the nobles." (Morgan)

    ii. "In this state of mind, the Lord will grant victory to his people, as he did to Nehemiah and his men who worked with 'sword and trowel' while praying to the Lord (Nehemiah 4:9, 16-23), believing that 'Our God will fight for us!' (Nehemiah 4:20)." (VanGemeren)

    iii. A saying among Americans came from the Second World War: *Praise the Lord and pass the ammunition.* Psalm 149:6 has something of that idea.

    iv. The combination of these two – **the high praises of God** and **the two-edged sword** – spiritually speaks to every leader among God's people. The gatherings of God's people should excel in *both* praise and the preaching of God's word. We should always press to have excellent **praises of God** and a right, sharp handling of the **sword** of the Spirit.

    v. "The word of God is all edge; whichever way we turn it, it strikes deadly blows at falsehood and wickedness. If we do not praise we shall grow sad in our conflict; and if we do not fight we shall become presumptuous in our song. The verse indicates a happy blending of the chorister and the crusader." (Spurgeon)

    vi. "If you had a sword of steel, you would fight with men; but that is no part of your business. You are not called to that cruel work; but, as you have the sword of the Spirit...go forth and praise God by the use of that two-edged sword which is the Word of God." (Spurgeon)

2. (7-9) The victory of God's people.

To execute vengeance on the nations,
And punishments on the peoples;
To bind their kings with chains,

And their nobles with fetters of iron;
To execute on them the written judgment—
This honor have all His saints.
Praise the LORD!

a. **To execute vengeance on the nations**: The power of praise and the word of God will ultimately see God's work accomplished among **the nations**. For those who persist in disobedience, it will be **vengeance** and **punishments** at the end of the age. Not even **kings** or **nobles** can escape this judgment to come.

i. "The stern close of the psalm strikes a note which many ears feel to be discordant…. [Yet] it is entirely free from any sentiment of personal vengeance." (Maclaren)

ii. **Execute vengeance**: "…for all their cruelties and injuries towards God's people. This was literally accomplished by David upon the Philistines, Ammonites, Syrians, and other neighbouring nations and princes, which were bitter enemies to God's people." (Poole)

iii. We see that in the immediate context of the psalmist, in some way Israel was to be the agent to **execute vengeance**. This means that their joyful praise had to connect itself to radical obedience, even to God's difficult and costly commands. As believers under the New Covenant, we don't battle flesh and blood enemies (Ephesians 6:12-18), yet we have the responsibility to be not only worshippers, but warriors in a spiritual warfare that at times will be difficult and costly. In a spiritual sense, we are to **execute vengeance** on every thing that would oppose Jesus Christ and the work of His kingdom in our lives.

iv. "Our equivalent of binding *kings with chains* (8) is to 'take every thought captive to obey Christ' (2 Cor. 10:5)." (Kidner)

v. **To execute on them the written judgment**: "It would be a sad thing for any one to misuse this text: lest any warlike believer should be led to do so, we would remind him that the execution must not go beyond the sentence and warrant; and we have received no warrant of execution against our fellow men." (Spurgeon)

vi. For the believer under the New Covenant, there is a **written judgment** against every spiritual enemy, and Jesus wrote it by His work on the cross (John 16:11, Colossians 2:14).

vii. **To execute vengeance**: "The history of this song is one of great sadness, due to grave misinterpretation, and grievous misapplication. Delitzsch has said: 'By means of this Psalm, Caspar Scioppius, in his *Classicum belli sacri*…. inflamed the Roman Catholic princes to the Thirty Years' Religious War and, within the Protestant Church, Thomas Münzer, by means of this Psalm, stirred up the War of the Peasants.'" (Morgan)

viii. Especially in light of how this verse has been abused, it is important to remember what Morgan noted: "There is no reference in this Psalm to the Church of God. As it specifically indicates, it has to do with 'Israel,' with 'the children of Zion.'"

b. **This honor have all His saints**: In some way beyond our present comprehension, God will use His people in setting right the wrongs of this present age. Even if our participation is only as an audience to the righteous judgments of God, it will be an **honor** to **all His saints**.

i. "They are redeemed from bondage that they may be God's warriors. The honour and obligation are universal." (Maclaren)

c. **Praise the LORD**: This sentence – one word in the Hebrew, *hallelujah* – is understood as either a declaration or an exhortation. Here especially it can be taken as an exhortation and encouragement for all those who reject and resist God to **praise** Him instead, to be among **His saints** and not among **the nations** who will receive God's vengeance.

Psalm 150 – Let All Things Praise the LORD

Each of the five divsions of the Book of Psalms closes with a doxology (Psalm 41:13, 72:18-19, 89:52, 106:48). This entire psalm can be seen as a doxology that not only closes the fifth and final volume of the collected psalms, but also closes the entire Book of Psalms.

Psalm 150 contains no argument, no real teaching, no real explanation. It is an eloquent, passionate cry to all creation to give Yahweh the praise due to Him.

"The psalm is more than an artistic close of the Psalter: it is a prophecy of the last result of the devout life, and, in its unclouded sunniness, as well as in its universality, it proclaims the certain end of the weary years for the individual and for the world." (Alexander Maclaren)

A. Unlimited praise to the God who is unlimited in His greatness.

1. (1) In every place, praise the LORD.

Praise the LORD!
Praise God in His sanctuary;
Praise Him in His mighty firmament!

a. **Praise the LORD**: This last of the five ending psalms shares the same beginning and ending line as the previous four. Yahweh is praised, and His people are encouraged, exhorted to praise Him. No crisis or enemy is in view; this is pure praise.

b. **Praise God in His sanctuary**: The **sanctuary** of God is a most fitting place for His **praise**. It is a place set apart for His honor, and involves special recognition of His presence. If Yahweh is to be praised anywhere, it should be in **His sanctuary**.

i. In light of the New Covenant, we realize that God's **sanctuary** is not fixed to a particular building in Jerusalem.

- Jesus serves His people in a sanctuary in the heavens (Hebrews 8:1-2).

313

- Jesus makes His sanctuary among His people collectively (2 Corinthians 6:16).

- Jesus makes His sanctuary in the individual believer (1 Corinthians 3:16).

- Ultimately, Jesus Himself will be the sanctuary of God among His people (Revelation 21:22).

ii. **Praise God in His sanctuary**: "In many places we have the compound word *halelu-yah*, praise ye Jehovah; but this is the first place in which we find *halelu-el*, praise God, or the strong God." (Clarke)

c. **Praise Him in His mighty firmament**: The wide expanse of sky, with all its might in storms and weather, is also a fitting place to praise God. Since the **firmament** stretches from horizon to horizon, it tells us that God should be praised in every place under the sky.

i. "His glory fills the universe; his praise must do no less." (Kidner)

ii. **In His mighty firmament**: "Through the whole expanse, to the utmost limits of his power.... Praise him whose power and goodness extend through all worlds; and let the inhabitants of all those worlds share in the grand chorus, that it may be universal." (Clarke)

2. (2) For every reason, praise the LORD.

Praise Him for His mighty acts;
Praise Him according to His excellent greatness!

a. **Praise Him for His mighty acts**: God's mighty acts are one reason to praise God in every place. He has done great and powerful things, especially what Jesus accomplished at the cross and the empty tomb. The singer of this psalm had only shadowy knowledge of it, but the ultimate demonstration of God's power would come in the resurrection of Jesus (Ephesians 1:19-20). For this and all **His mighty acts**, we should **praise Him**.

i. "'His mighty deeds' might be rendered 'His heroic [or, valiant] acts.' The reference is to His deliverance of His people as a clear manifestation of prowess or conquering might." (Maclaren)

ii. "'Mighty' were the 'acts' which God wrought for Israel; and 'great' was the Holy One in the midst of his ancient people; but mightier acts did he perform in Christ Jesus, for the redemption of the world." (Horne)

b. **Praise Him according to His excellent greatness**: While it is right to ~aise God for the mighty things He does, there is perhaps something even 'er in praising Him for *who He is*, in all the excellence of His **greatness**. 'eatness surpasses all else in the entire universe, **excellent** above all.

i. **His excellent greatness**: "…or, Greatness of greatness; which yet can never be done, but must be endeavoured." (Trapp)

3. (3-5) With every expression, praise the LORD.

Praise Him with the sound of the trumpet;
Praise Him with the lute and harp!
Praise Him with the timbrel and dance;
Praise Him with stringed instruments and flutes!
Praise Him with loud cymbals;
Praise Him with clashing cymbals!

a. **Praise Him with the sound of the trumpet**: The psalmist referred to an orchestra of God's people and conducted their music in praise to God. There was to be no instrument left out. Brass, string, wind, and percussion must all join in the praise of a God so great.

i. There was good reason to mention **the trumpet** first in this long list. "The sound of trumpet is associated with the grandest and most solemn events, such as the giving of the law, the proclamation of jubilee, the coronation of Jewish kings, and the raging of war. It is to be thought of in reference to the coming of our Lord in his second advent and the raising of the dead." (Spurgeon)

ii. Adam Clarke described what he believed each musical instrument here mentioned to be.

- **Trumpet**: "*Sophar*, from its noble, cheering, and majestic sound."

- **Lute**: "*Nebel*; the nabla, a hollow stringed instrument; perhaps like the *guitar*."

- **Harp**: "*Kinnor*, another *stringed* instrument, played on with the *hands* or *fingers*."

- **Timbrel**: "*Toph, drum, tabret*, or *tomtom*, or *tympanum* of the ancients; a skin stretched over a broad hoop; perhaps something like the *tambourine*."

- **Dance**: "*Machol*, the *pipe*…it never means *dance*; see note on Psalm 149:3."

- **Stringed instruments**: "*Minnim*. This literally signifies *strings put in order*; perhaps a *triangular kind of hollow instrument* on which the strings were regularly placed, growing *shorter* and *shorter* till they came to a *point*."

- **Flutes**: "*Ugab*. Very likely the *syrinx* or *mouth organ; Pan's pipe*; both of the ancients and moderns."

- **Loud cymbals**: "*Tseltselim.* Two hollow plates of brass, which, being struck together, produced a sharp clanging sound."

- **Clashing cymbals**: "[Perhaps] those of a *larger make*, struck above the head, and consequently emitting a louder sound."

iii. "The list of instruments is not meant to be comprehensive, though it may be. We do not know what instruments the ancient Jews had. The point is actually that everything you have can be used to worship God." (Boice)

iv. The broad list of musical instruments tells us that God wants *every* class and group of people to praise Him, because these instruments were normally played by different types of people. "The horn was the curved '*Shophar,*' blown by the priests; harp and psaltery were played by the Levites, timbrels were struck by women [as they were] dancing, playing on stringed instruments, and pipes and cymbals, were not reserved for the Levites." (Maclaren)

b. **Praise Him with loud cymbals**: The individual instruments must be played with strength and celebration, and the collection of them together would fill the room with sound. This was not halting or hesitant praise – just like the love and goodness of God are not halting or hesitant toward us in any way.

i. "Let's be done with worship that is *always* weak and unexciting. If you cannot sing loudly and make loud music to praise the God who has redeemed you in Jesus Christ and is preparing you for heaven, perhaps it is because you do not really know God or the gospel at all. If you do know him, hallelujah." (Boice)

4. (6) With every available breath, praise the Lord.

Let everything that has breath praise the Lord.
Praise the Lord!

a. **Let everything that has breath praise the Lord**: This is a remarkably fitting conclusion to this psalm and to the entire Book of Psalms. Everything that breathes should give its praise to the One who gave it **breath**. Every breath is the gift of God and praise is the worthy response we should make for that gift.

i. Derek Kidner noted that the literal phrase is, "Let all breath praise the Lord."

ii. John Trapp wrote, "Or, Let every breath praise the Lord.... We have all as much reason to praise God as we have need to draw breath."

iii. "The word *nesamah* [**has breath**] denotes all living creatures, endowed with life by the Creator (Genesis 1:24-25; 7:21-22), but always in distinction from the Creator." (VanGemeren)

iv. "The one condition of praise is the possession of breath, that is to say, life received from Him must return in praise to Him." (Morgan)

v. Revelation 5:13 tells us that this *will* happen: *And every creature which is in heaven and on the earth and under the earth and such as are in the sea, and all that are in them, I heard saying: "Blessing and honor and glory and power be to Him who sits on the throne, and to the Lamb, forever and ever!"*

b. **Praise the LORD:** The last line of the Psalter could be nothing else than *Hallelujah!* Yahweh is to be praised and honored, and will be so among His people and all creation.

i. "The psalter begins with 'Blessed,' and ends with 'Hallelujah.'" (Meyer)

ii. "Your life may resemble the psalter with its varying moods, its light and shadow, its sob and smile; but it will end with hallelujahs, if only you will keep true to the will and way and work of the Most Holy." (Meyer)

Psalms 119-150 – Bibliography

Boice, James Montgomery *Psalms, Volume 3 – Psalms 107-150* (Grand Rapids, Michigan: Baker Books, 1999)

Bridges, Charles *Psalm 119: An Exposition* (Edinburgh: Banner of Truth, 1974)

Chappell, Clovis G. *Sermons from the Psalms* (Nashville, Tennessee: Cokesbury Press, 1931)

Clarke, Adam *The Holy Bible, Containing the Old and New Testaments, with A Commentary and Critical Notes, Volume III – Job to Song of Solomon* (New York: Eaton and Mains, 1827?)

Harris, Arthur Emerson *The Psalms Outlined* (Philadelphia: The Judson Press, 1925)

Horne, George *Commentary on the Psalms* (Audubon, New Jersey: Old Paths Publications, 1997 reprint of a 1771 edition)

Kidner, Derek *Psalms 73-150, A Commentary* (Leicester, England: Inter-Varsity Press, 1975)

Maclaren, Alexander *The Psalms, Volume III – Psalms 90-150* (London: Hodder and Stoughton, 1892)

Meyer, F.B. *Our Daily Homily* (Westwood, New Jersey: Revell, 1966)

Morgan, G. Campbell *Searchlights from the Word* (New York: Revell, 1926)

Morgan, G. Campbell *An Exposition of the Whole Bible* (Old Tappan, New Jersey: Revell, 1959)

Poole, Matthew *A Commentary on the Holy Bible, Volume 2* (London: The Banner of Truth Trust, 1968)

Spurgeon, Charles Haddon *The Treasury of David, Volume 3 – Psalms 111-150* (Peabody, Massachusetts: Hendrickson, 1988)

Spurgeon, Charles Haddon *The New Park Street Pulpit, Volumes 1-6* and *The Metropolitan Tabernacle Pulpit, Volumes 7-63* (Pasadena, Texas: Pilgrim Publications, 1990)

Trapp, John *A Commentary on the Old and New Testaments, Volume 3 – Proverbs to Daniel* (Eureka, California: Tanski Publications, 1997)

VanGemeren, Willem A. "Psalms," *The Expositor's Bible Commentary, Volume 5: Psalms-Song of Songs* (Grand Rapids, Michigan: Zondervan, 1991)

As the years pass I love the work of studying, learning, and teaching the Bible more than ever. I'm so grateful that God is faithful to meet me in His Word.

Mary Osgood is doing a wonderful work in proofreading and with editorial suggestions for these volumes of commentary on Psalms. Mary, thank you for helping me to write clearer and better!

Thanks to Brian Procedo for the cover design and the graphics work.

Most especially, thanks to my wife Inga-Lill. She is my loved and valued partner in life and in service to God and His people.

David Guzik

David Guzik's Bible commentary is regularly used and trusted by many thousands who want to know the Bible better. Pastors, teachers, class leaders, and everyday Christians find his commentary helpful for their own understanding and explanation of the Bible. David and his wife Inga-Lill live in Santa Barbara, California.

You can email David at
david@enduringword.com

For more resources by David Guzik,
go to www.enduringword.com